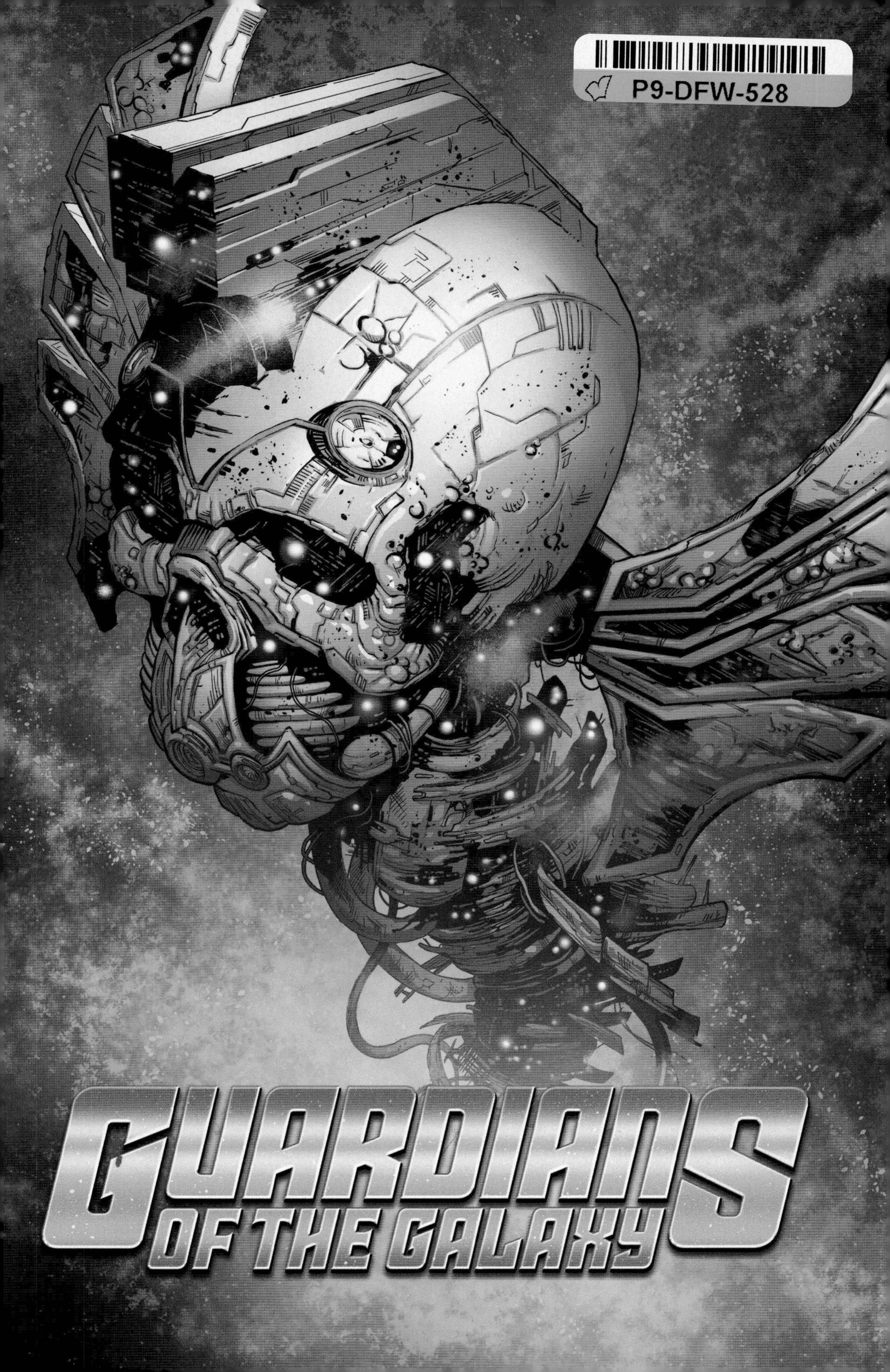
GUARDIANS
OF THE GALAXY

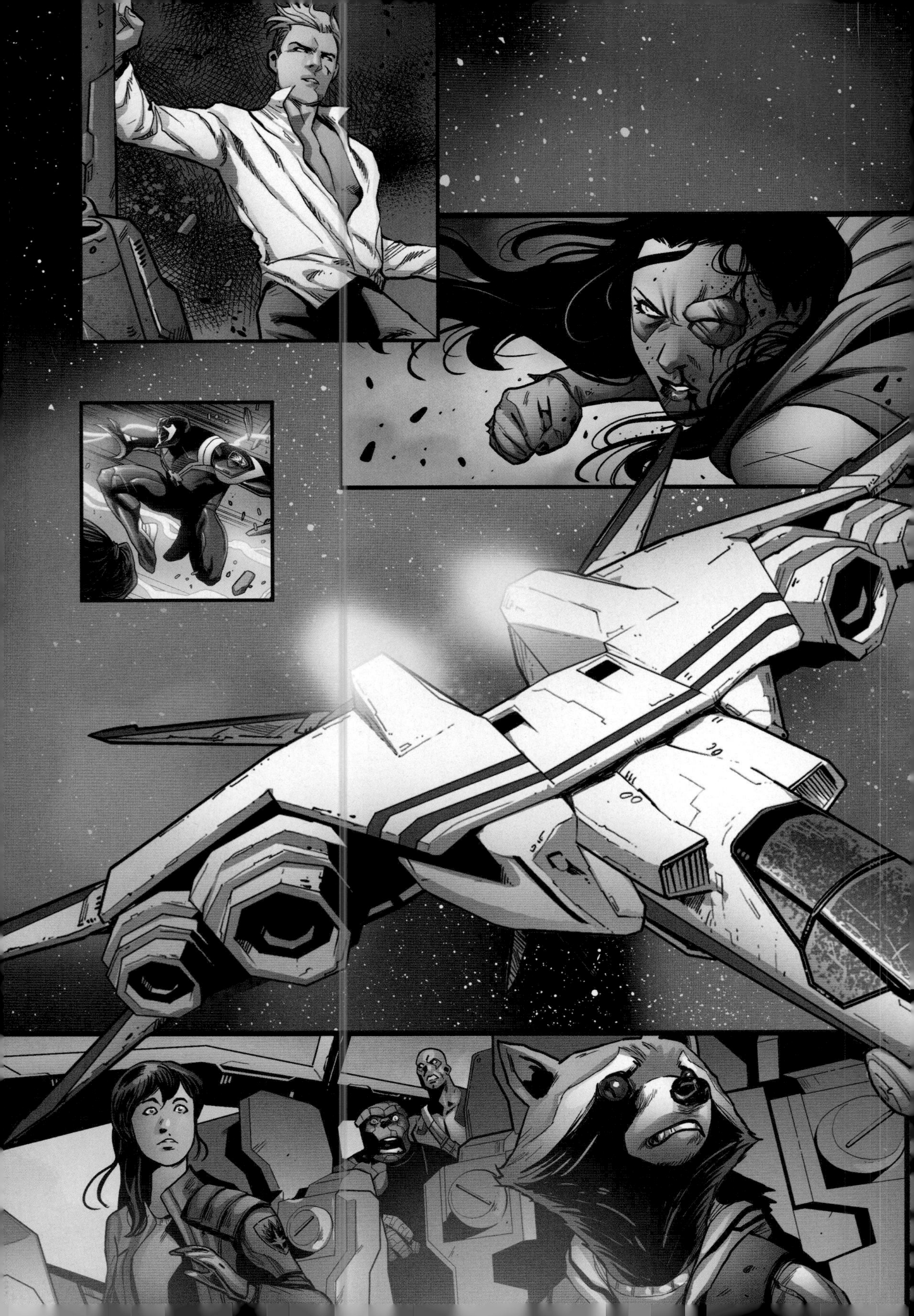

# GUARDIANS OF THE GALAXY

## EMPEROR QUILL

**BRIAN MICHAEL BENDIS**
WRITER

**VALERIO SCHITI**
ARTIST

**RICHARD ISANOVE**
COLOR ARTIST

**VC'S CORY PETIT**
LETTERER

**ART ADAMS** COVER ARTIST

**DAVE STEWART** (#1), **JASON KEITH** (#2, #4-5) & **PETER STEIGERWALD** (#3)
COVER COLORISTS

**KATHLEEN WISNESKI**
ASSISTANT EDITOR

**JAKE THOMAS**
ASSOCIATE EDITOR

**NICK LOWE**
EDITOR

COLLECTION EDITOR: *JENNIFER GRÜNWALD*
ASSOCIATE MANAGING EDITOR: *KATERI WOODY*
ASSOCIATE EDITOR: *SARAH BRUNSTAD*
EDITOR, SPECIAL PROJECTS: *MARK D. BEAZLEY*
VP PRODUCTION & SPECIAL PROJECTS: *JEFF YOUNGQUIST*
SVP PRINT, SALES & MARKETING: *DAVID GABRIEL*
BOOK DESIGNER: *JAY BOWEN*

EDITOR IN CHIEF: *AXEL ALONSO*
CHIEF CREATIVE OFFICER: *JOE QUESADA*
PUBLISHER: *DAN BUCKLEY*
EXECUTIVE PRODUCER: *ALAN FINE*

GUARDIANS OF THE GALAXY: NEW GUARD VOL. 1 — EMPEROR QUILL. Contains material originally published in magazine form as GUARDIANS OF THE GALAXY #1-5. First printing 2016. ISBN# 978-0-7851-9950-2. Published by MARVEL WORLDWIDE, INC., a subsidiary of MARVEL ENTERTAINMENT, LLC. OFFICE OF PUBLICATION: 135 West 50th Street, New York, NY 10020. Copyright © 2016 MARVEL No similarity between any of the names, characters, persons, and/or institutions in this magazine with those of any living or dead person or institution is intended, and any such similarity which may exist is purely coincidental. **Printed in the U.S.A.** ALAN FINE, President, Marvel Entertainment; DAN BUCKLEY, President, TV, Publishing & Brand Management; JOE QUESADA, Chief Creative Officer; TOM BREVOORT, SVP of Publishing; DAVID BOGART, SVP of Business Affairs & Operations, Publishing & Partnership; C.B. CEBULSKI, VP of Brand Management & Development, Asia; DAVID GABRIEL, SVP of Sales & Marketing, Publishing; JEFF YOUNGQUIST, VP of Production & Special Projects; DAN CARR, Executive Director of Publishing Technology; ALEX MORALES, Director of Publishing Operations; SUSAN CRESPI, Production Manager; STAN LEE, Chairman Emeritus. For information regarding advertising in Marvel Comics or on Marvel.com, please contact Vit DeBellis, Integrated Sales Manager, at vdebellis@marvel.com. For Marvel subscription inquiries, please call 888-511-5480. **Manufactured between 10/21/2016 and 11/28/2016 by LSC COMMUNICATIONS INC., SALEM, VA, USA.**

0 9 8 7 6 5 4 3 2 1

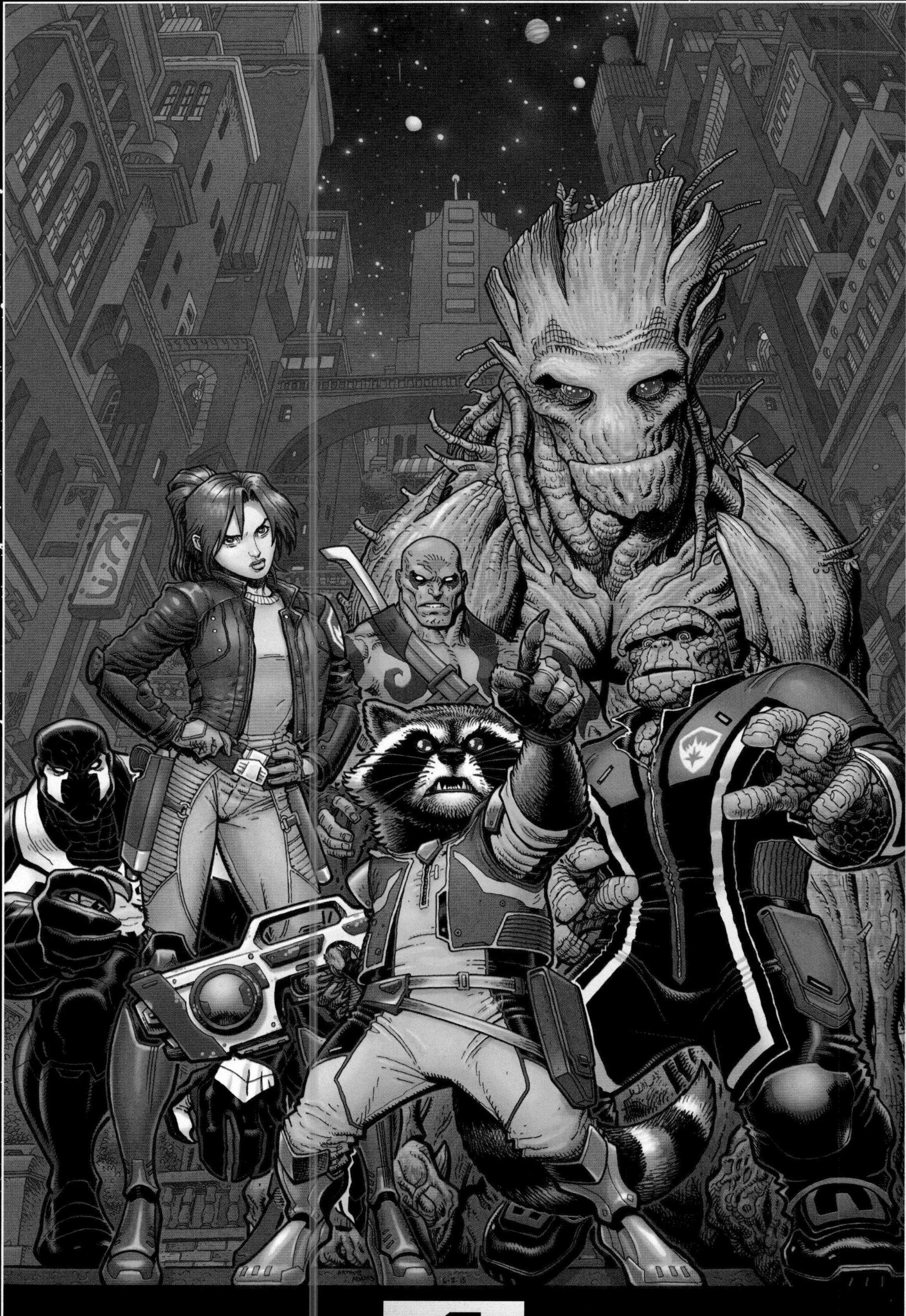

# 1

The entire galaxy is a mess. Warring empires and cosmic terrorists plague every corner. Someone has to rise above it all and fight for those who have no one to fight for them. Against their natures, a group of misanthropes and misfits came together to serve a higher cause. **Drax the Destroyer**, **Gamora**, the most dangerous woman in the universe, **Rocket Raccoon**, **Groot**, and **Flash Thompson**, a.k.a. **Venom** all joined together under the leadership of **Peter Quill, Star-Lord** to be the saviors of the spaceways, the conservators of the cosmos, the…

**GUARDIANS OF THE GALAXY**

But things have changed.

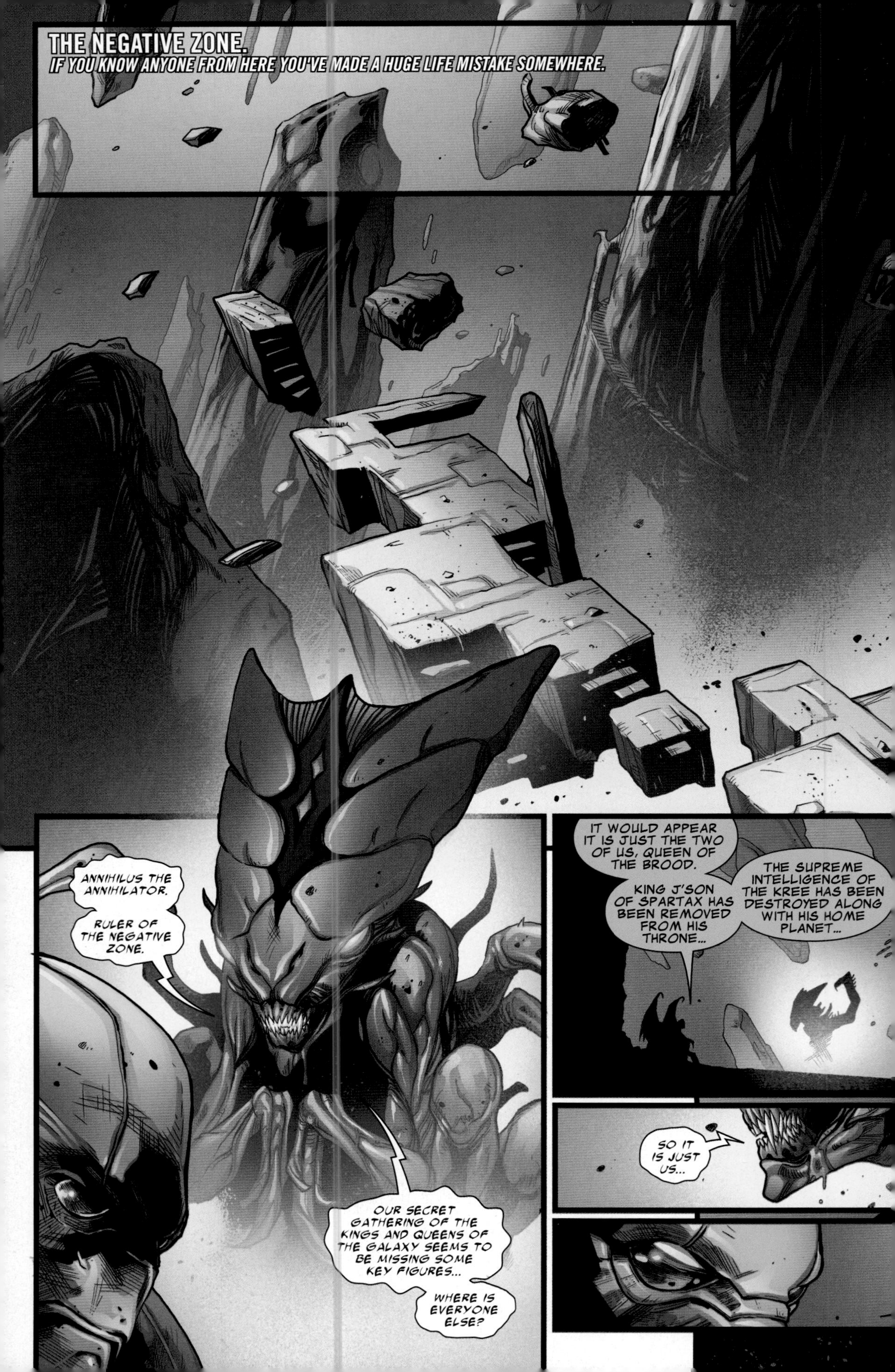
THE NEGATIVE ZONE.
IF YOU KNOW ANYONE FROM HERE YOU'VE MADE A HUGE LIFE MISTAKE SOMEWHERE.
ANNIHILUS THE ANNIHILATOR.
RULER OF THE NEGATIVE ZONE.
OUR SECRET GATHERING OF THE KINGS AND QUEENS OF THE GALAXY SEEMS TO BE MISSING SOME KEY FIGURES...
WHERE IS EVERYONE ELSE?
IT WOULD APPEAR IT IS JUST THE TWO OF US, QUEEN OF THE BROOD.
KING J'SON OF SPARTAX HAS BEEN REMOVED FROM HIS THRONE...
THE SUPREME INTELLIGENCE OF THE KREE HAS BEEN DESTROYED ALONG WITH HIS HOME PLANET...
SO IT IS JUST US...

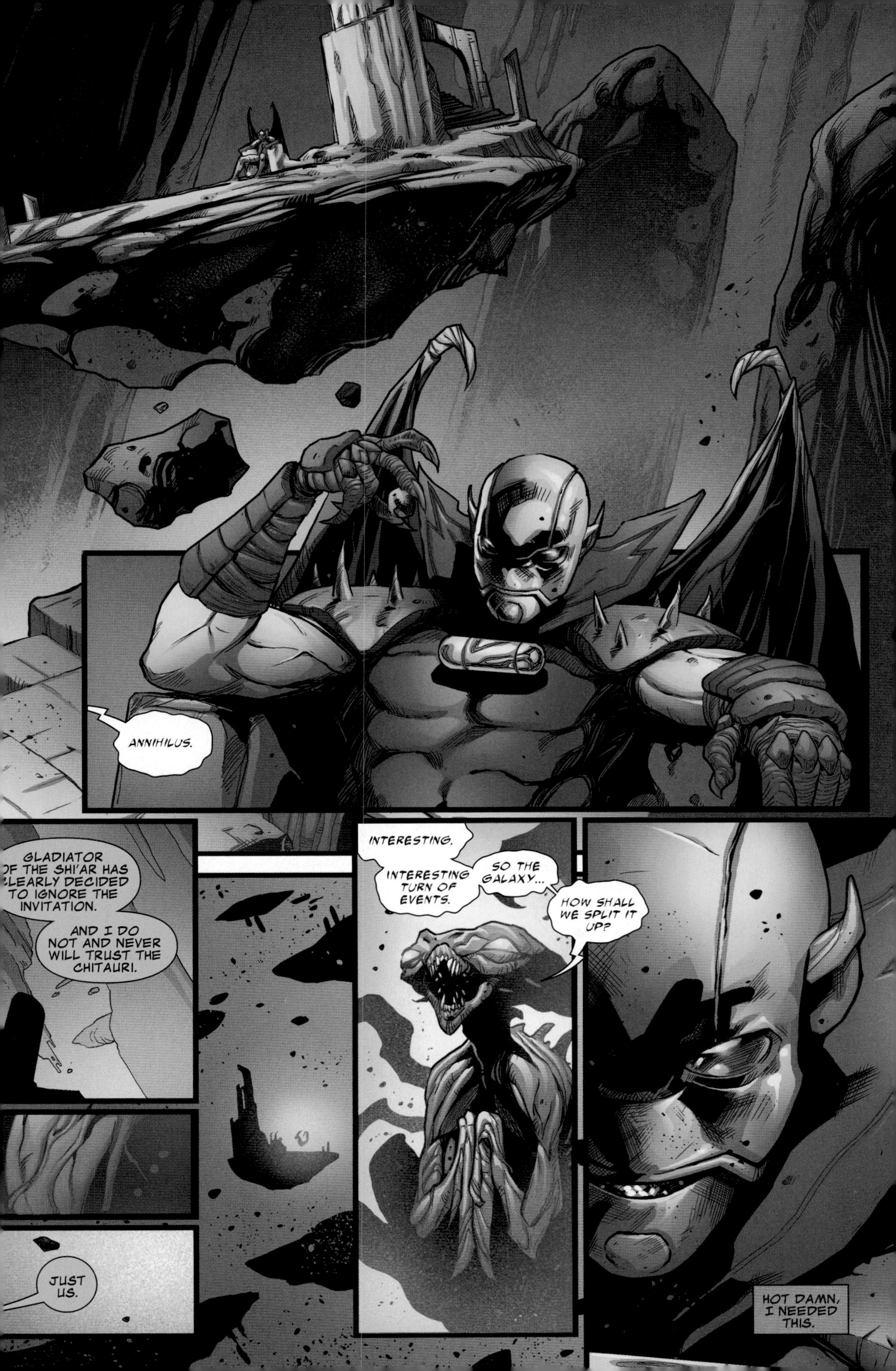
ANNIHILUS.
GLADIATOR OF THE SHI'AR HAS CLEARLY DECIDED TO IGNORE THE INVITATION.
AND I DO NOT AND NEVER WILL TRUST THE CHITAURI.
JUST US.
INTERESTING.
INTERESTING TURN OF EVENTS.
SO THE GALAXY...
HOW SHALL WE SPLIT IT UP?
HOT DAMN, I NEEDED THIS.

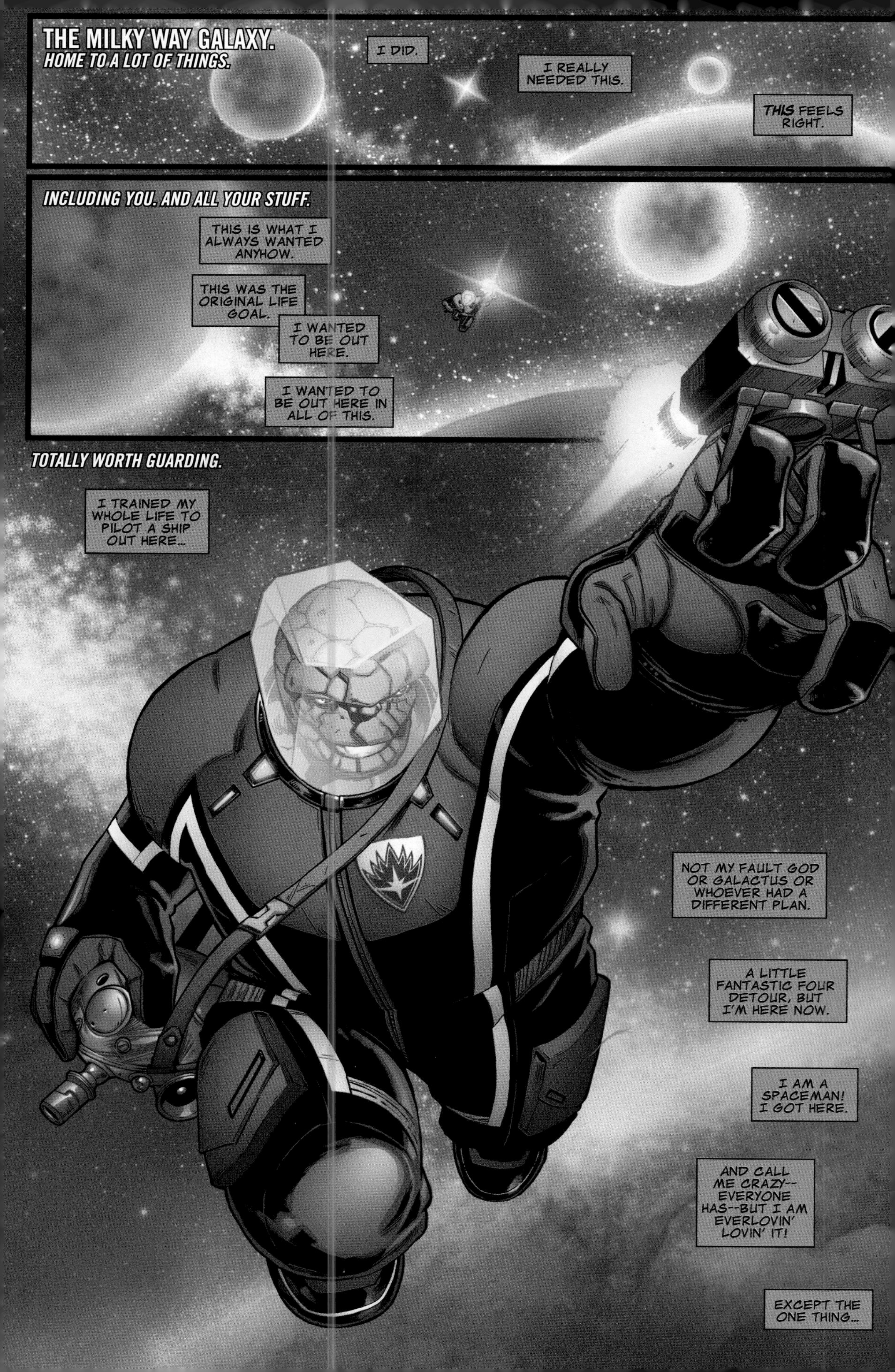
THE MILKY WAY GALAXY.
HOME TO A LOT OF THINGS.
I DID.
I REALLY NEEDED THIS.
THIS FEELS RIGHT.
INCLUDING YOU. AND ALL YOUR STUFF.
THIS IS WHAT I ALWAYS WANTED ANYHOW.
THIS WAS THE ORIGINAL LIFE GOAL.
I WANTED TO BE OUT HERE.
I WANTED TO BE OUT HERE IN ALL OF THIS.
TOTALLY WORTH GUARDING.
I TRAINED MY WHOLE LIFE TO PILOT A SHIP OUT HERE...
NOT MY FAULT GOD OR GALACTUS OR WHOEVER HAD A DIFFERENT PLAN.
A LITTLE FANTASTIC FOUR DETOUR, BUT I'M HERE NOW.
I AM A SPACEMAN! I GOT HERE.
AND CALL ME CRAZY-- EVERYONE HAS--BUT I AM EVERLOVIN' LOVIN' IT!
EXCEPT THE ONE THING...

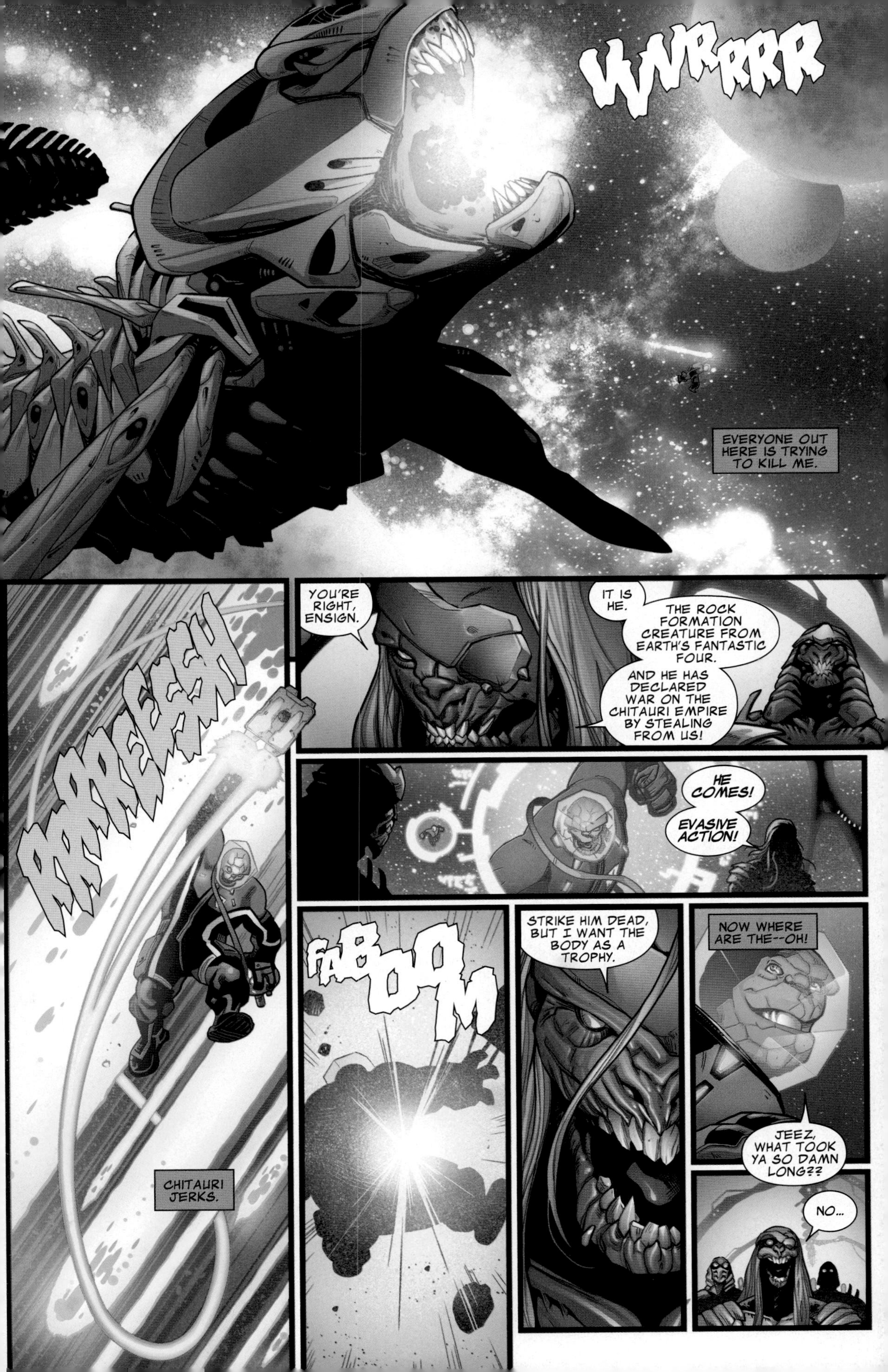
WVRRRR
EVERYONE OUT HERE IS TRYING TO KILL ME.
RARREEESH
CHITAURI JERKS.
YOU'RE RIGHT, ENSIGN.
IT IS HE.
THE ROCK FORMATION CREATURE FROM EARTH'S FANTASTIC FOUR.
AND HE HAS DECLARED WAR ON THE CHITAURI EMPIRE BY STEALING FROM US!
HE COMES!
EVASIVE ACTION!
FABOOM
STRIKE HIM DEAD, BUT I WANT THE BODY AS A TROPHY.
NOW WHERE ARE THE--OH!
JEEZ, WHAT TOOK YA SO DAMN LONG??
NO...

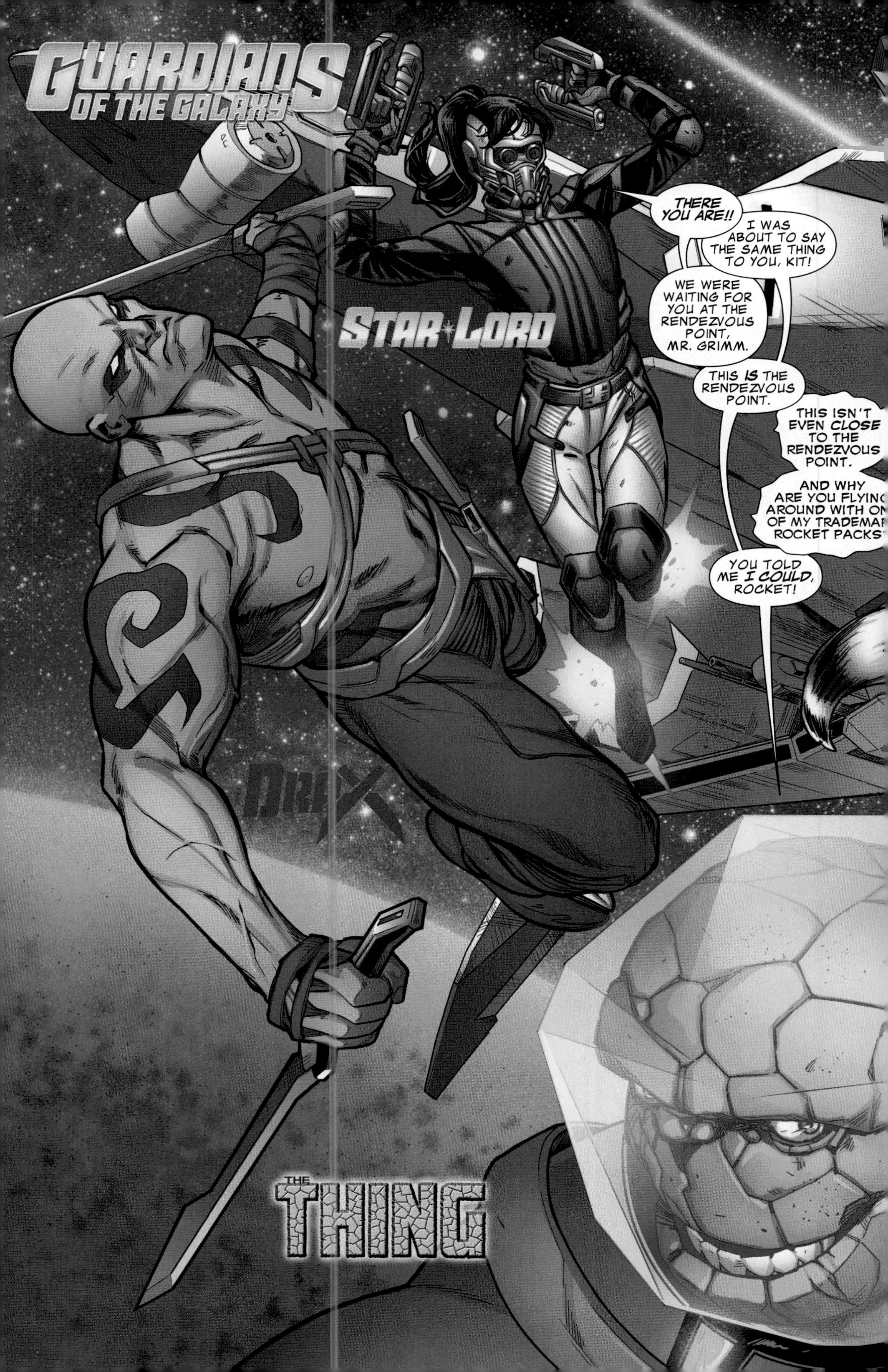
GUARDIANS OF THE GALAXY
STAR-LORD
THERE YOU ARE!!
I WAS ABOUT TO SAY THE SAME THING TO YOU, KIT!
WE WERE WAITING FOR YOU AT THE RENDEZVOUS POINT, MR. GRIMM.
THIS IS THE RENDEZVOUS POINT.
THIS ISN'T EVEN CLOSE TO THE RENDEZVOUS POINT.
YOU TOLD ME I COULD, ROCKET!
DRAX
THE THING

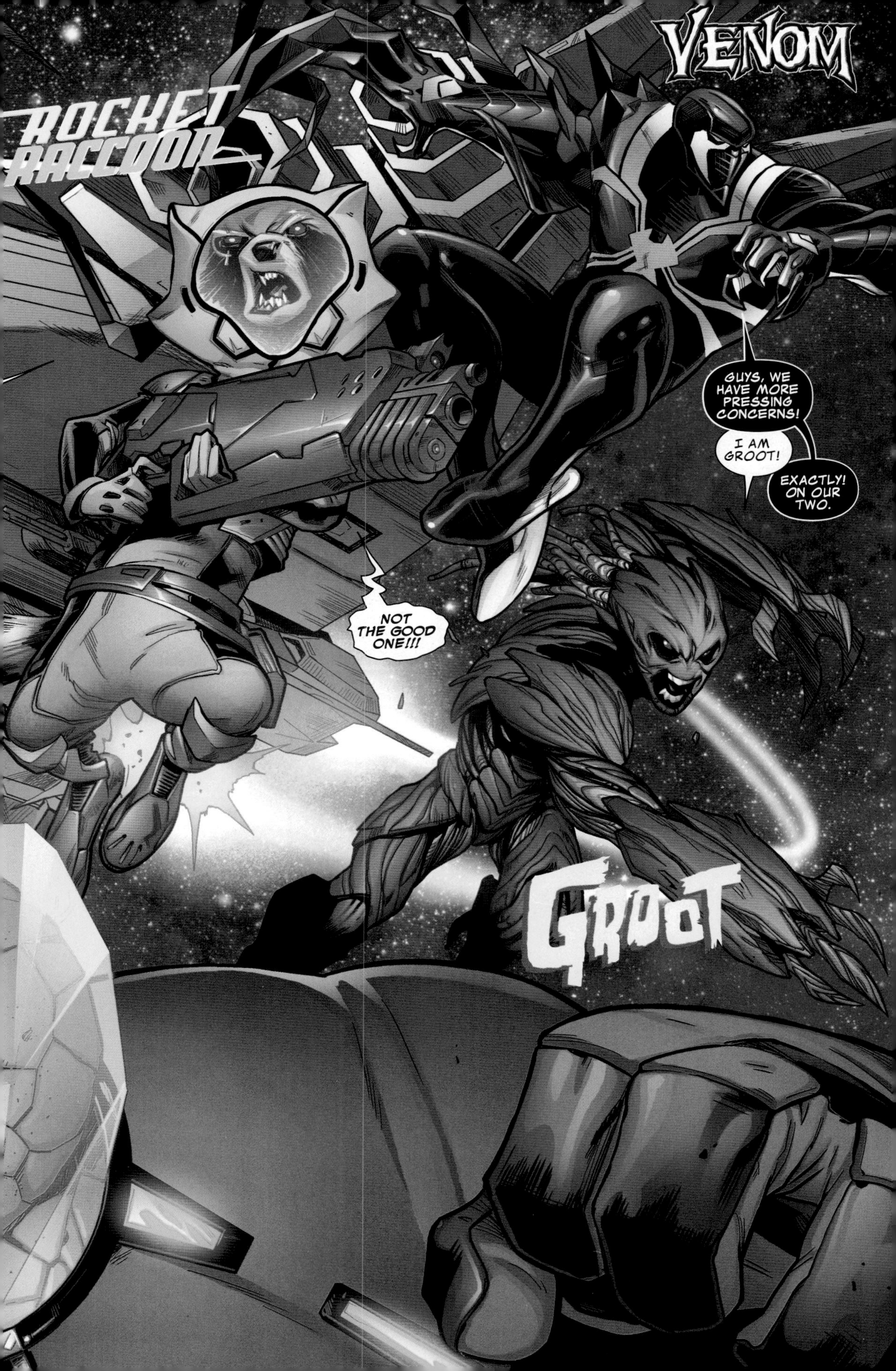
VENOM
ROCKET RACCOON
GUYS, WE HAVE MORE PRESSING CONCERNS!
I AM GROOT!
EXACTLY! ON OUR TWO.
NOT THE GOOD ONE!!!
GROOT

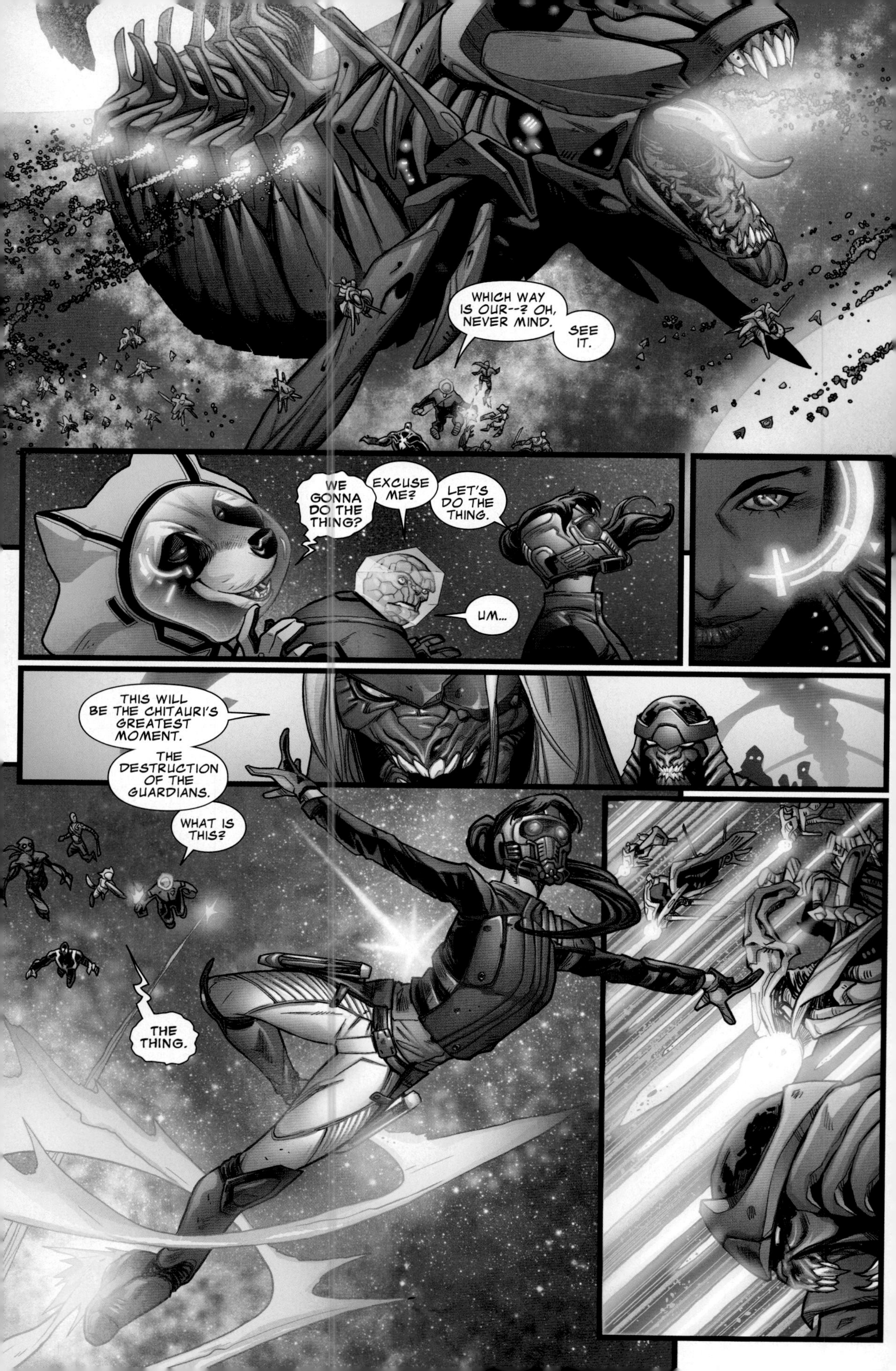
WHICH WAY IS OUR--? OH, NEVER MIND.
SEE IT.
WE GONNA DO THE THING?
EXCUSE ME?
LET'S DO THE THING.
UM...
THIS WILL BE THE CHITAURI'S GREATEST MOMENT.
THE DESTRUCTION OF THE GUARDIANS.
WHAT IS THIS?
THE THING.

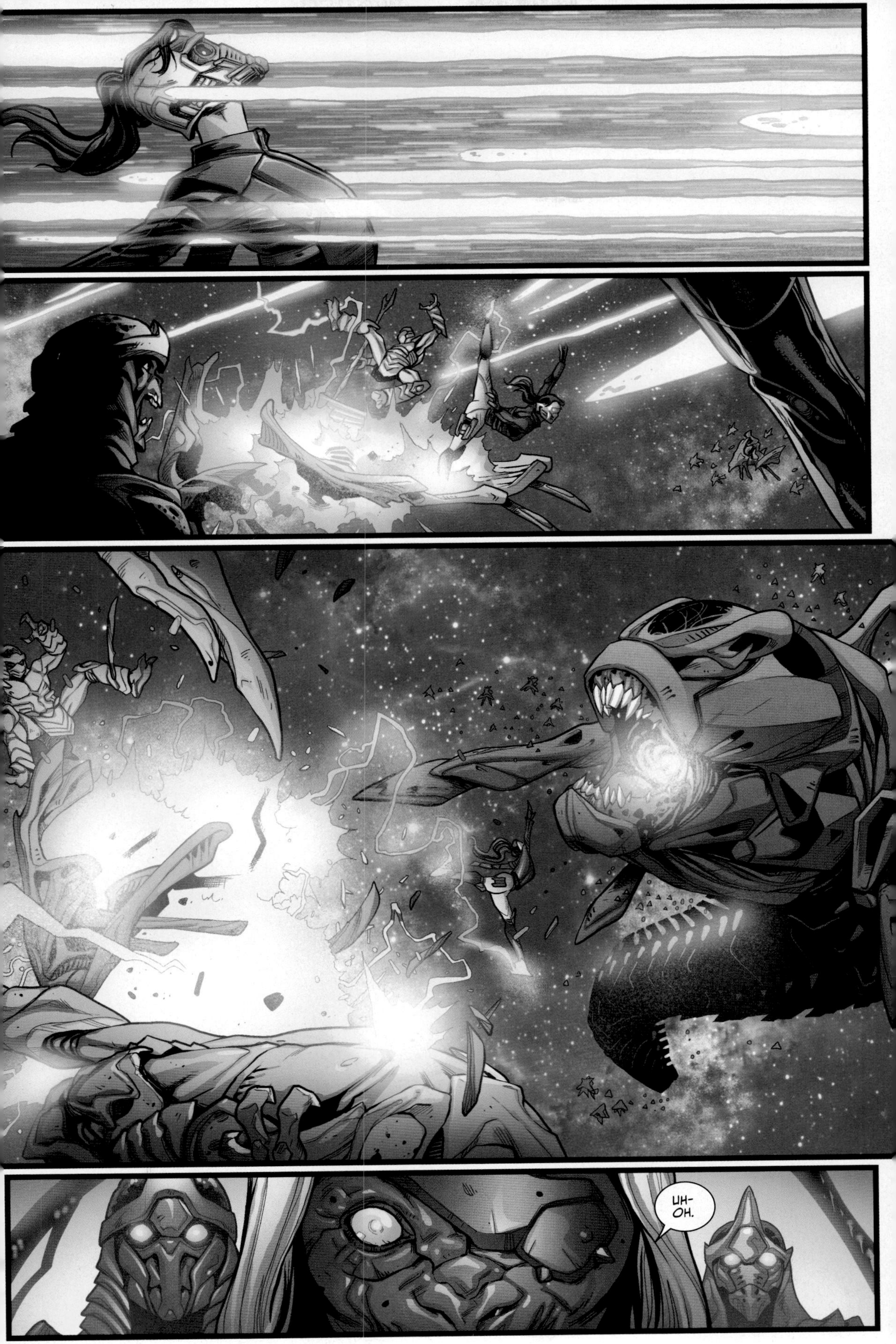
UH-OH.

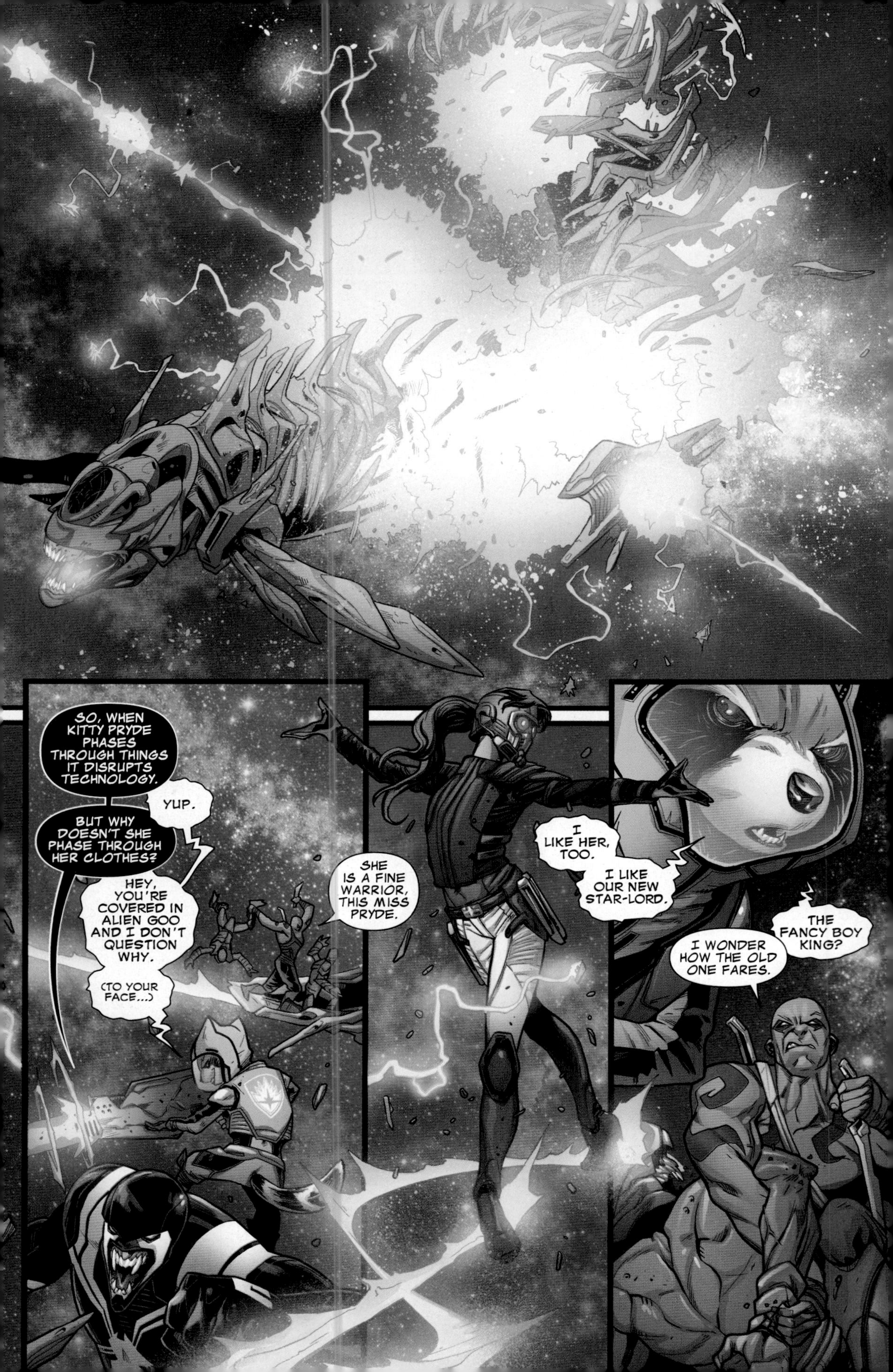
SO, WHEN KITTY PRYDE PHASES THROUGH THINGS IT DISRUPTS TECHNOLOGY.
YUP.
BUT WHY DOESN'T SHE PHASE THROUGH HER CLOTHES?
HEY, YOU'RE COVERED IN ALIEN GOO AND I DON'T QUESTION WHY.
(TO YOUR FACE...)
SHE IS A FINE WARRIOR, THIS MISS PRYDE.
I LIKE HER, TOO.
I LIKE OUR NEW STAR-LORD.
I WONDER HOW THE OLD ONE FARES.
THE FANCY BOY KING?

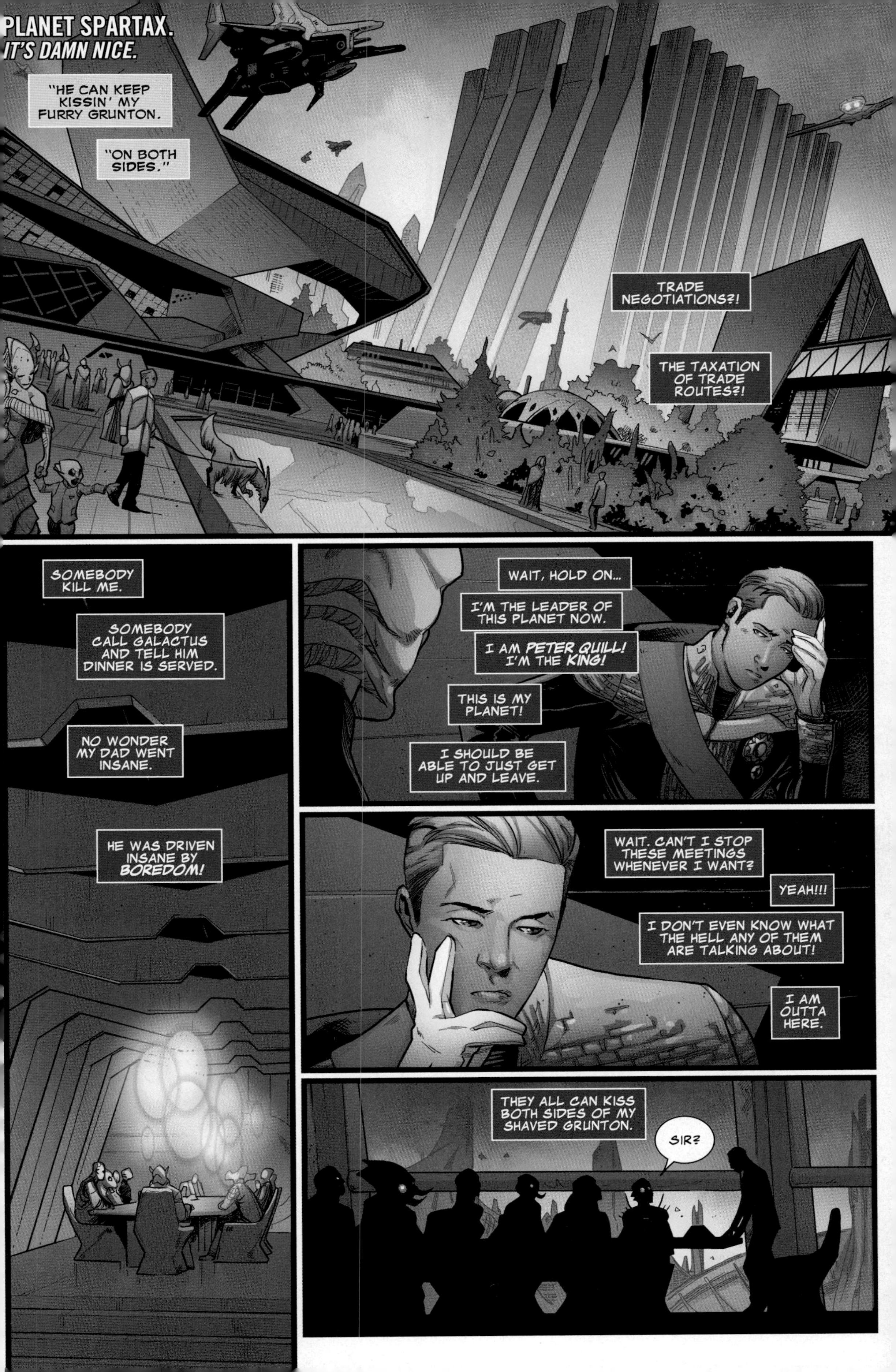

PLANET SPARTAX.
IT'S DAMN NICE.
"HE CAN KEEP KISSIN' MY FURRY GRUNTON.
"ON BOTH SIDES."
TRADE NEGOTIATIONS?!
THE TAXATION OF TRADE ROUTES?!
SOMEBODY KILL ME.
SOMEBODY CALL GALACTUS AND TELL HIM DINNER IS SERVED.
NO WONDER MY DAD WENT INSANE.
HE WAS DRIVEN INSANE BY BOREDOM!
WAIT, HOLD ON...
I'M THE LEADER OF THIS PLANET NOW.
I AM PETER QUILL! I'M THE KING!
THIS IS MY PLANET!
I SHOULD BE ABLE TO JUST GET UP AND LEAVE.
WAIT. CAN'T I STOP THESE MEETINGS WHENEVER I WANT?
YEAH!!!
I DON'T EVEN KNOW WHAT THE HELL ANY OF THEM ARE TALKING ABOUT!
I AM OUTTA HERE.
THEY ALL CAN KISS BOTH SIDES OF MY SHAVED GRUNTON.
SIR?

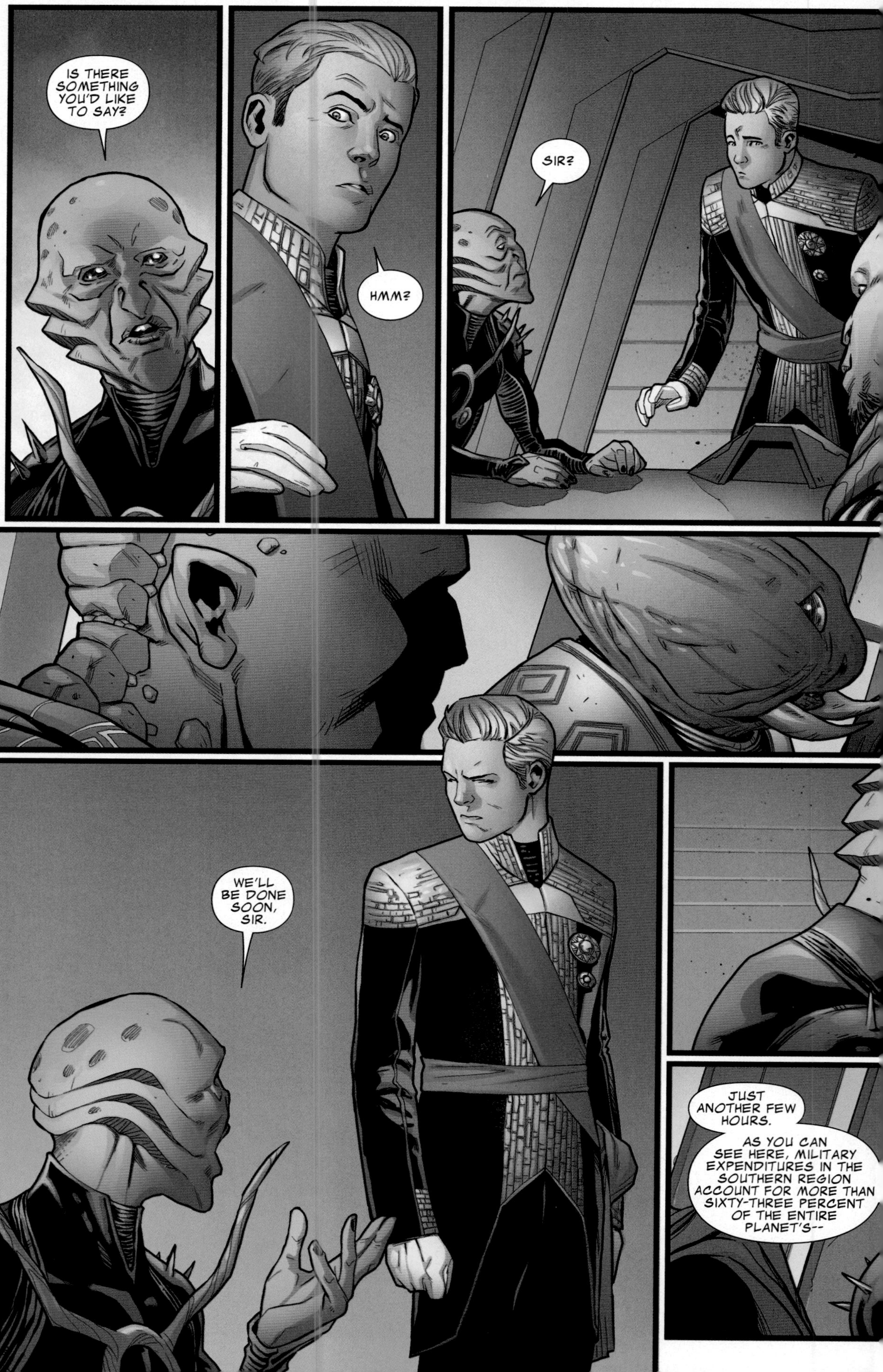
IS THERE SOMETHING YOU'D LIKE TO SAY?
HMM?
SIR?
WE'LL BE DONE SOON, SIR.
JUST ANOTHER FEW HOURS.
AS YOU CAN SEE HERE, MILITARY EXPENDITURES IN THE SOUTHERN REGION ACCOUNT FOR MORE THAN SIXTY-THREE PERCENT OF THE ENTIRE PLANET'S--

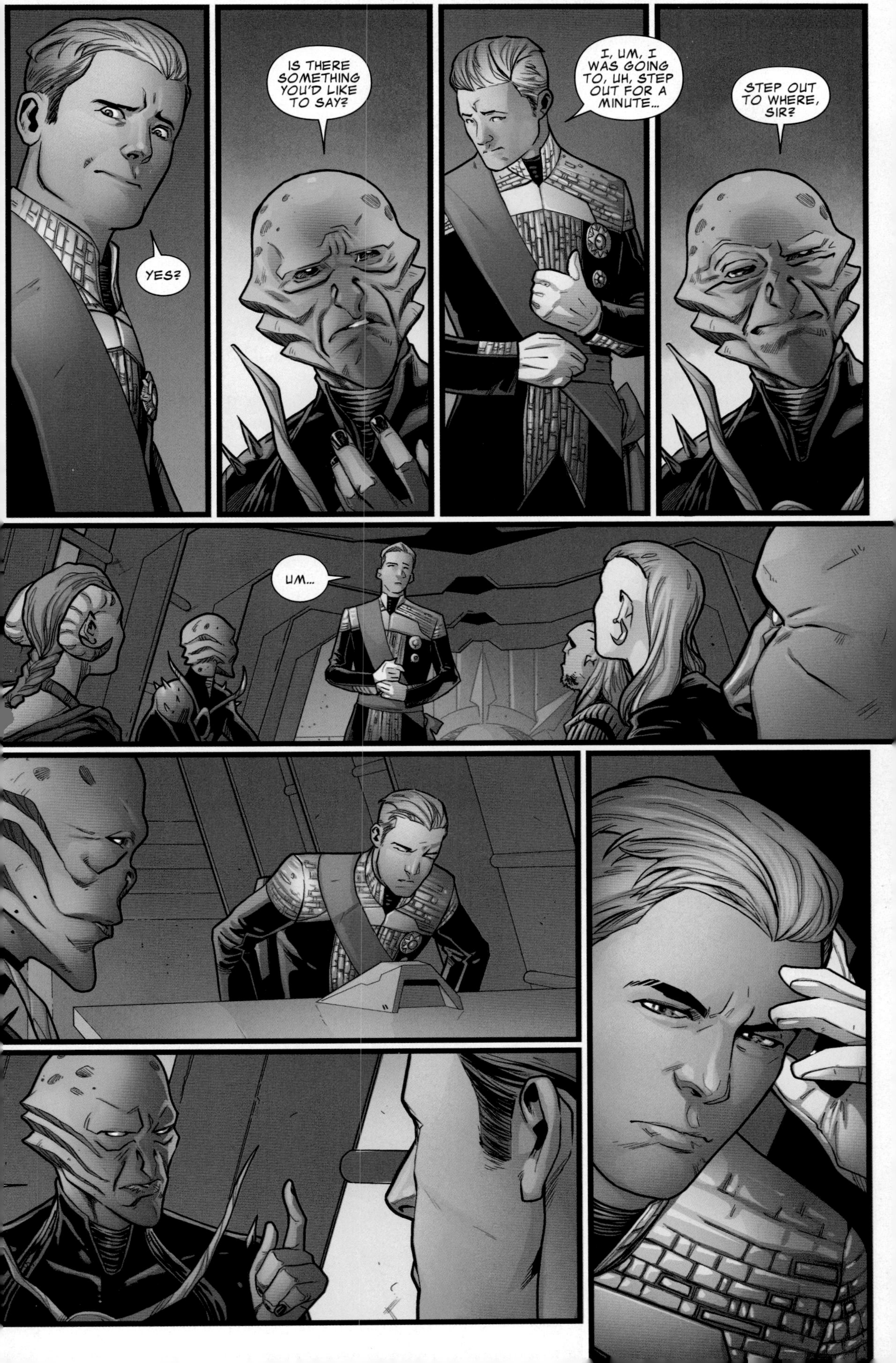
YES?
IS THERE SOMETHING YOU'D LIKE TO SAY?
I, UM, I WAS GOING TO, UH, STEP OUT FOR A MINUTE...
STEP OUT TO WHERE, SIR?
UM...

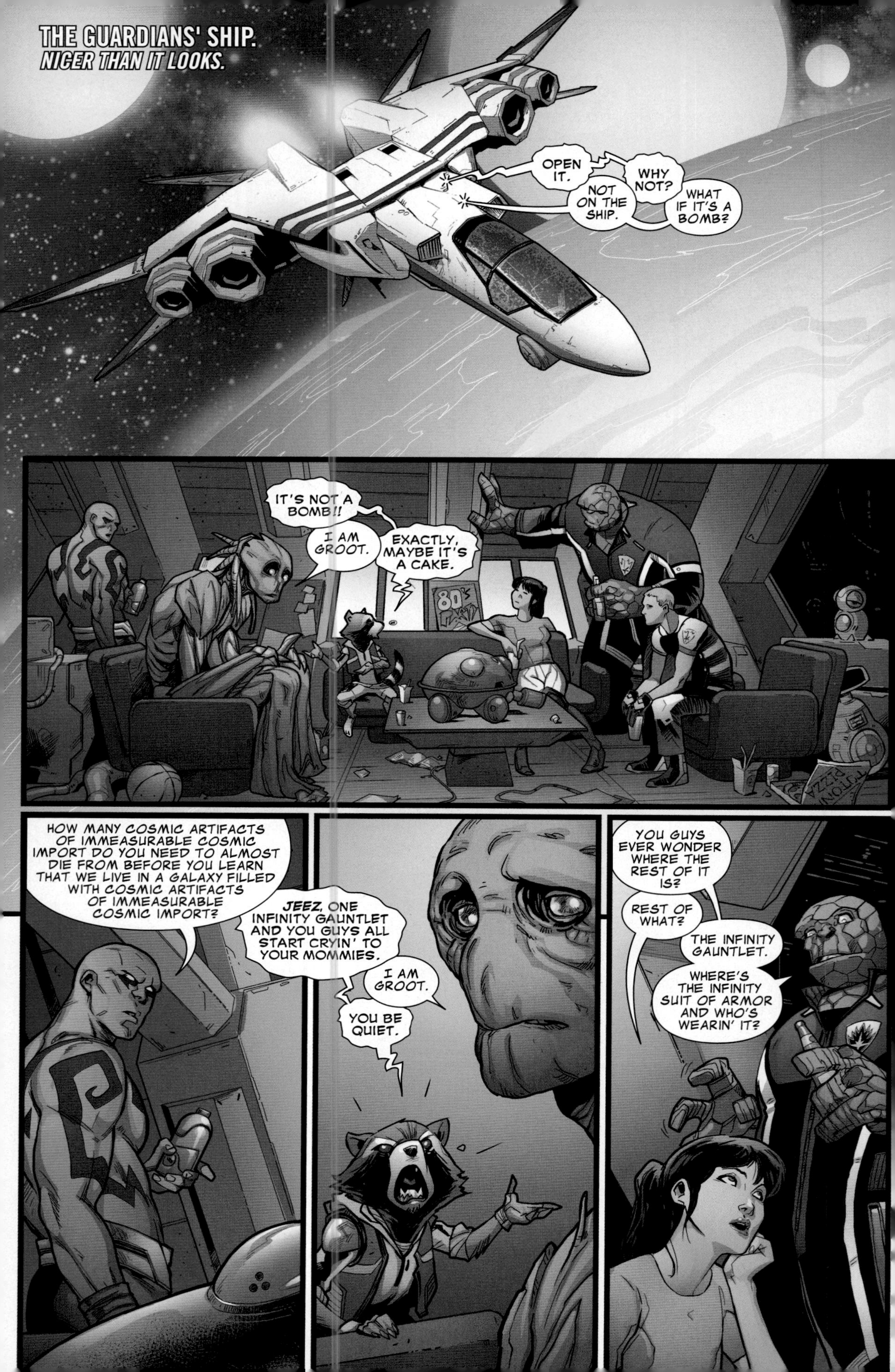
THE GUARDIANS' SHIP.
NICER THAN IT LOOKS.
OPEN IT.
WHY NOT?
NOT ON THE SHIP.
WHAT IF IT'S A BOMB?
IT'S NOT A BOMB!!
I AM GROOT.
EXACTLY, MAYBE IT'S A CAKE.
80's
HOW MANY COSMIC ARTIFACTS OF IMMEASURABLE COSMIC IMPORT DO YOU NEED TO ALMOST DIE FROM BEFORE YOU LEARN THAT WE LIVE IN A GALAXY FILLED WITH COSMIC ARTIFACTS OF IMMEASURABLE COSMIC IMPORT?
JEEZ, ONE INFINITY GAUNTLET AND YOU GUYS ALL START CRYIN' TO YOUR MOMMIES.
I AM GROOT.
YOU BE QUIET.
YOU GUYS EVER WONDER WHERE THE REST OF IT IS?
REST OF WHAT?
THE INFINITY GAUNTLET.
WHERE'S THE INFINITY SUIT OF ARMOR AND WHO'S WEARIN' IT?

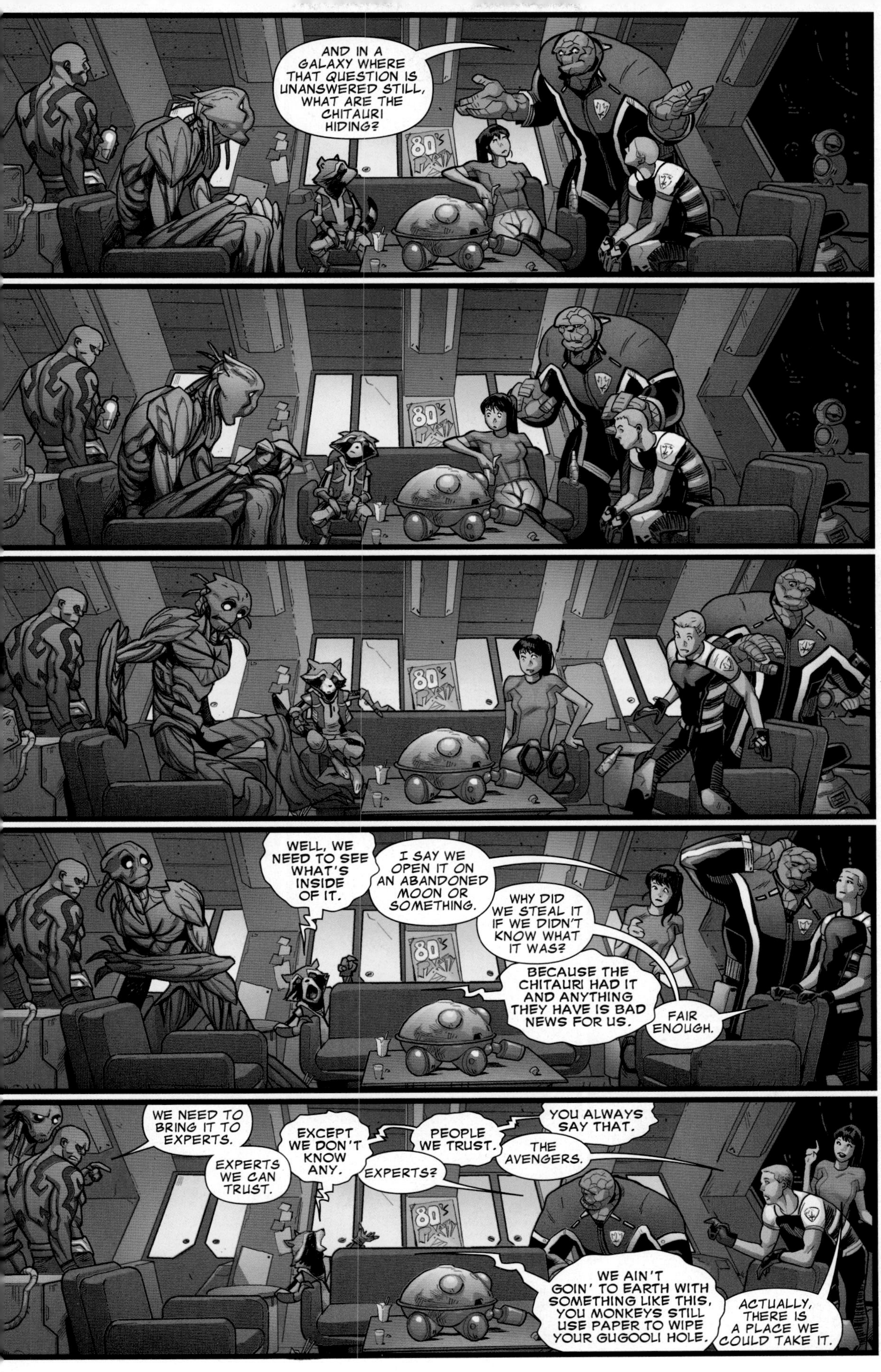
AND IN A GALAXY WHERE THAT QUESTION IS UNANSWERED STILL, WHAT ARE THE CHITAURI HIDING?
80's
WELL, WE NEED TO SEE WHAT'S INSIDE OF IT.
I SAY WE OPEN IT ON AN ABANDONED MOON OR SOMETHING.
WHY DID WE STEAL IT IF WE DIDN'T KNOW WHAT IT WAS?
BECAUSE THE CHITAURI HAD IT AND ANYTHING THEY HAVE IS BAD NEWS FOR US.
FAIR ENOUGH.
WE NEED TO BRING IT TO EXPERTS.
EXPERTS WE CAN TRUST.
EXCEPT WE DON'T KNOW ANY.
PEOPLE WE TRUST.
YOU ALWAYS SAY THAT.
EXPERTS?
THE AVENGERS.
WE AIN'T GOIN' TO EARTH WITH SOMETHING LIKE THIS, YOU MONKEYS STILL USE PAPER TO WIPE YOUR GUGOOLI HOLE.
ACTUALLY, THERE IS A PLACE WE COULD TAKE IT.

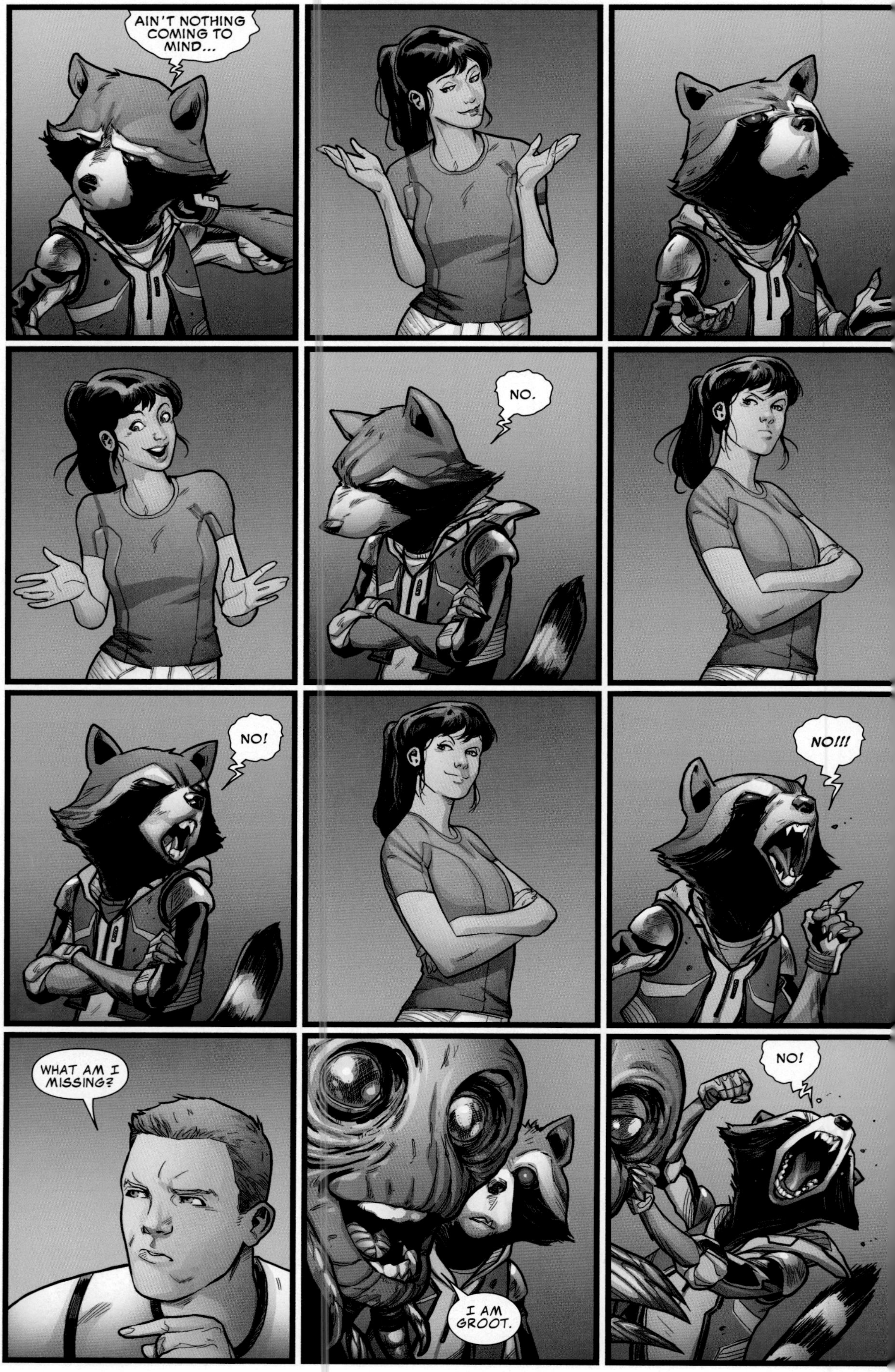
AIN'T NOTHING COMING TO MIND...
NO.
NO!
NO!!!
WHAT AM I MISSING?
I AM GROOT.
NO!

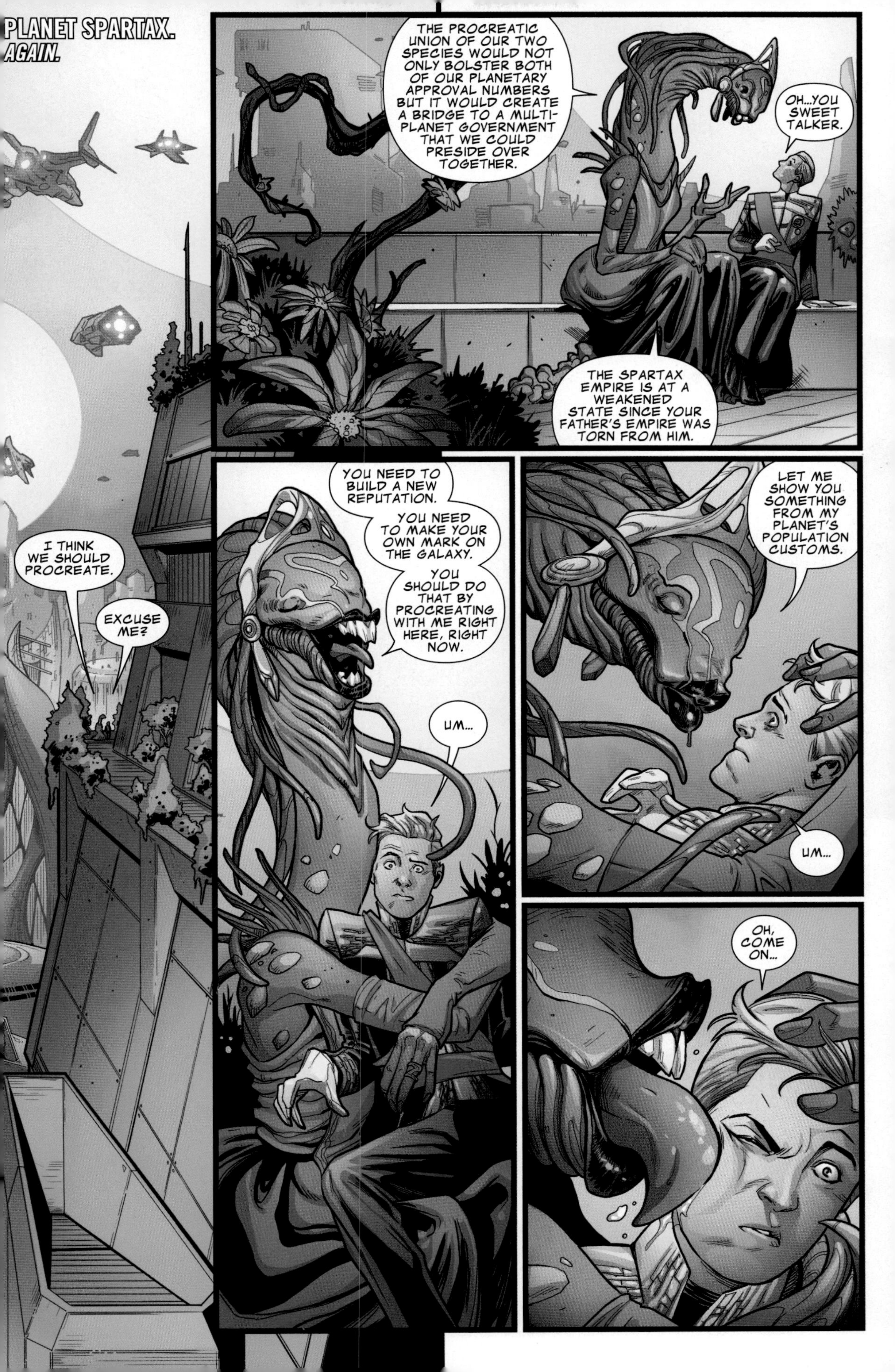
PLANET SPARTAX.
AGAIN.
THE PROCREATIC UNION OF OUR TWO SPECIES WOULD NOT ONLY BOLSTER BOTH OF OUR PLANETARY APPROVAL NUMBERS BUT IT WOULD CREATE A BRIDGE TO A MULTI-PLANET GOVERNMENT THAT WE COULD PRESIDE OVER TOGETHER.
OH...YOU SWEET TALKER.
THE SPARTAX EMPIRE IS AT A WEAKENED STATE SINCE YOUR FATHER'S EMPIRE WAS TORN FROM HIM.
I THINK WE SHOULD PROCREATE.
EXCUSE ME?
YOU NEED TO BUILD A NEW REPUTATION.
YOU NEED TO MAKE YOUR OWN MARK ON THE GALAXY.
YOU SHOULD DO THAT BY PROCREATING WITH ME RIGHT HERE, RIGHT NOW.
UM...
LET ME SHOW YOU SOMETHING FROM MY PLANET'S POPULATION CUSTOMS.
UM...
OH, COME ON...

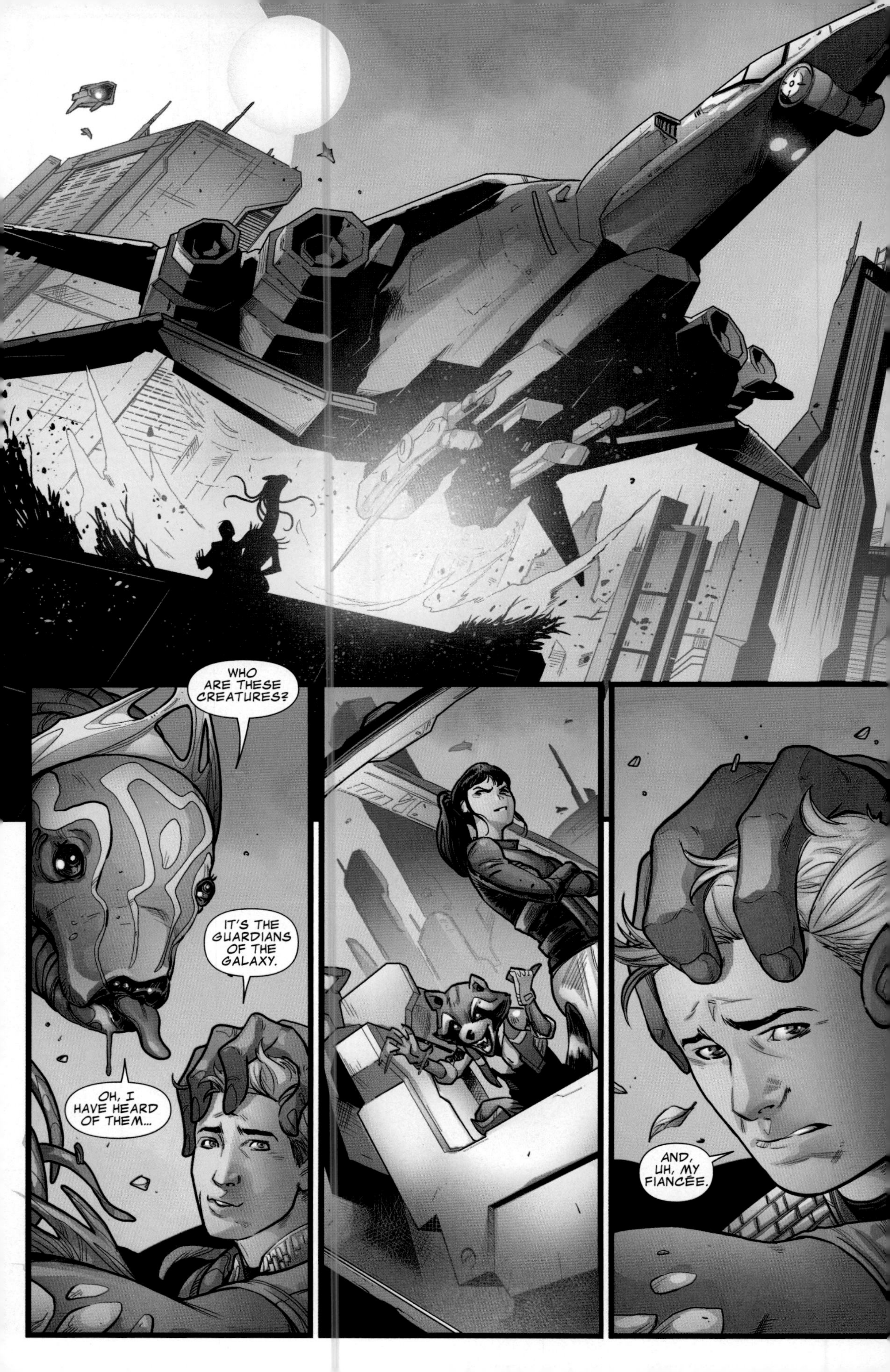
WHO ARE THESE CREATURES?
IT'S THE GUARDIANS OF THE GALAXY.
OH, I HAVE HEARD OF THEM...
AND, UH, MY FIANCÉE.

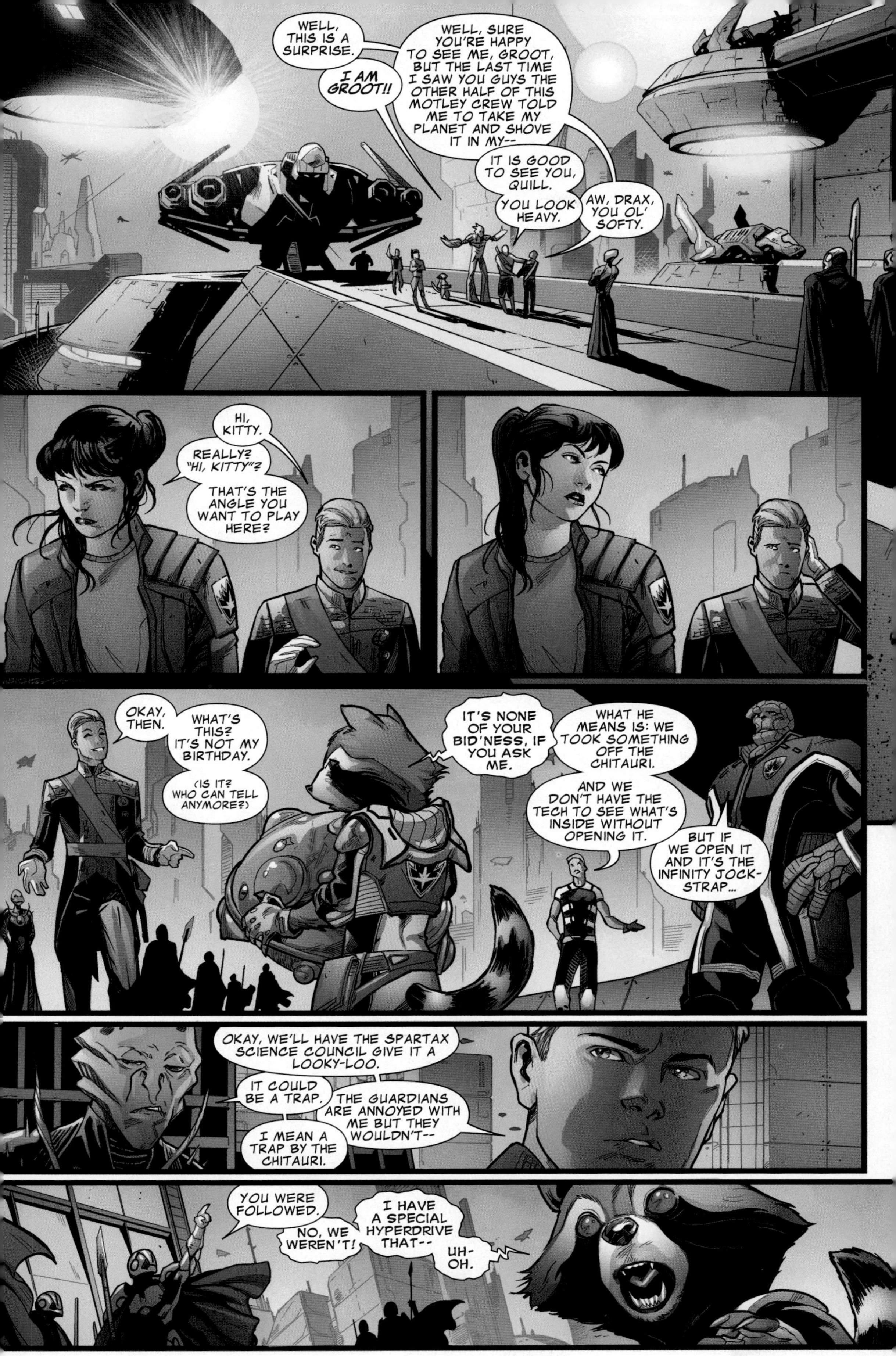
WELL, THIS IS A SURPRISE.
I AM GROOT!!
WELL, SURE YOU'RE HAPPY TO SEE ME, GROOT, BUT THE LAST TIME I SAW YOU GUYS THE OTHER HALF OF THIS MOTLEY CREW TOLD ME TO TAKE MY PLANET AND SHOVE IT IN MY--
IT IS GOOD TO SEE YOU, QUILL.
YOU LOOK HEAVY.
AW, DRAX, YOU OL' SOFTY.
HI, KITTY.
REALLY? "HI, KITTY"?
THAT'S THE ANGLE YOU WANT TO PLAY HERE?
OKAY, THEN.
WHAT'S THIS? IT'S NOT MY BIRTHDAY.
(IS IT? WHO CAN TELL ANYMORE?)
IT'S NONE OF YOUR BID'NESS, IF YOU ASK ME.
WHAT HE MEANS IS: WE TOOK SOMETHING OFF THE CHITAURI.
AND WE DON'T HAVE THE TECH TO SEE WHAT'S INSIDE WITHOUT OPENING IT.
BUT IF WE OPEN IT AND IT'S THE INFINITY JOCK-STRAP...
OKAY, WE'LL HAVE THE SPARTAX SCIENCE COUNCIL GIVE IT A LOOKY-LOO.
IT COULD BE A TRAP.
THE GUARDIANS ARE ANNOYED WITH ME BUT THEY WOULDN'T--
I MEAN A TRAP BY THE CHITAURI.
YOU WERE FOLLOWED.
NO, WE WEREN'T!
I HAVE A SPECIAL HYPERDRIVE THAT--
UH-OH.

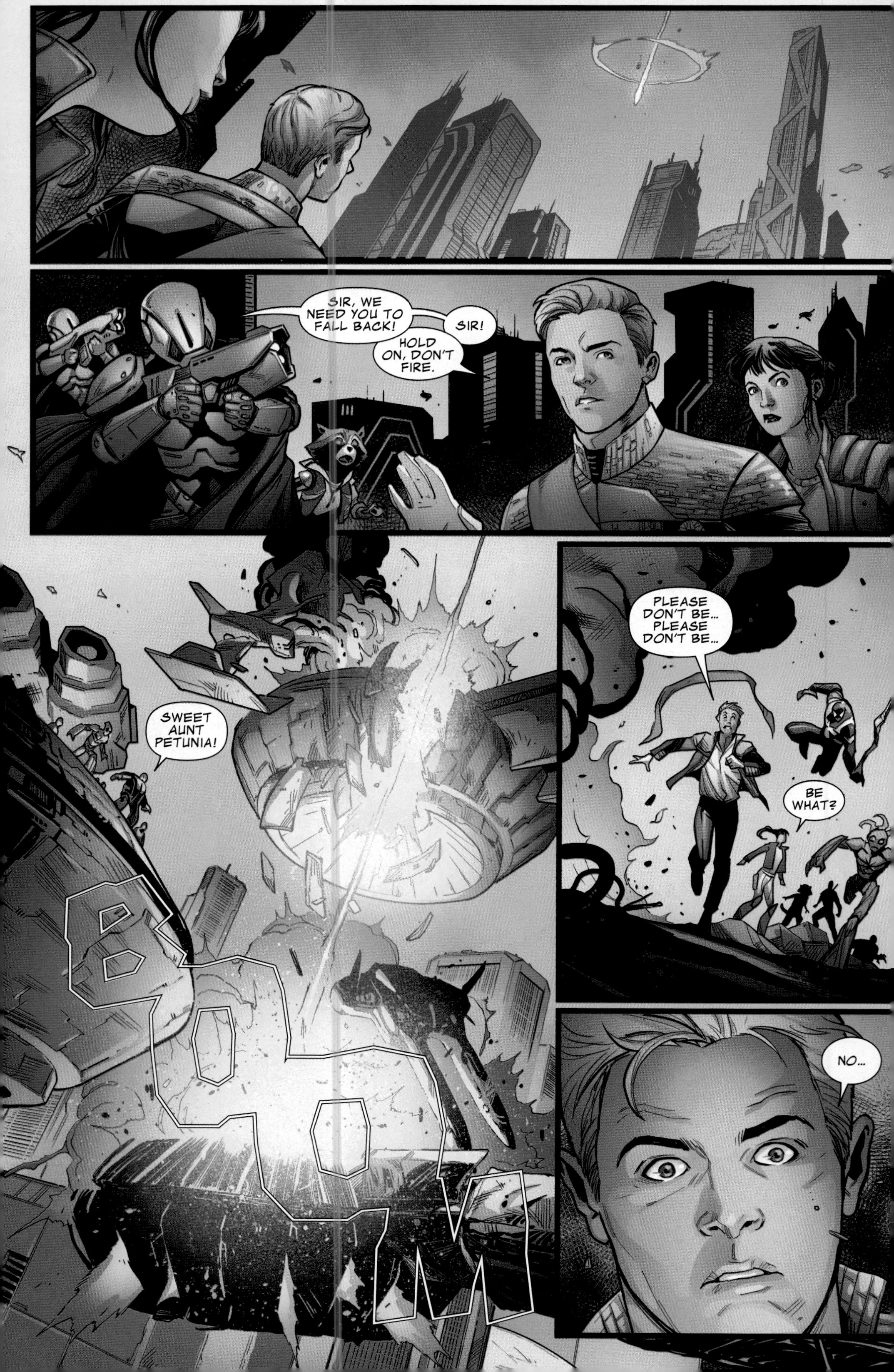
SIR, WE NEED YOU TO FALL BACK!
SIR!
HOLD ON, DON'T FIRE.
SWEET AUNT PETUNIA!
BOOM
PLEASE DON'T BE... PLEASE DON'T BE...
BE WHAT?
NO...

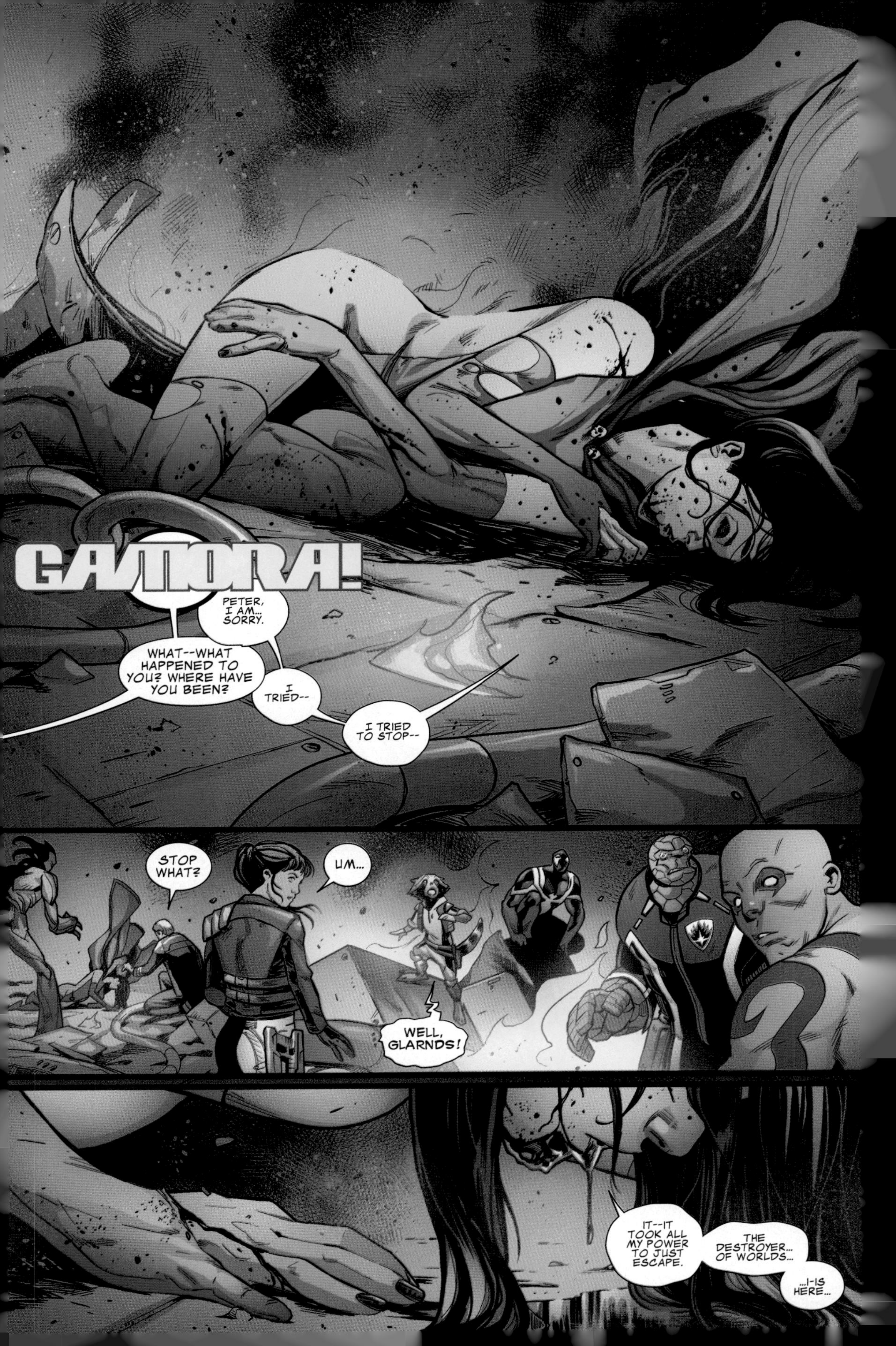
GAMORA!
WHAT--WHAT HAPPENED TO YOU? WHERE HAVE YOU BEEN?
PETER, I AM... SORRY.
I TRIED--
I TRIED TO STOP--
STOP WHAT?
UM...
WELL, GLARNDS!
IT--IT TOOK ALL MY POWER TO JUST ESCAPE.
THE DESTROYER... OF WORLDS...
...I-IS HERE...

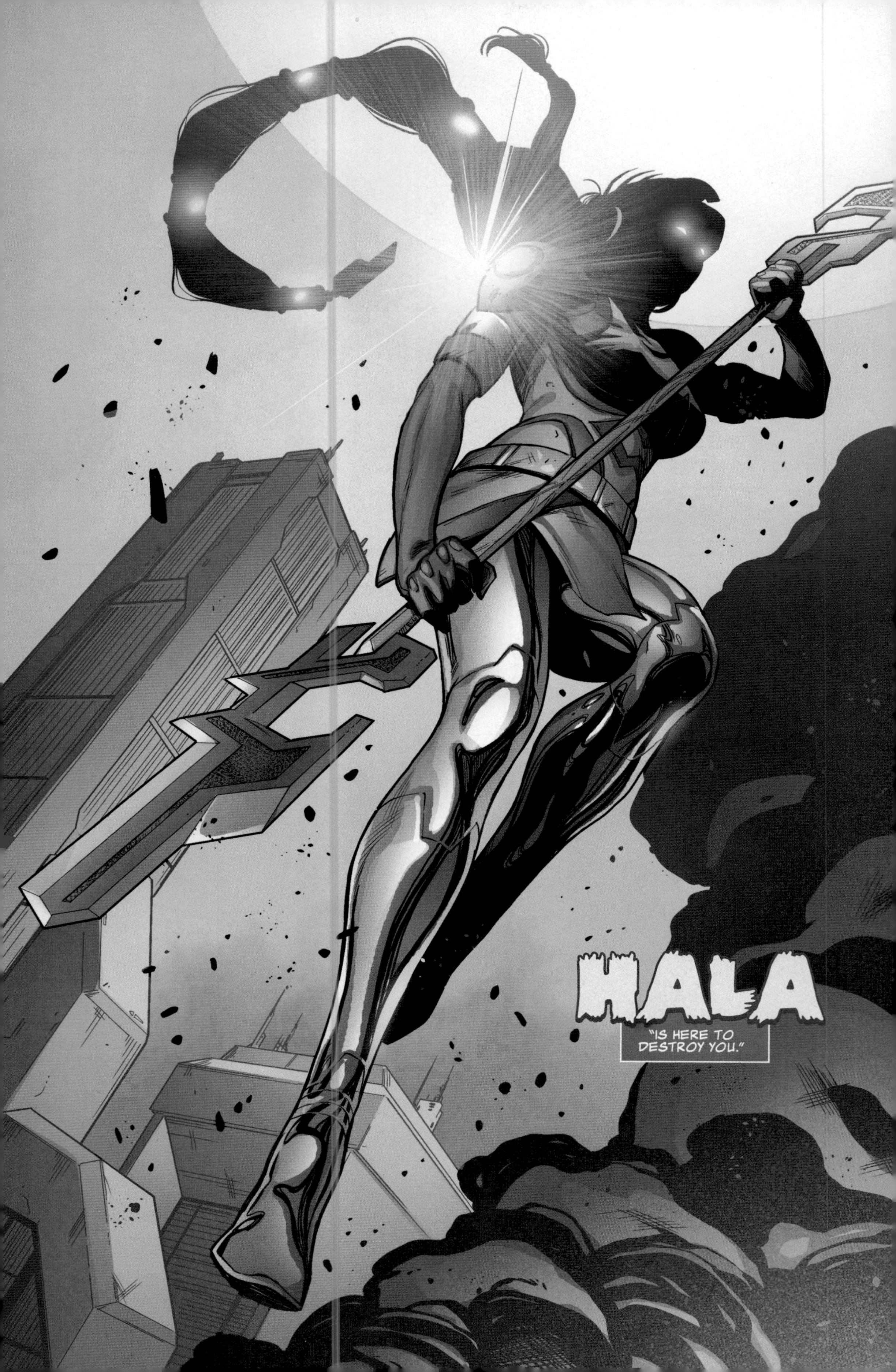
HALA
"IS HERE TO DESTROY YOU."

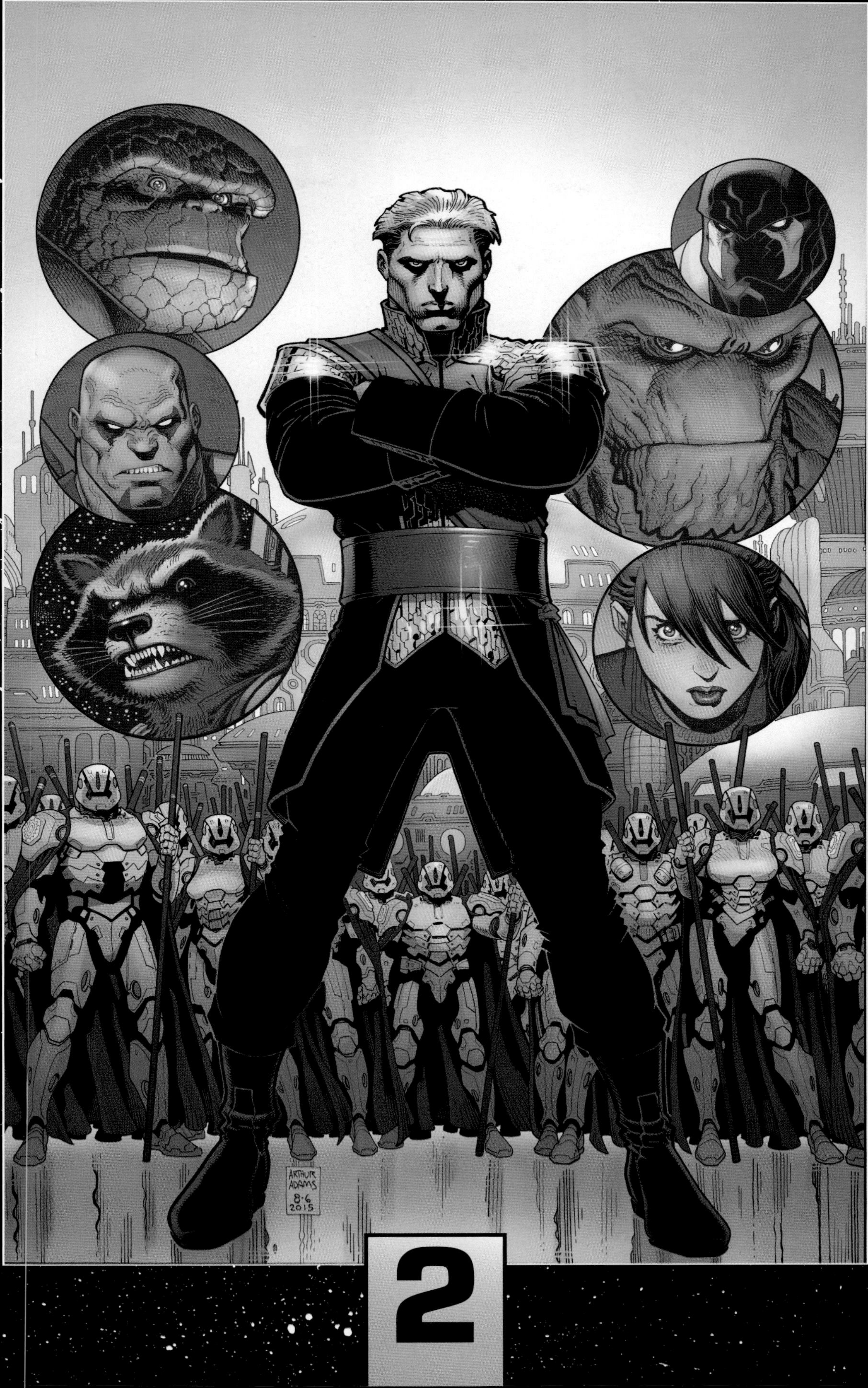
ARTHUR ADAMS 8·6 2015
2

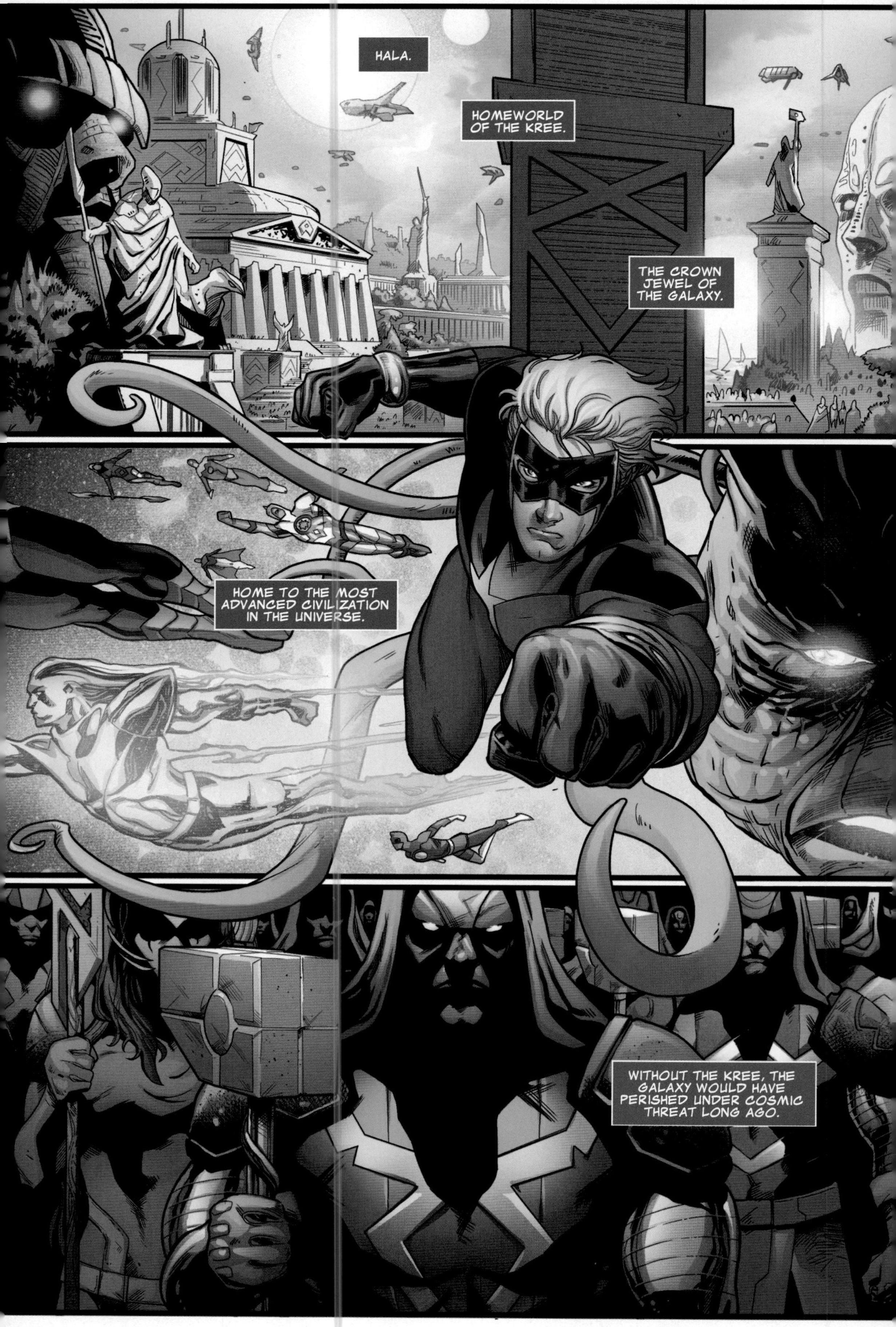
HALA.
HOMEWORLD OF THE KREE.
THE CROWN JEWEL OF THE GALAXY.
HOME TO THE MOST ADVANCED CIVILIZATION IN THE UNIVERSE.
WITHOUT THE KREE, THE GALAXY WOULD HAVE PERISHED UNDER COSMIC THREAT LONG AGO.

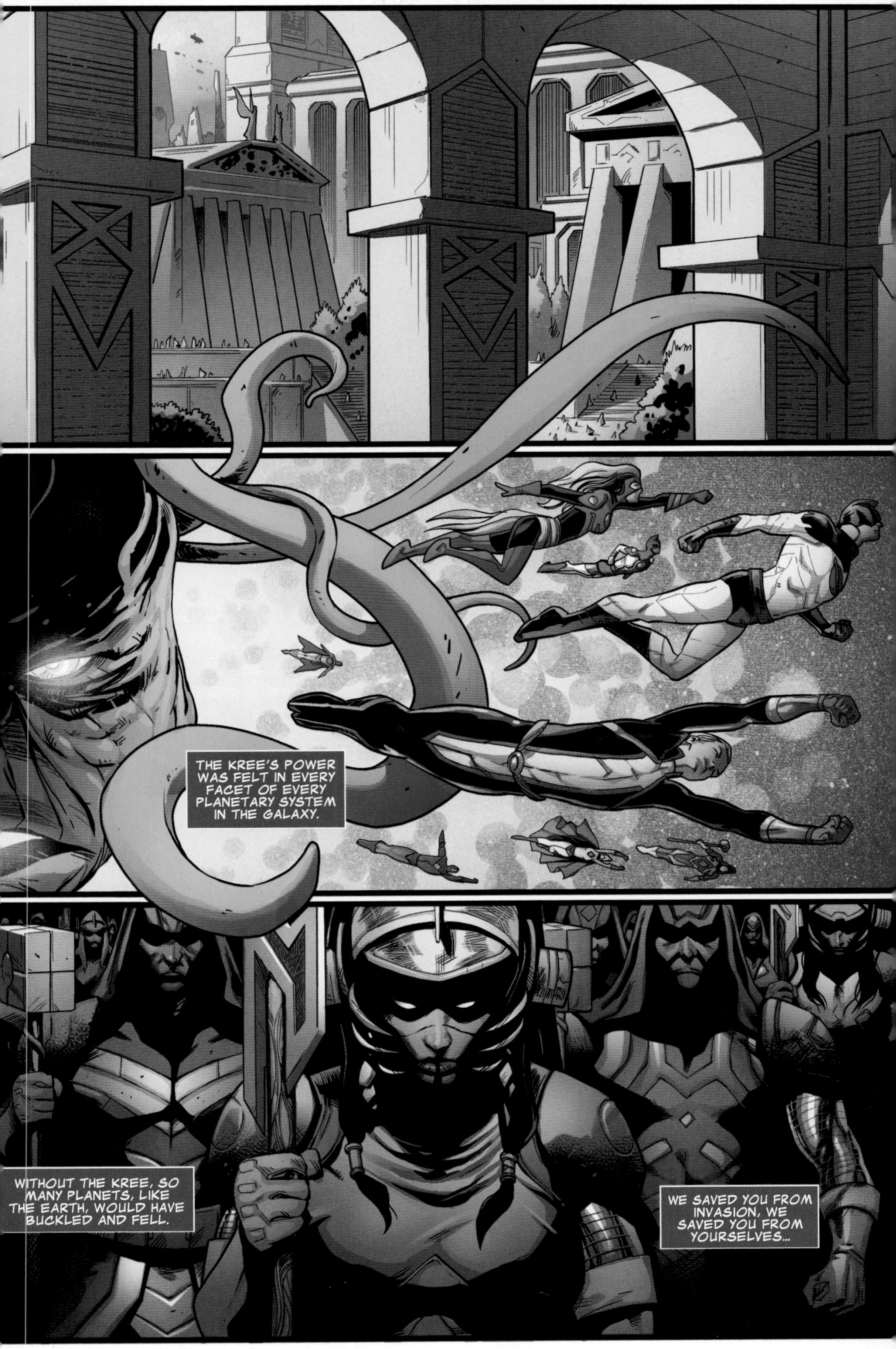
THE KREE'S POWER WAS FELT IN EVERY FACET OF EVERY PLANETARY SYSTEM IN THE GALAXY.
WITHOUT THE KREE, SO MANY PLANETS, LIKE THE EARTH, WOULD HAVE BUCKLED AND FELL.
WE SAVED YOU FROM INVASION, WE SAVED YOU FROM YOURSELVES...

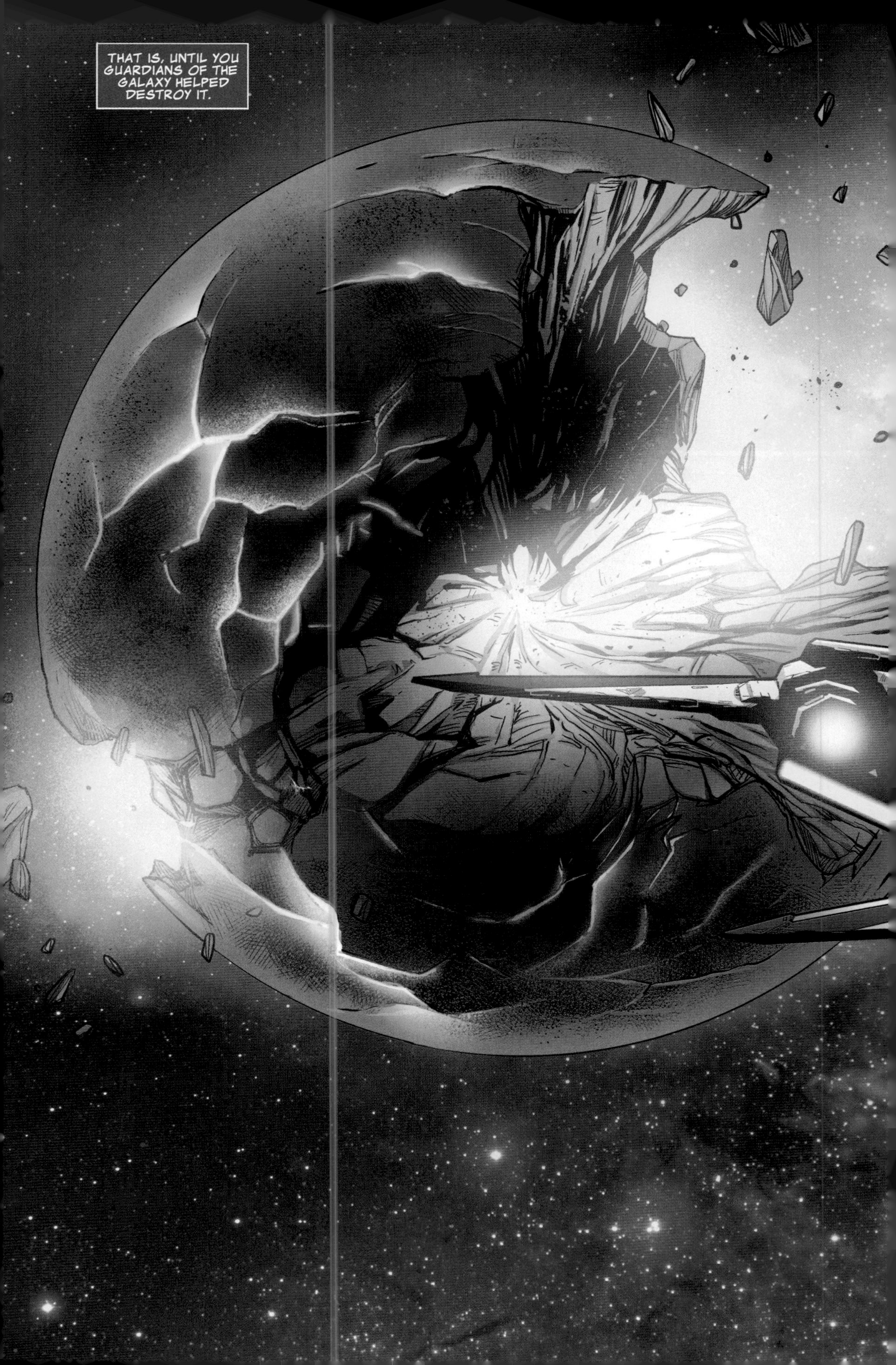
THAT IS, UNTIL YOU GUARDIANS OF THE GALAXY HELPED DESTROY IT.

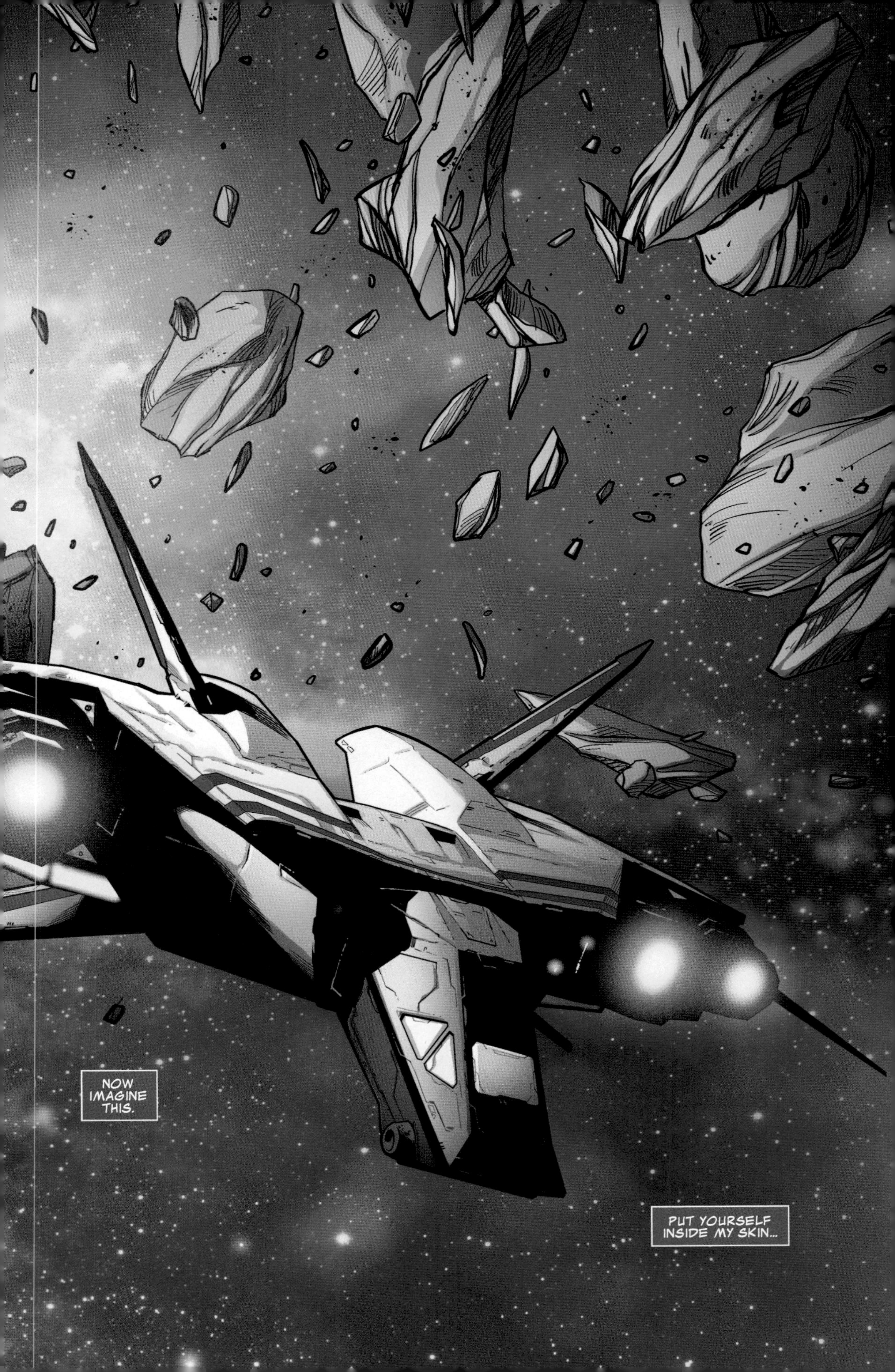
NOW IMAGINE THIS.
PUT YOURSELF INSIDE MY SKIN...

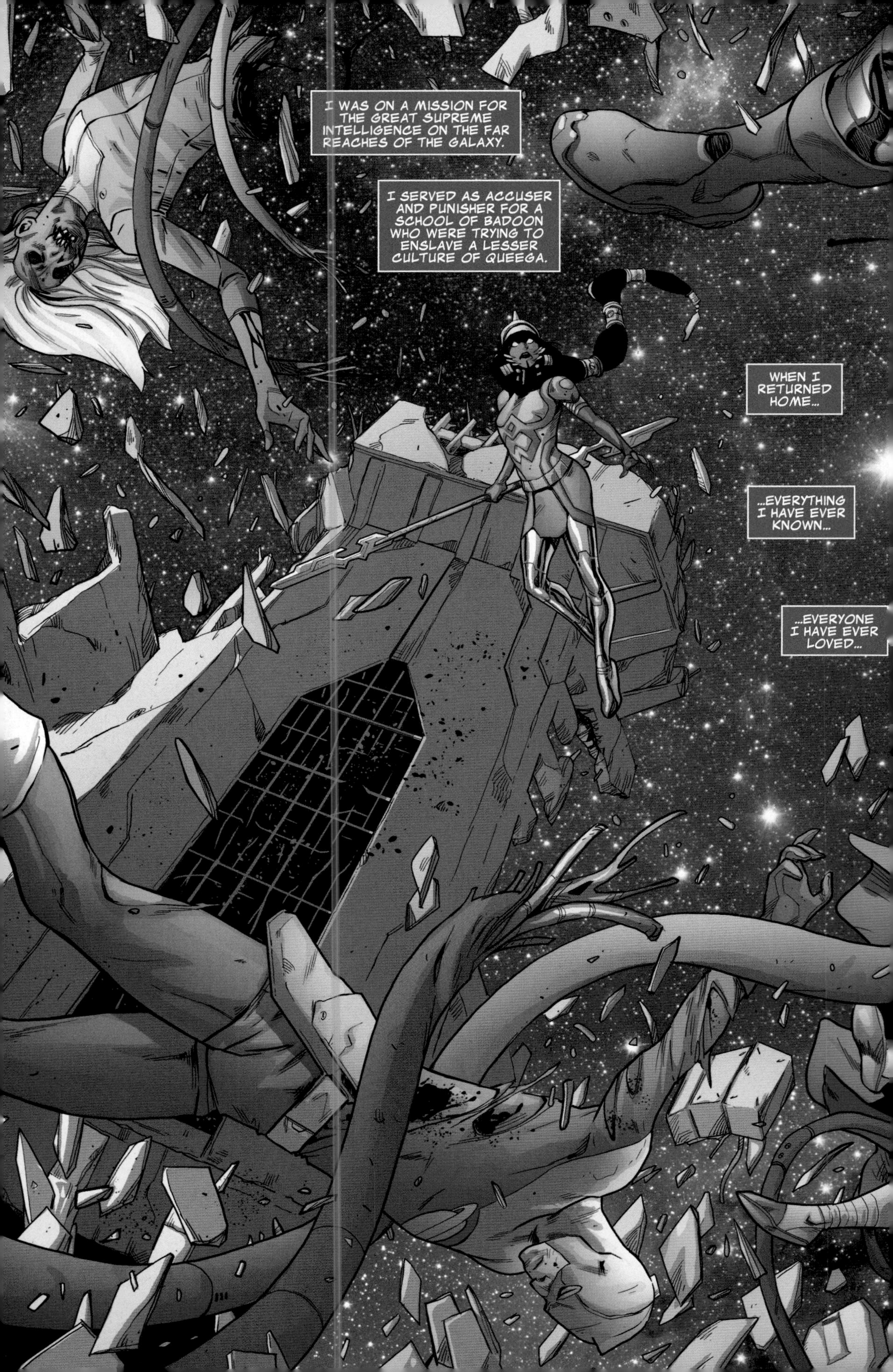
I WAS ON A MISSION FOR THE GREAT SUPREME INTELLIGENCE ON THE FAR REACHES OF THE GALAXY.
I SERVED AS ACCUSER AND PUNISHER FOR A SCHOOL OF BADOON WHO WERE TRYING TO ENSLAVE A LESSER CULTURE OF QUEEGA.
WHEN I RETURNED HOME...
...EVERYTHING I HAVE EVER KNOWN...
...EVERYONE I HAVE EVER LOVED...

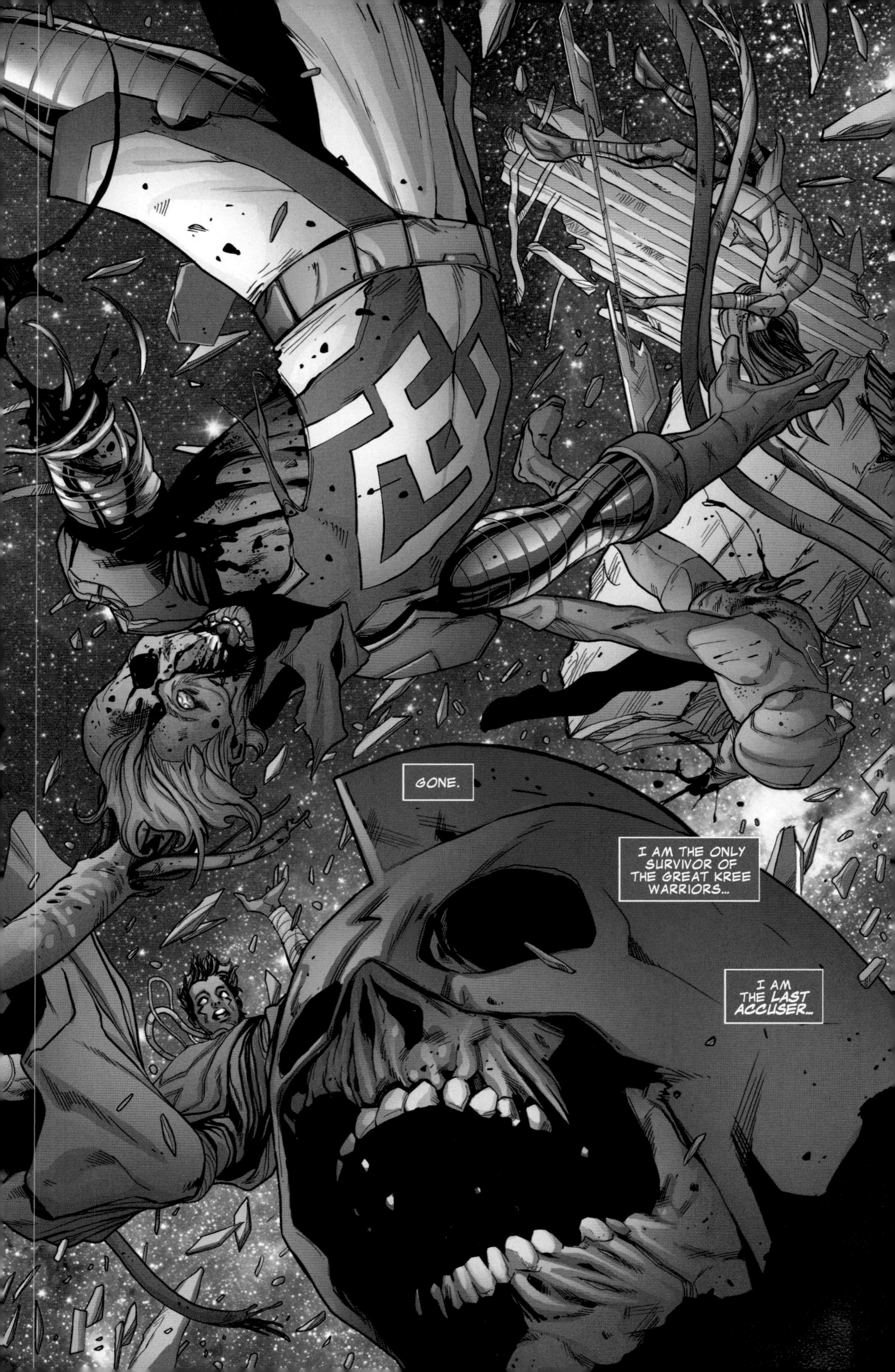
GONE.
I AM THE ONLY SURVIVOR OF THE GREAT KREE WARRIORS...
I AM THE LAST ACCUSER...

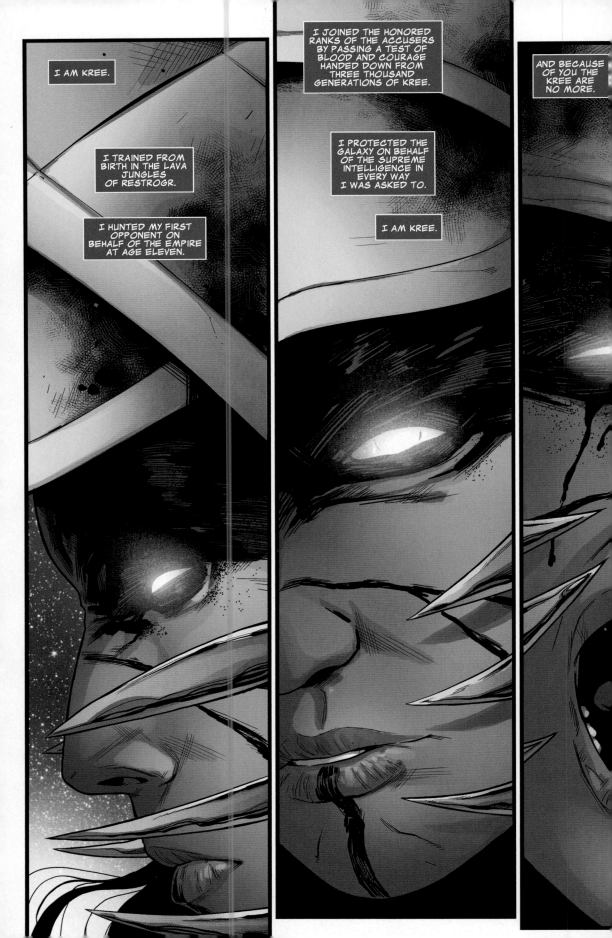

I AM KREE.

I TRAINED FROM BIRTH IN THE LAVA JUNGLES OF RESTROGR.

I HUNTED MY FIRST OPPONENT ON BEHALF OF THE EMPIRE AT AGE ELEVEN.

I JOINED THE HONORED RANKS OF THE ACCUSERS BY PASSING A TEST OF BLOOD AND COURAGE HANDED DOWN FROM THREE THOUSAND GENERATIONS OF KREE.

I PROTECTED THE GALAXY ON BEHALF OF THE SUPREME INTELLIGENCE IN EVERY WAY I WAS ASKED TO.

I AM KREE.

AND BECAUSE OF YOU THE KREE ARE NO MORE.

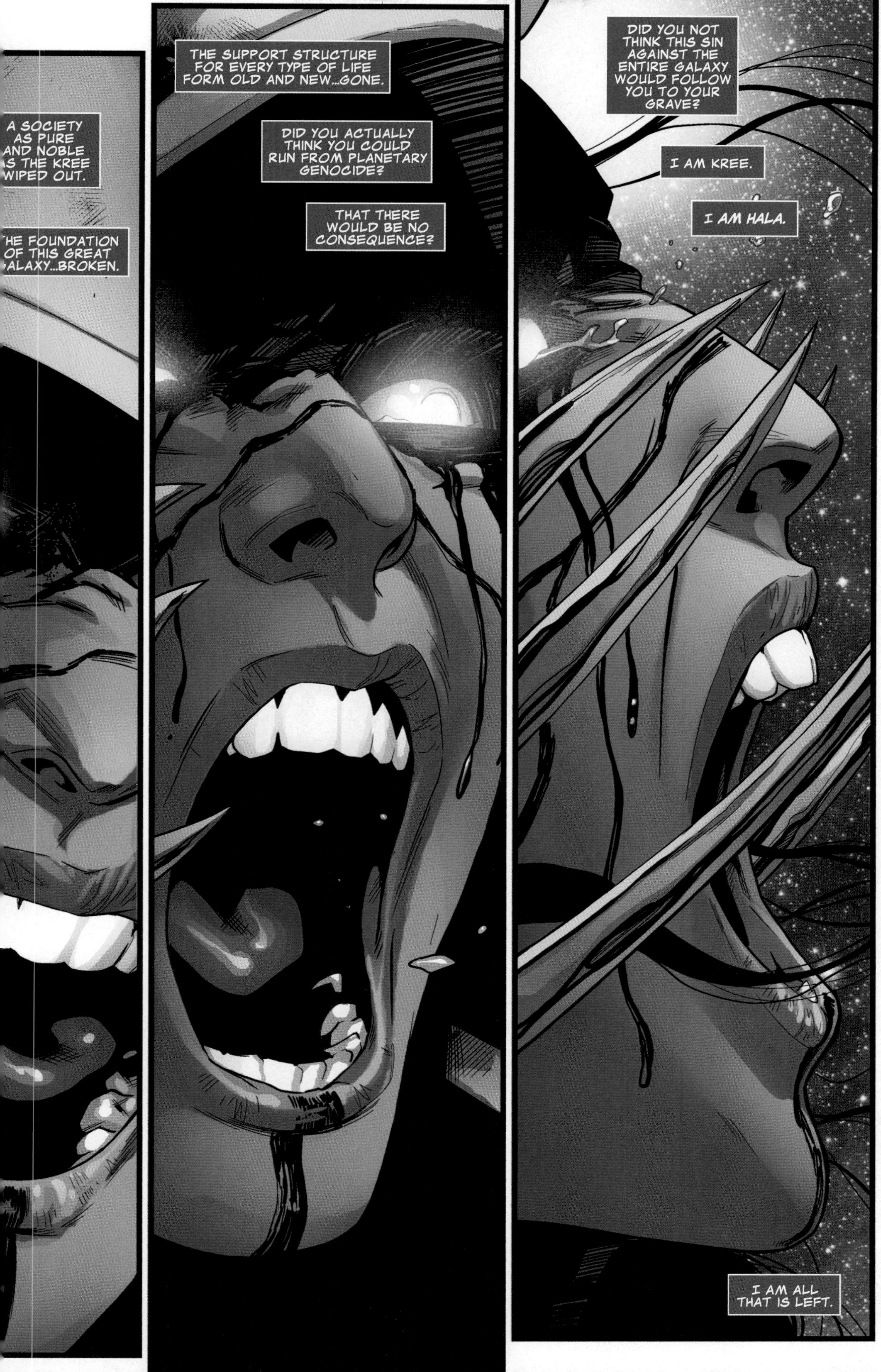
A SOCIETY AS PURE AND NOBLE S THE KREE WIPED OUT.
HE FOUNDATION OF THIS GREAT ALAXY...BROKEN.
THE SUPPORT STRUCTURE FOR EVERY TYPE OF LIFE FORM OLD AND NEW...GONE.
DID YOU ACTUALLY THINK YOU COULD RUN FROM PLANETARY GENOCIDE?
THAT THERE WOULD BE NO CONSEQUENCE?
DID YOU NOT THINK THIS SIN AGAINST THE ENTIRE GALAXY WOULD FOLLOW YOU TO YOUR GRAVE?
I AM KREE.
I AM HALA.
I AM ALL THAT IS LEFT.

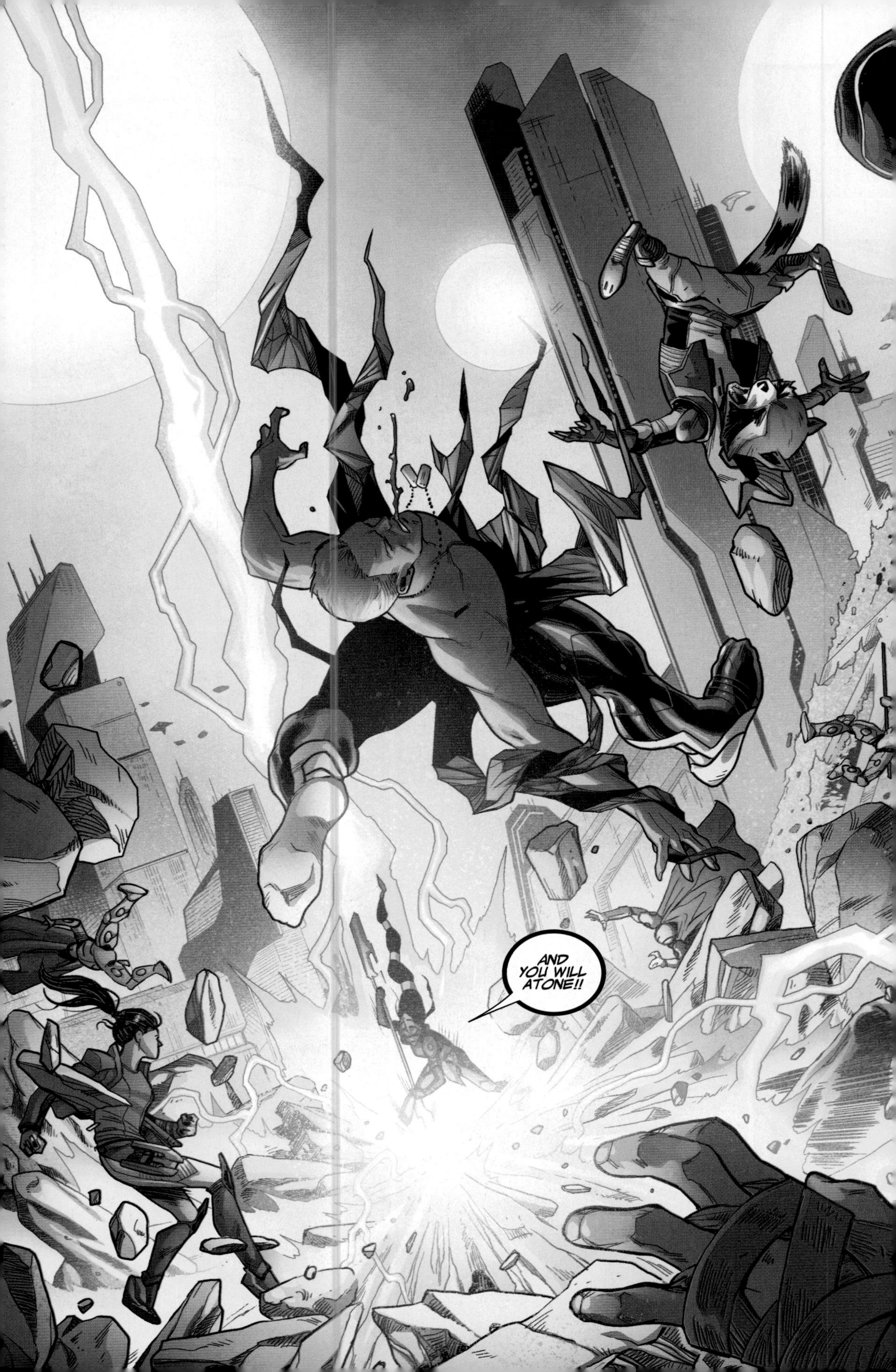
AND YOU WILL ATONE!!

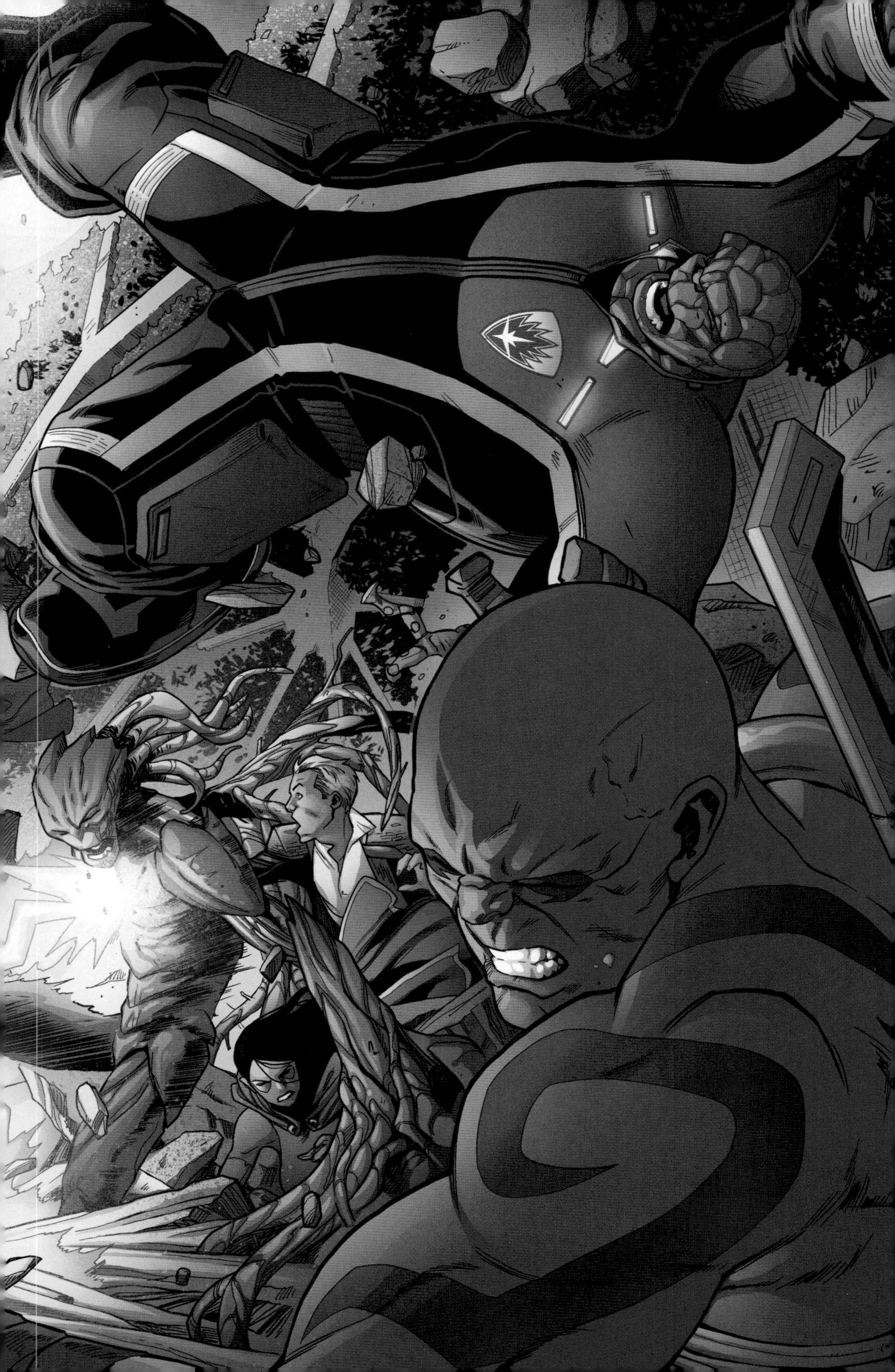

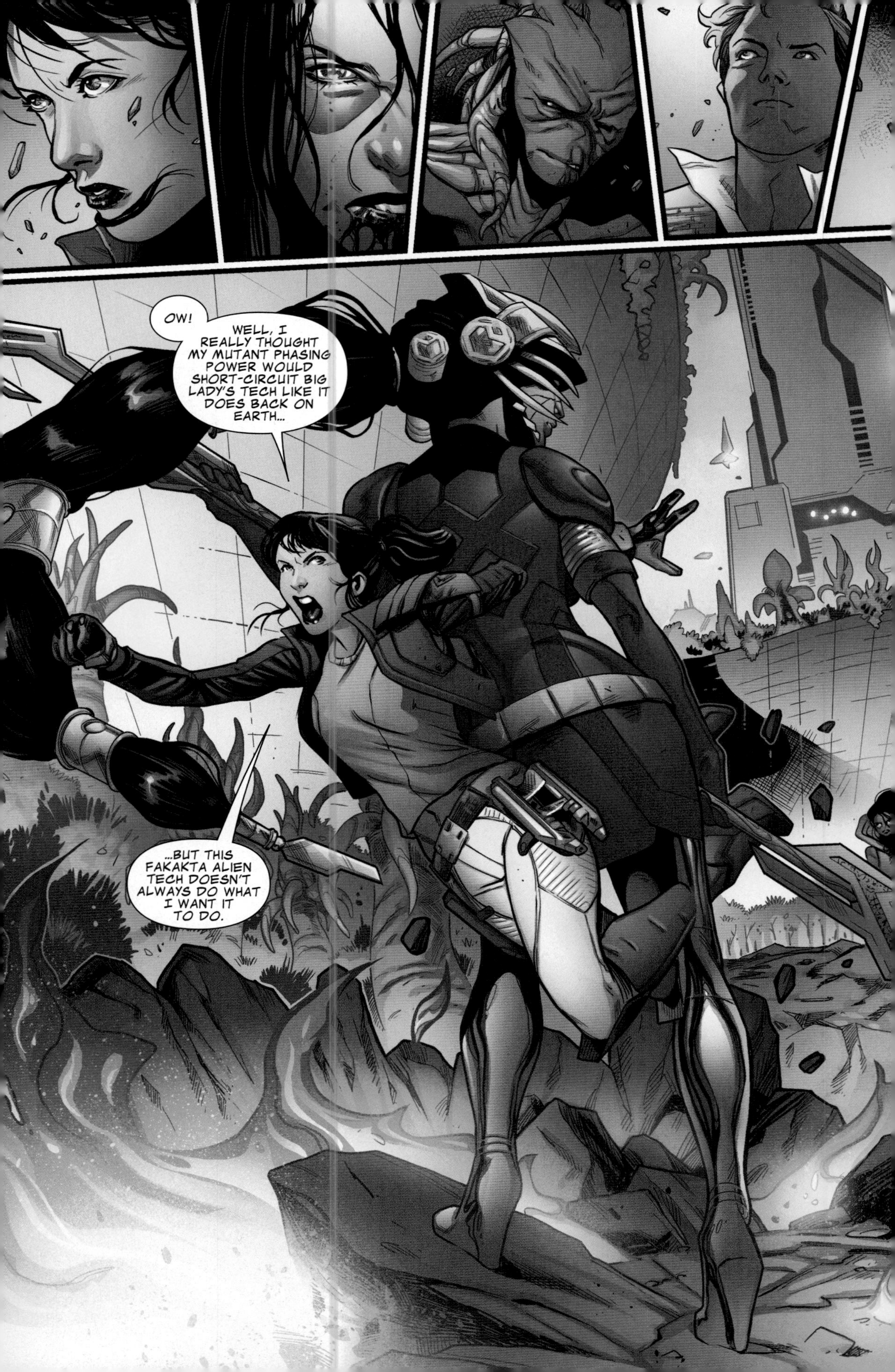
OW!
WELL, I REALLY THOUGHT MY MUTANT PHASING POWER WOULD SHORT-CIRCUIT BIG LADY'S TECH LIKE IT DOES BACK ON EARTH...
...BUT THIS FAKAKTA ALIEN TECH DOESN'T ALWAYS DO WHAT I WANT IT TO DO.

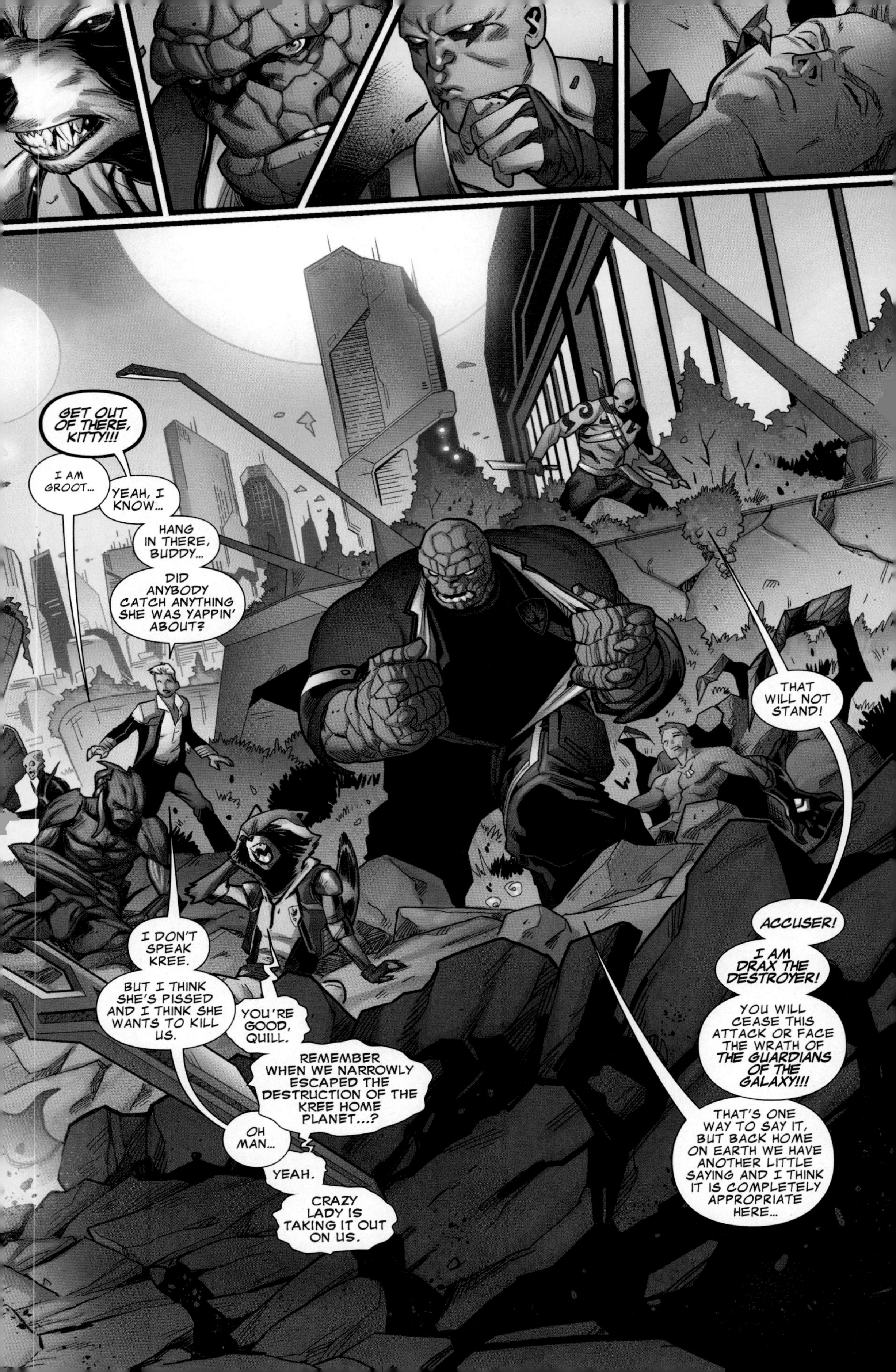
GET OUT OF THERE, KITTY!!!
I AM GROOT...
YEAH, I KNOW...
HANG IN THERE, BUDDY...
DID ANYBODY CATCH ANYTHING SHE WAS YAPPIN' ABOUT?
THAT WILL NOT STAND!
ACCUSER!
I AM DRAX THE DESTROYER!
YOU WILL CEASE THIS ATTACK OR FACE THE WRATH OF THE GUARDIANS OF THE GALAXY!!!
I DON'T SPEAK KREE.
BUT I THINK SHE'S PISSED AND I THINK SHE WANTS TO KILL US.
YOU'RE GOOD, QUILL.
REMEMBER WHEN WE NARROWLY ESCAPED THE DESTRUCTION OF THE KREE HOME PLANET...?
OH MAN...
YEAH.
CRAZY LADY IS TAKING IT OUT ON US.
THAT'S ONE WAY TO SAY IT, BUT BACK HOME ON EARTH WE HAVE ANOTHER LITTLE SAYING AND I THINK IT IS COMPLETELY APPROPRIATE HERE...

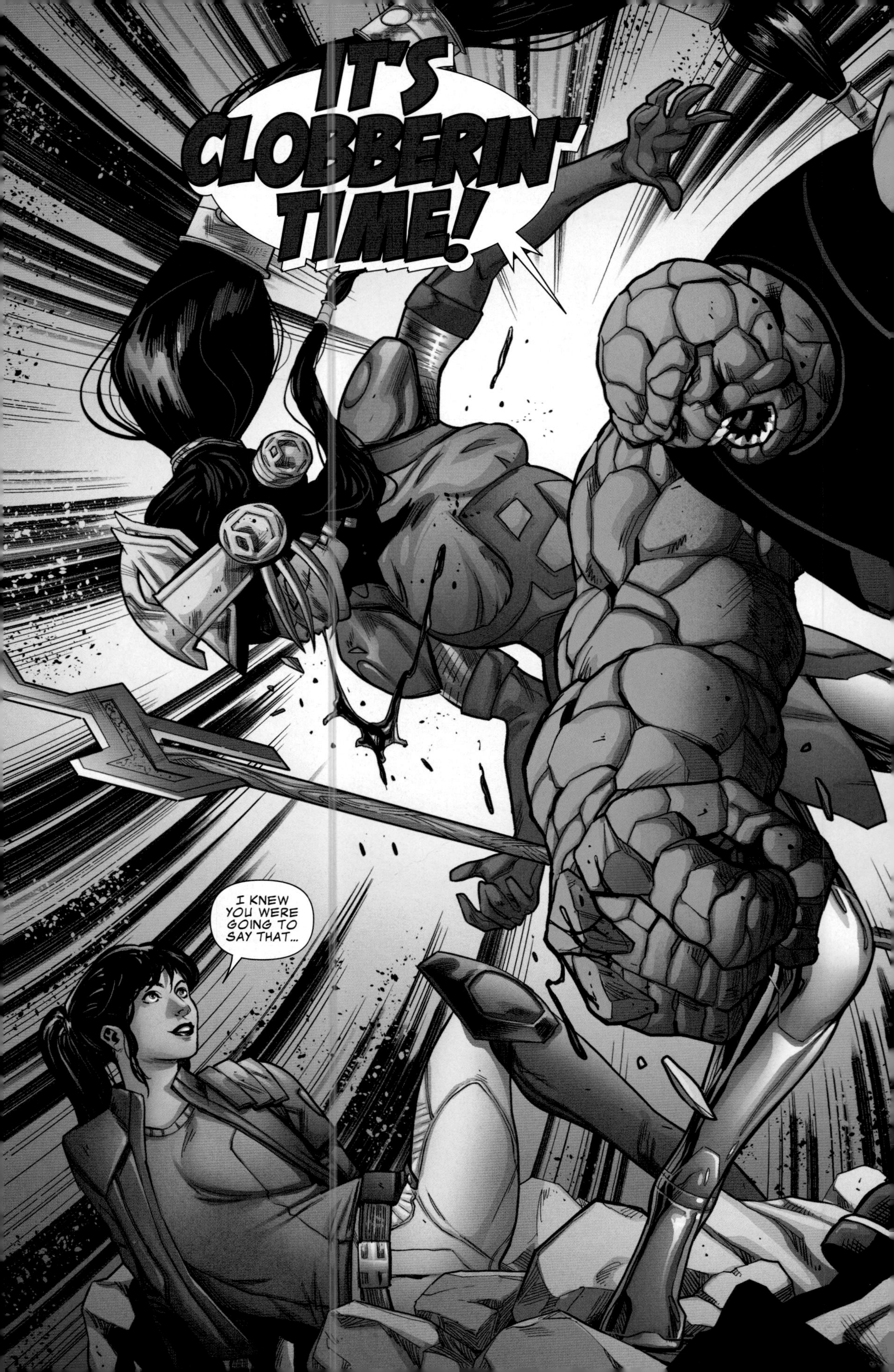
IT'S CLOBBERIN' TIME!
I KNEW YOU WERE GOING TO SAY THAT...

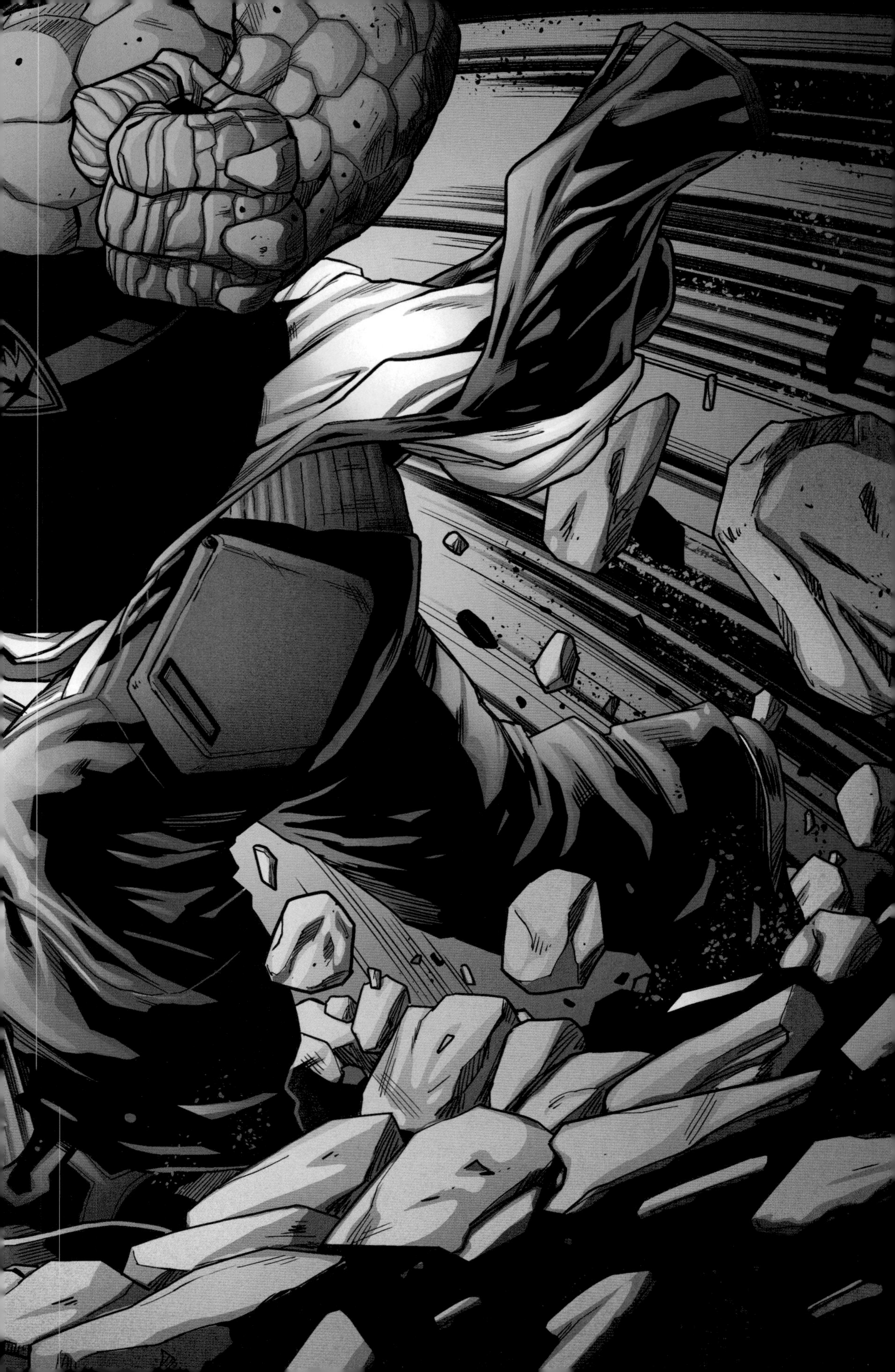

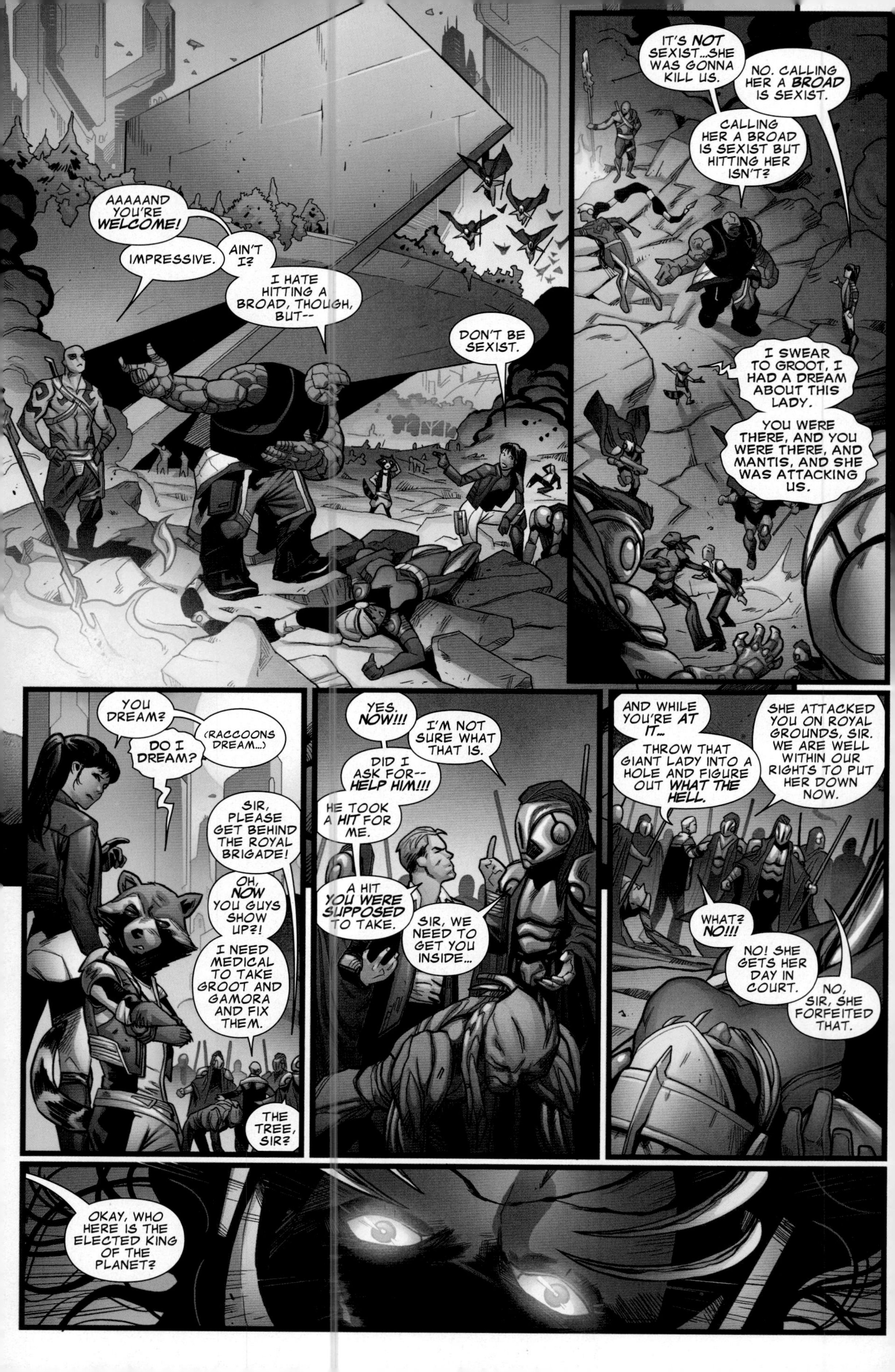

AAAAAND YOU'RE WELCOME!
IMPRESSIVE.
AIN'T I?
I HATE HITTING A BROAD, THOUGH, BUT--
DON'T BE SEXIST.
IT'S NOT SEXIST...SHE WAS GONNA KILL US.
NO. CALLING HER A BROAD IS SEXIST.
CALLING HER A BROAD IS SEXIST BUT HITTING HER ISN'T?
I SWEAR TO GROOT, I HAD A DREAM ABOUT THIS LADY.
YOU WERE THERE, AND YOU WERE THERE, AND MANTIS, AND SHE WAS ATTACKING US.
YOU DREAM?
DO I DREAM?
(RACCOONS DREAM...)
SIR, PLEASE GET BEHIND THE ROYAL BRIGADE!
OH, NOW YOU GUYS SHOW UP?!
I NEED MEDICAL TO TAKE GROOT AND GAMORA AND FIX THEM.
THE TREE, SIR?
YES. NOW!!!
I'M NOT SURE WHAT THAT IS.
DID I ASK FOR-- HELP HIM!!!
HE TOOK A HIT FOR ME.
A HIT YOU WERE SUPPOSED TO TAKE.
SIR, WE NEED TO GET YOU INSIDE...
AND WHILE YOU'RE AT IT...
THROW THAT GIANT LADY INTO A HOLE AND FIGURE OUT WHAT THE HELL.
SHE ATTACKED YOU ON ROYAL GROUNDS, SIR. WE ARE WELL WITHIN OUR RIGHTS TO PUT HER DOWN NOW.
WHAT? NO!!!
NO! SHE GETS HER DAY IN COURT.
NO, SIR, SHE FORFEITED THAT.
OKAY, WHO HERE IS THE ELECTED KING OF THE PLANET?

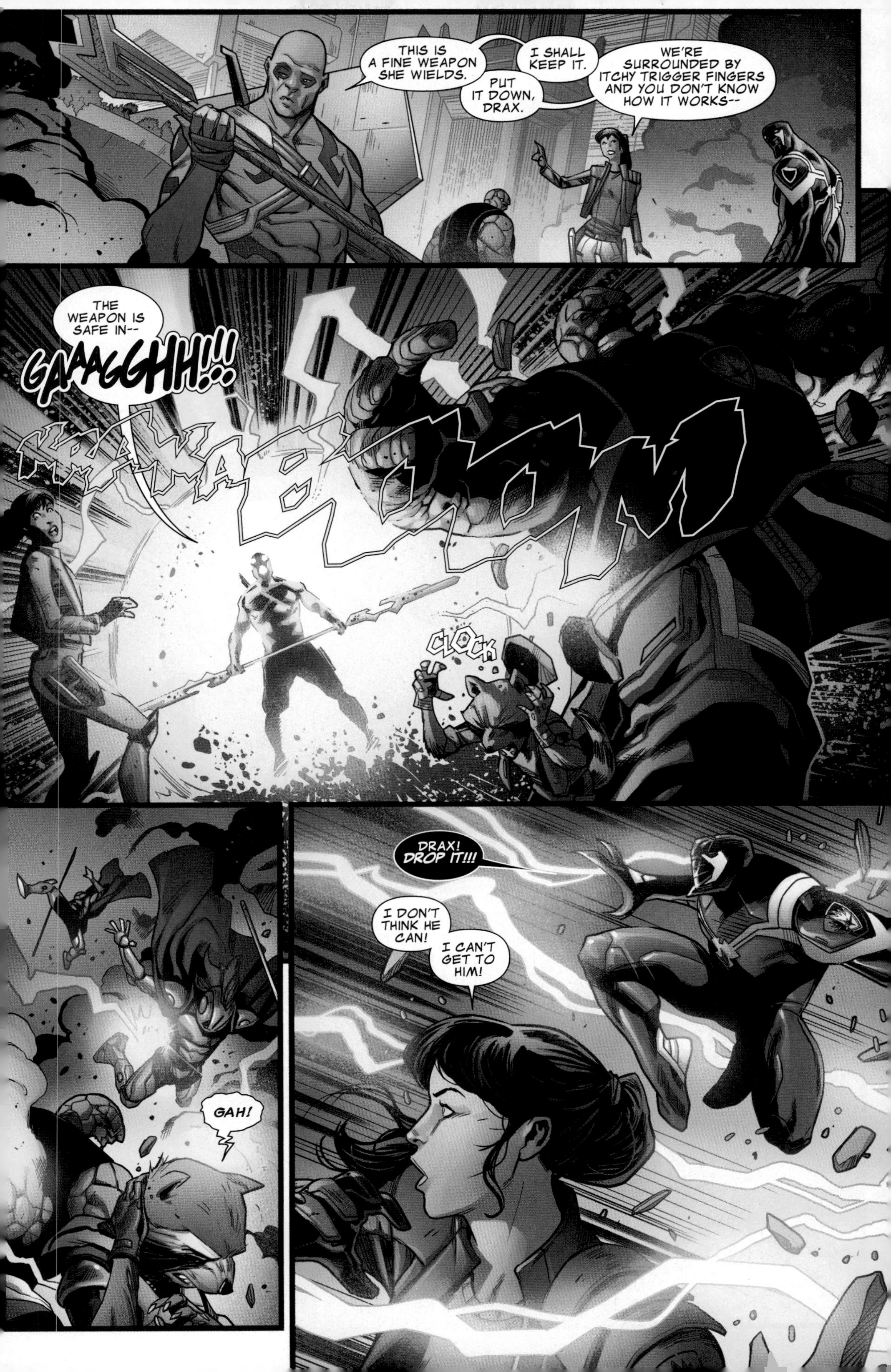
THIS IS A FINE WEAPON SHE WIELDS.
I SHALL KEEP IT.
PUT IT DOWN, DRAX.
WE'RE SURROUNDED BY ITCHY TRIGGER FINGERS AND YOU DON'T KNOW HOW IT WORKS--
THE WEAPON IS SAFE IN--
GAAAGGHH!!!
KA-BOOM
CLOCK
DRAX! DROP IT!!!
I DON'T THINK HE CAN!
I CAN'T GET TO HIM!
GAH!

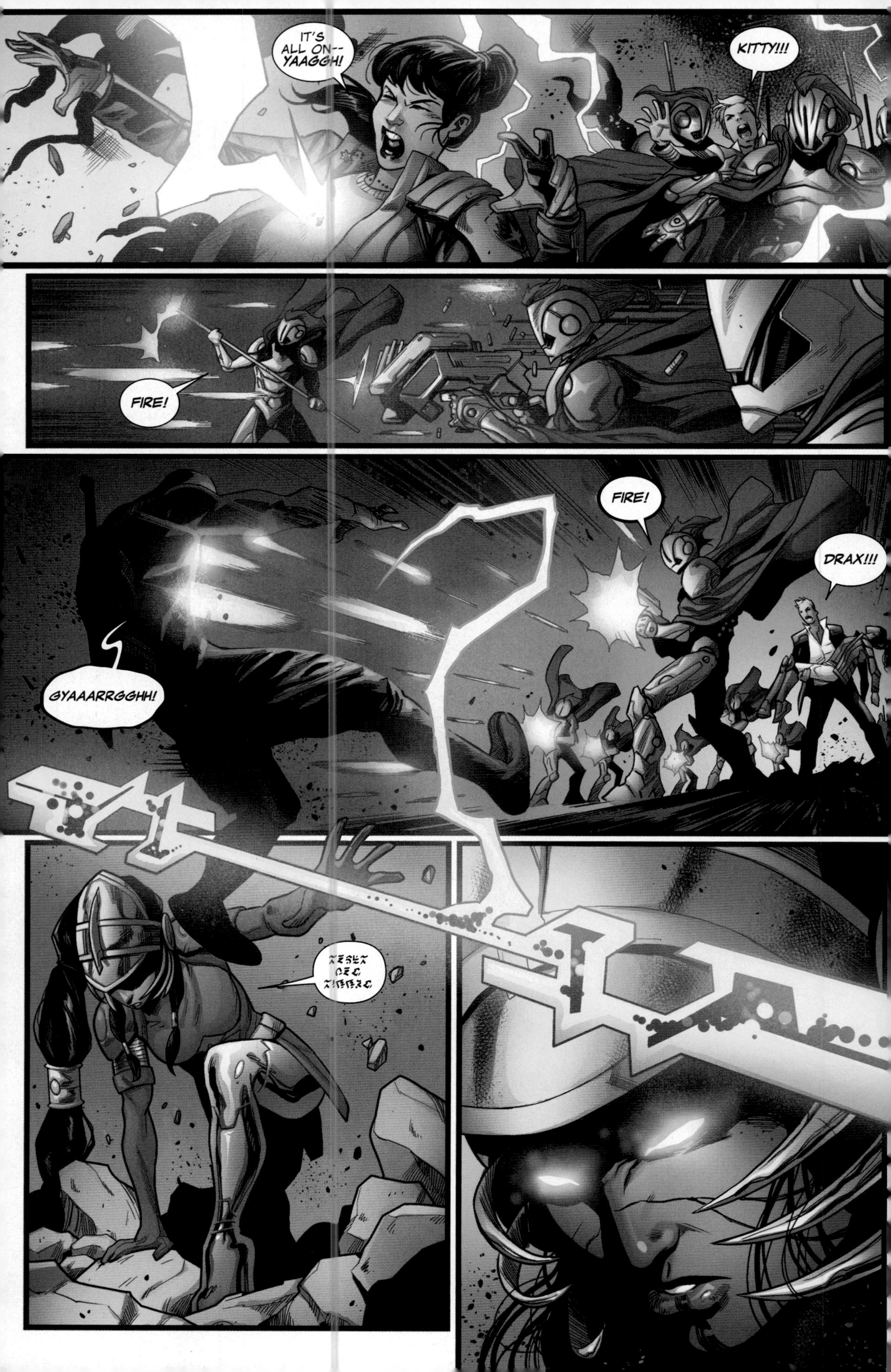
IT'S ALL ON-- YAAGGH!
KITTY!!!
FIRE!
FIRE!
DRAX!!!
GYAAARRGGHH!

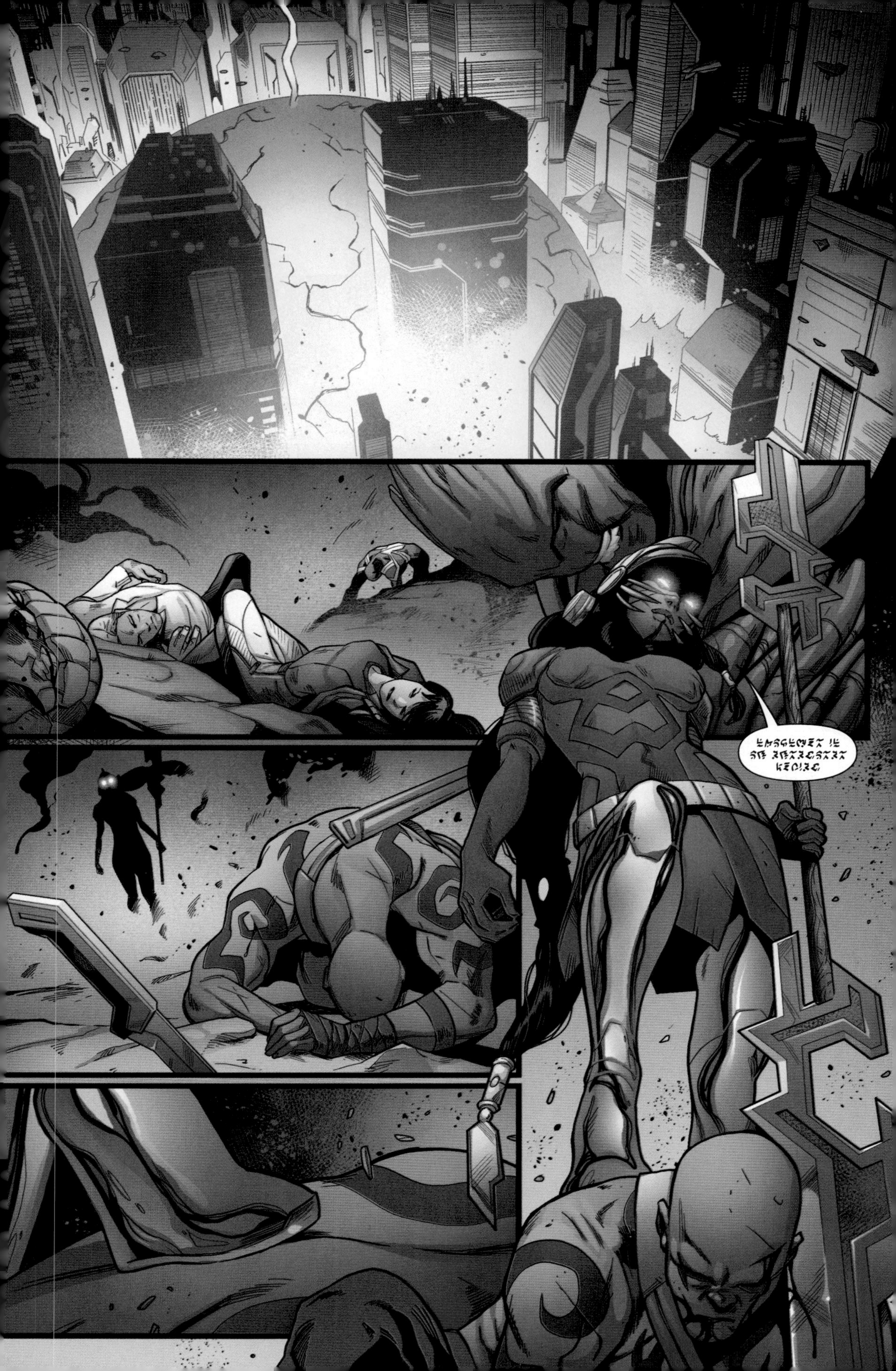

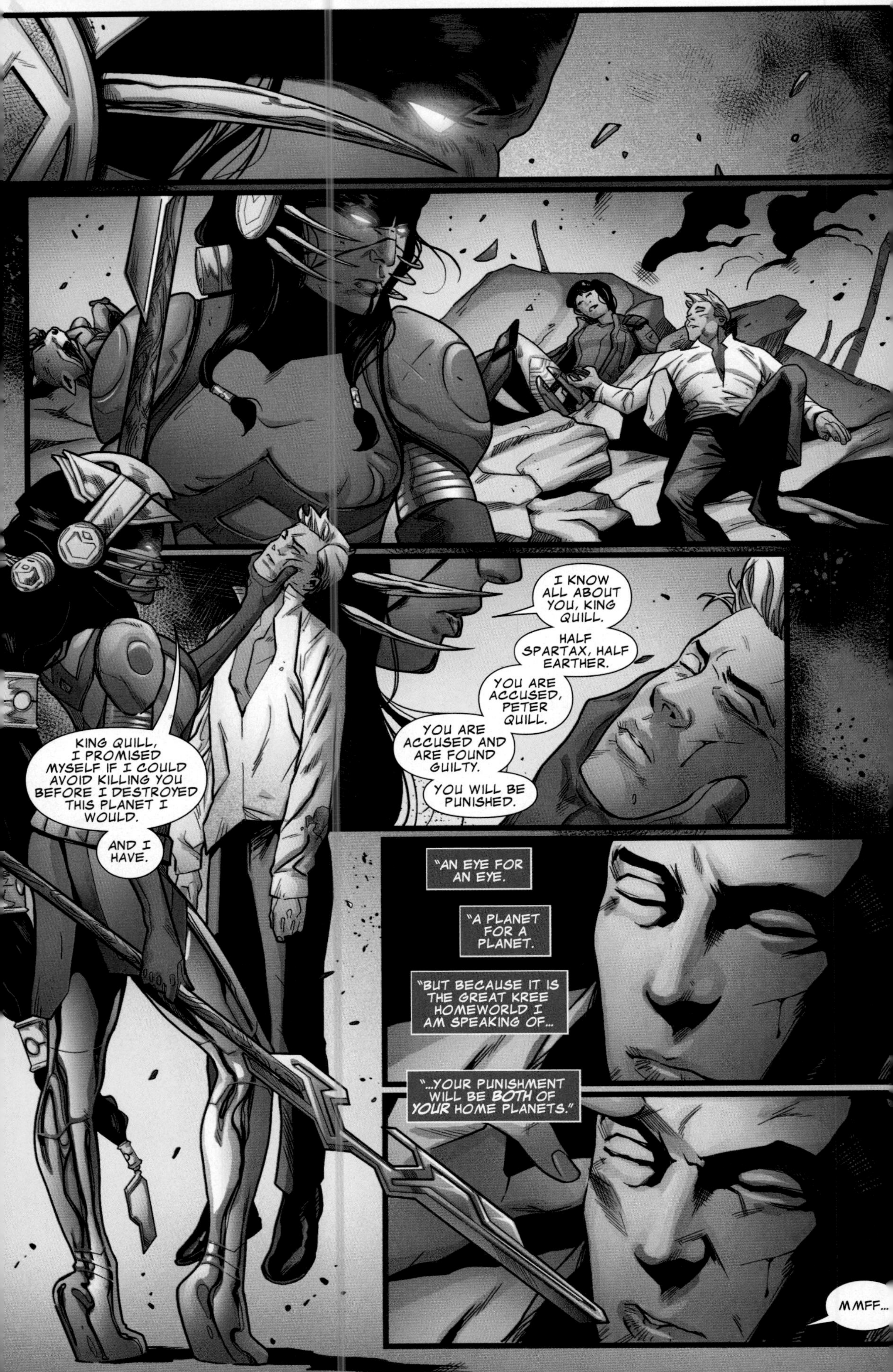
I KNOW ALL ABOUT YOU, KING QUILL.
HALF SPARTAX, HALF EARTHER.
YOU ARE ACCUSED, PETER QUILL.
YOU ARE ACCUSED AND ARE FOUND GUILTY.
YOU WILL BE PUNISHED.
KING QUILL, I PROMISED MYSELF IF I COULD AVOID KILLING YOU BEFORE I DESTROYED THIS PLANET I WOULD.
AND I HAVE.
"AN EYE FOR AN EYE.
"A PLANET FOR A PLANET.
"BUT BECAUSE IT IS THE GREAT KREE HOMEWORLD I AM SPEAKING OF...
"...YOUR PUNISHMENT WILL BE *BOTH* OF *YOUR* HOME PLANETS."
MMFF...

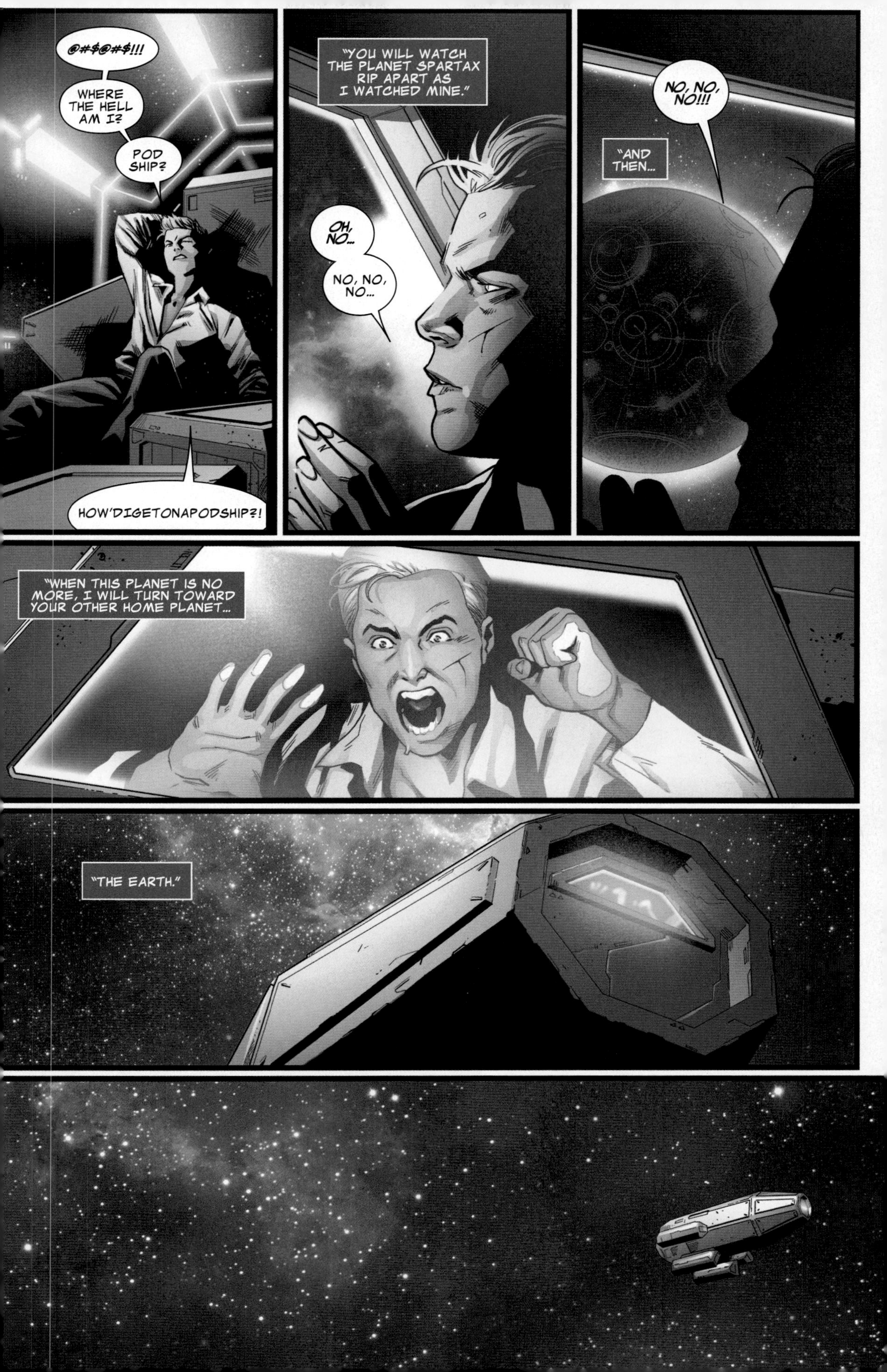

@#$@#$!!!
WHERE THE HELL AM I?
POD SHIP?
HOW'DIGETONAPODSHIP?!
"YOU WILL WATCH THE PLANET SPARTAX RIP APART AS I WATCHED MINE."
OH, NO...
NO, NO, NO...
NO, NO, NO!!!
"AND THEN...
"WHEN THIS PLANET IS NO MORE, I WILL TURN TOWARD YOUR OTHER HOME PLANET...
"THE EARTH."

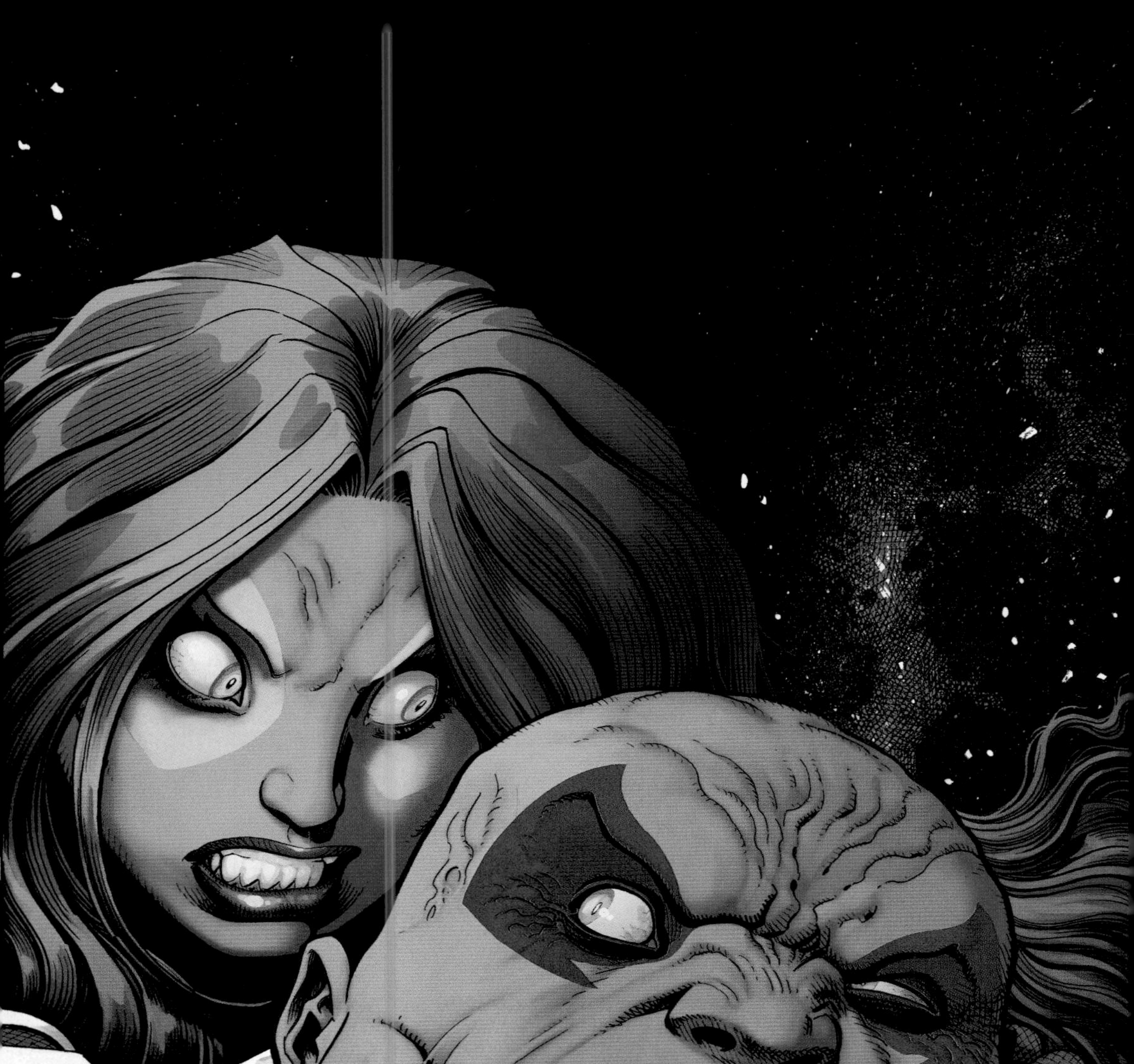
ARTHUR ADAMS
8-29
2015

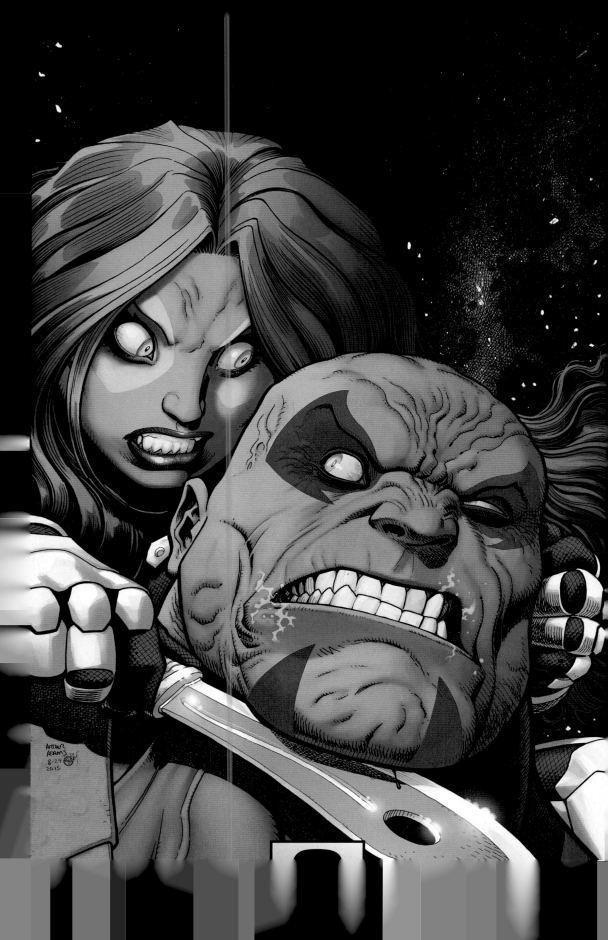

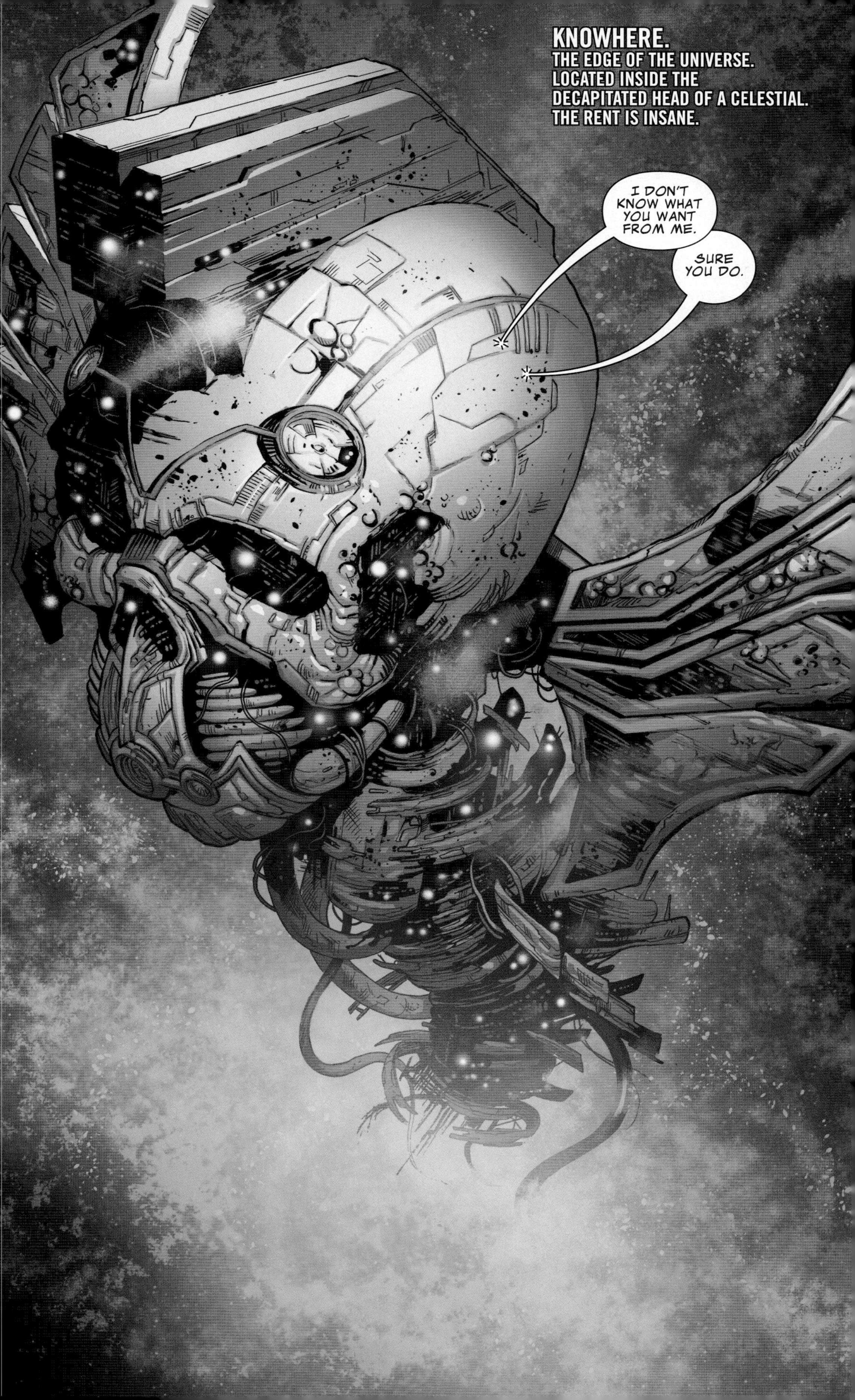
KNOWHERE.
THE EDGE OF THE UNIVERSE.
LOCATED INSIDE THE
DECAPITATED HEAD OF A CELESTIAL.
THE RENT IS INSANE.
I DON'T KNOW WHAT YOU WANT FROM ME.
SURE YOU DO.

**THE MARKETPLACE.**
WE TOLD YOU NOT TO EAT AT THE STREET
VENDOR GLARKIN AND YOU NEVER LISTEN.

I-I REALLY DON'T.

I DON'T KNOW YOU.

I DON'T KNOW WHAT YOU WANT.

GET THE FLARK OUT OF MY STORE BEFORE I CALL THE COSMO DOG ON YOU!

OR BETTER YET, IF YOU DON'T GET OUT OF HERE I'M GOING TO GIVE YOU A VERY PERSONAL DEMONSTRATION OF MY LATEST WEAPONS SYSTEM...

AND SEE HOW YOU LIKE SUCKING GLREEDO OUT OF A STRAW FROM YOUR HOSPICE HOLO-BED.

**FRUNTA'S HOUSE OF SELF-DEFENSERY.**
HE HAS ONLY A TWO-STAR RATING IN DROGON'S MARKET GUIDE.
HE THINKS IT'S BECAUSE HIS COMPETITION ON THE OTHER
SIDE OF THE MARKET IS SPAMMING HIM WITH NEGATIVE
REVIEWS, BUT IT IS REALLY HIS SISTER.
SHE DRINKS.

I MEAN IT!

DRAX. THE DESTROYER.

DON'T KNOW HIM.

EVERYONE KNOWS HIM.

WHAT ABOUT HIM?

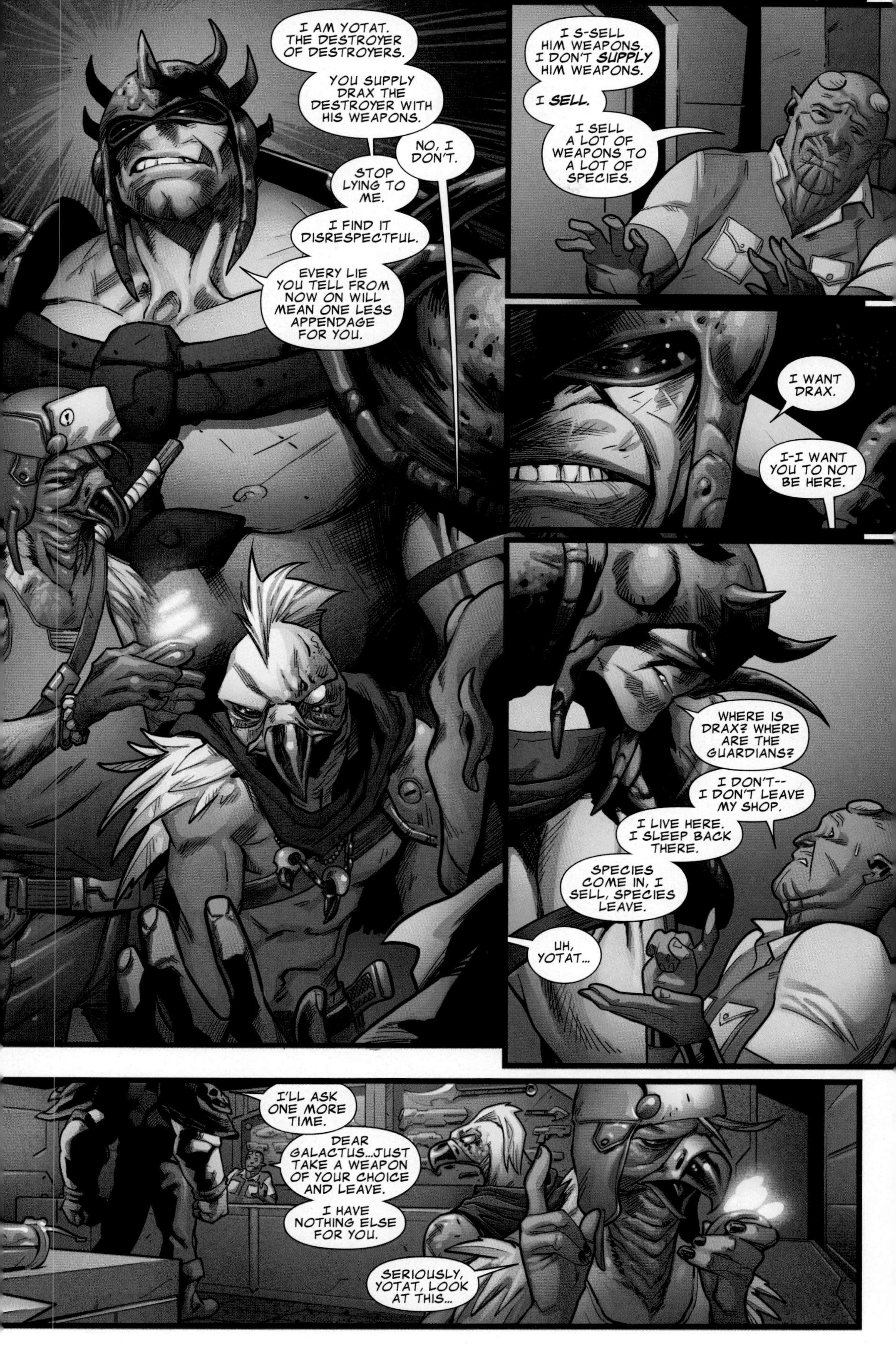
I AM YOTAT. THE DESTROYER OF DESTROYERS.
YOU SUPPLY DRAX THE DESTROYER WITH HIS WEAPONS.
NO, I DON'T.
STOP LYING TO ME.
I FIND IT DISRESPECTFUL.
EVERY LIE YOU TELL FROM NOW ON WILL MEAN ONE LESS APPENDAGE FOR YOU.
I S-SELL HIM WEAPONS. I DON'T **SUPPLY** HIM WEAPONS.
I **SELL.**
I SELL A LOT OF WEAPONS TO A LOT OF SPECIES.
I WANT DRAX.
I-I WANT YOU TO NOT BE HERE.
WHERE IS DRAX? WHERE ARE THE GUARDIANS?
I DON'T-- I DON'T LEAVE MY SHOP.
I LIVE HERE. I SLEEP BACK THERE.
SPECIES COME IN, I SELL, SPECIES LEAVE.
UH, YOTAT...
I'LL ASK ONE MORE TIME.
DEAR GALACTUS...JUST TAKE A WEAPON OF YOUR CHOICE AND LEAVE.
I HAVE NOTHING ELSE FOR YOU.
SERIOUSLY, YOTAT, LOOK AT THIS...

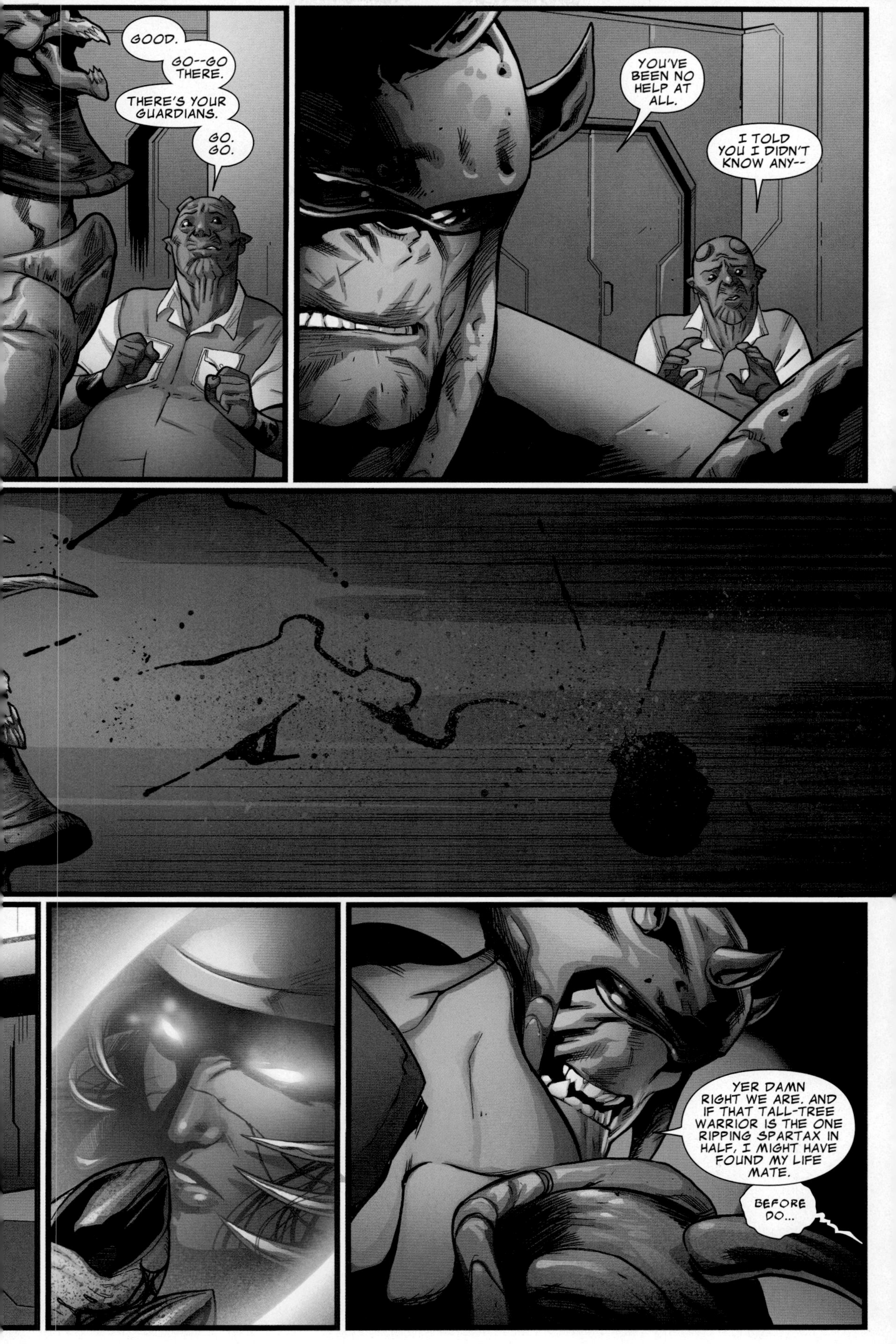
GOOD.
GO--GO THERE.
THERE'S YOUR GUARDIANS.
GO. GO.
YOU'VE BEEN NO HELP AT ALL.
I TOLD YOU I DIDN'T KNOW ANY--
YER DAMN RIGHT WE ARE. AND IF THAT TALL-TREE WARRIOR IS THE ONE RIPPING SPARTAX IN HALF, I MIGHT HAVE FOUND MY LIFE MATE.
BEFORE DO...

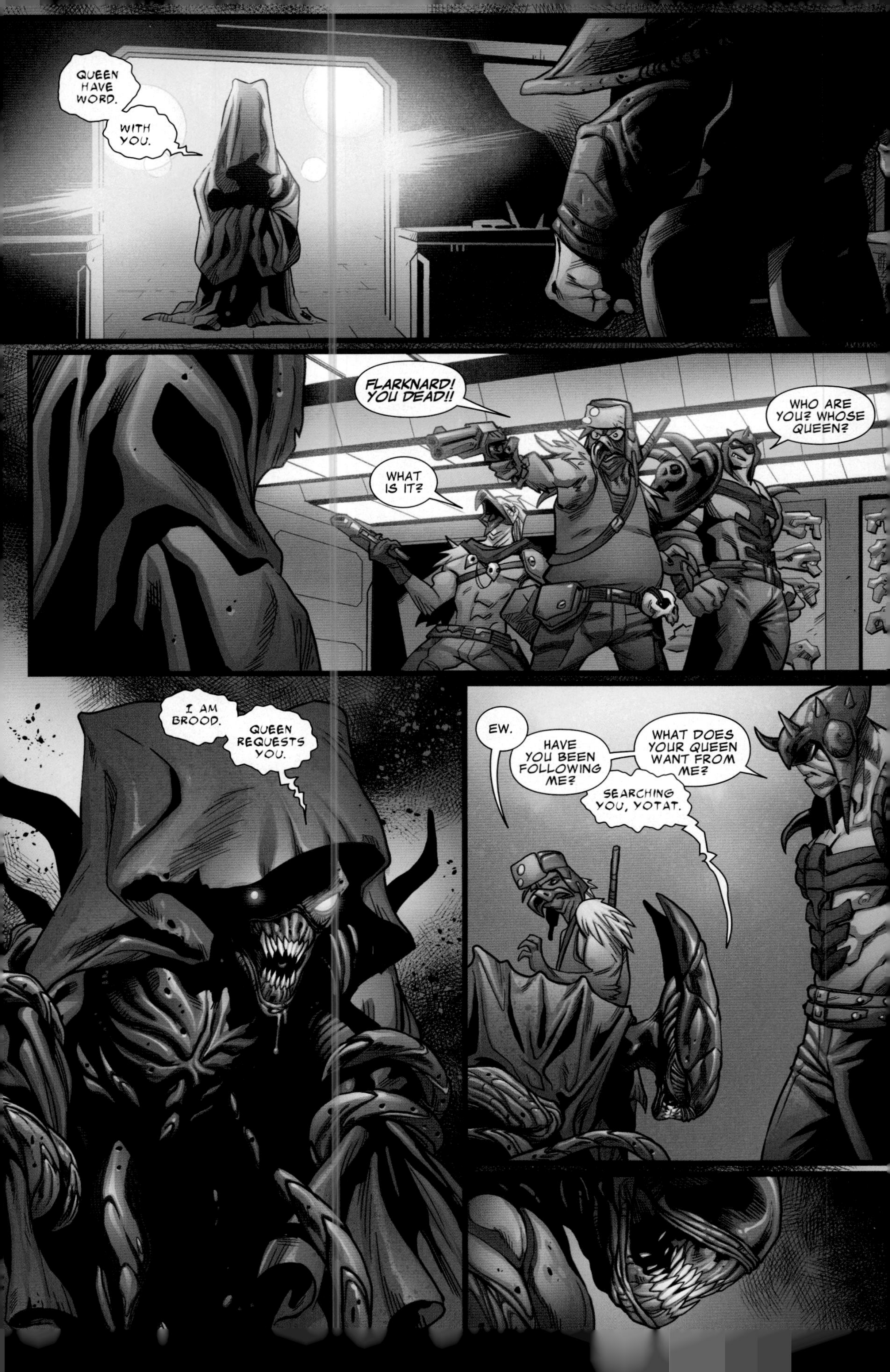
QUEEN HAVE WORD.
WITH YOU.
FLARKNARD! YOU DEAD!!
WHO ARE YOU? WHOSE QUEEN?
WHAT IS IT?
I AM BROOD.
QUEEN REQUESTS YOU.
EW.
HAVE YOU BEEN FOLLOWING ME?
WHAT DOES YOUR QUEEN WANT FROM ME?
SEARCHING YOU, YOTAT.

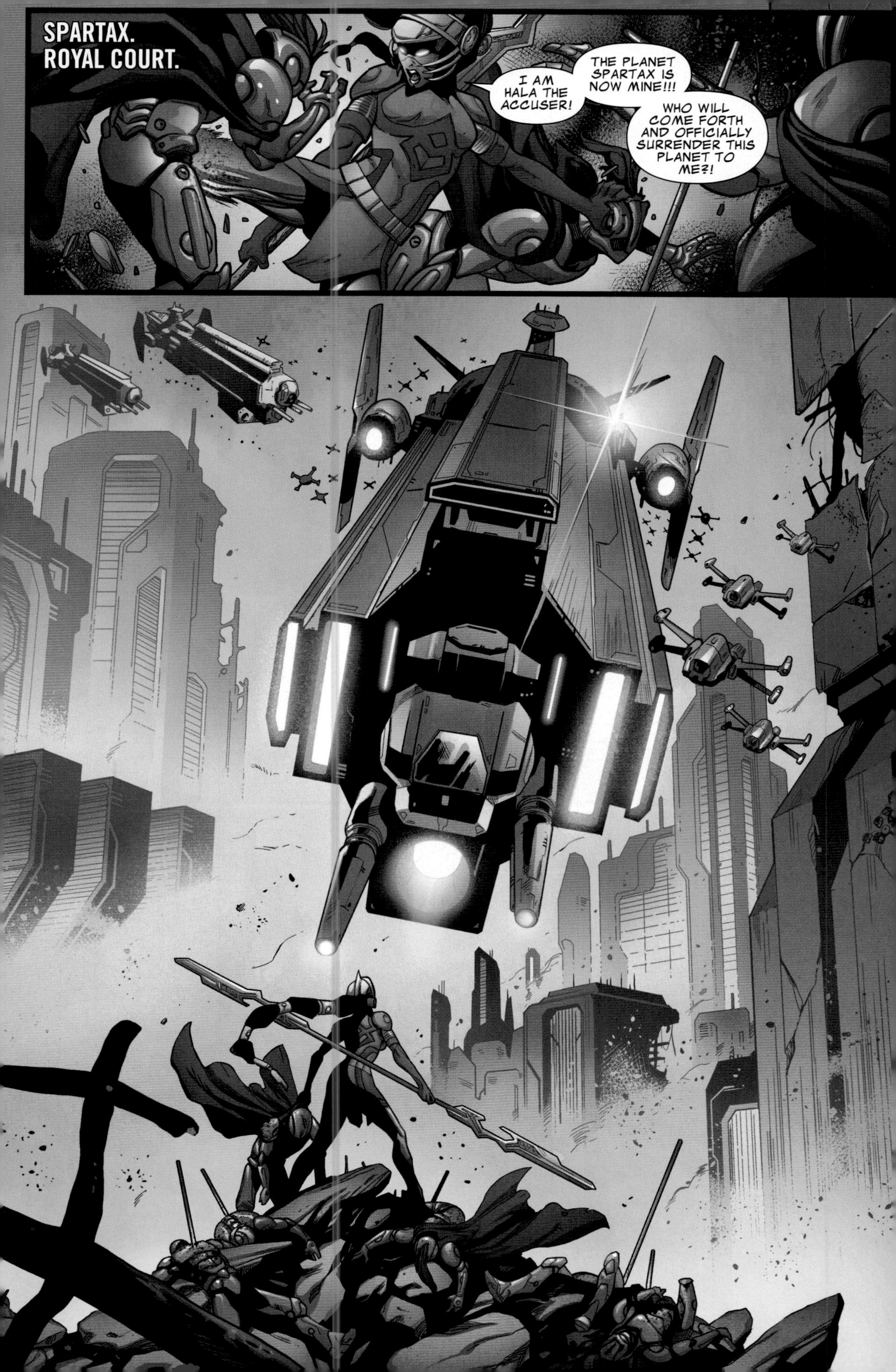
SPARTAX.
ROYAL COURT.
I AM HALA THE ACCUSER!
THE PLANET SPARTAX IS NOW MINE!!!
WHO WILL COME FORTH AND OFFICIALLY SURRENDER THIS PLANET TO ME?!

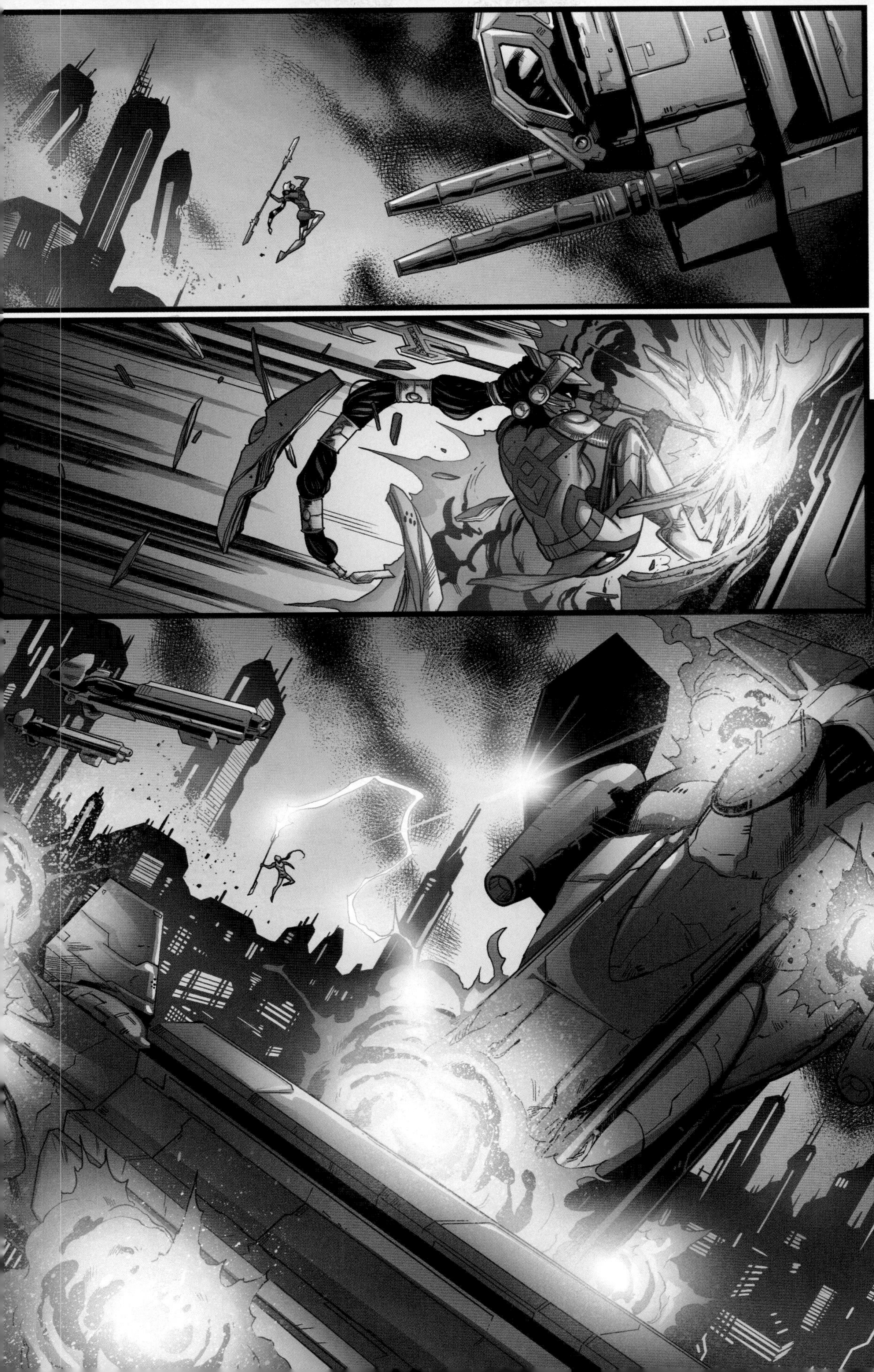

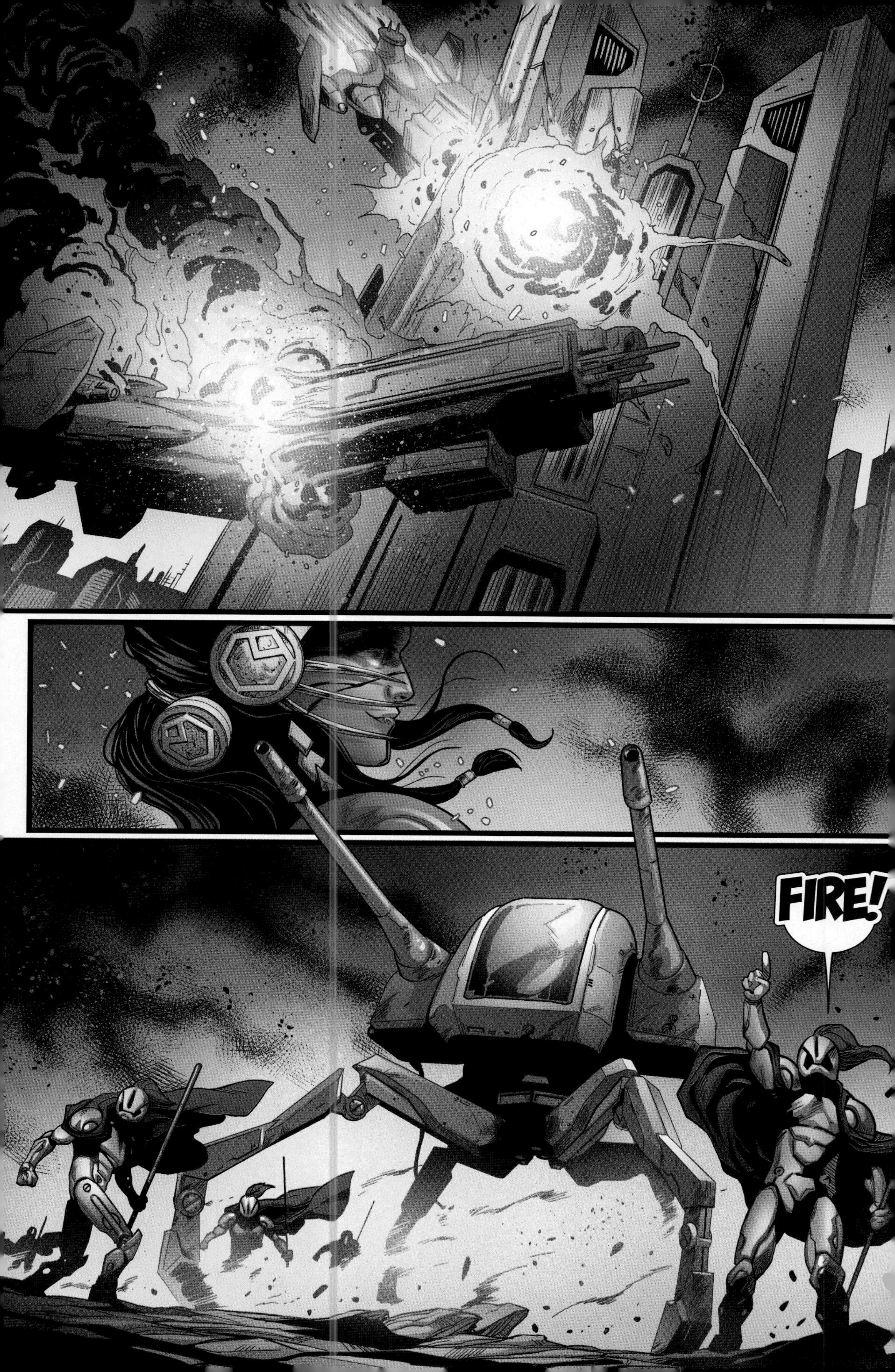
FIRE!

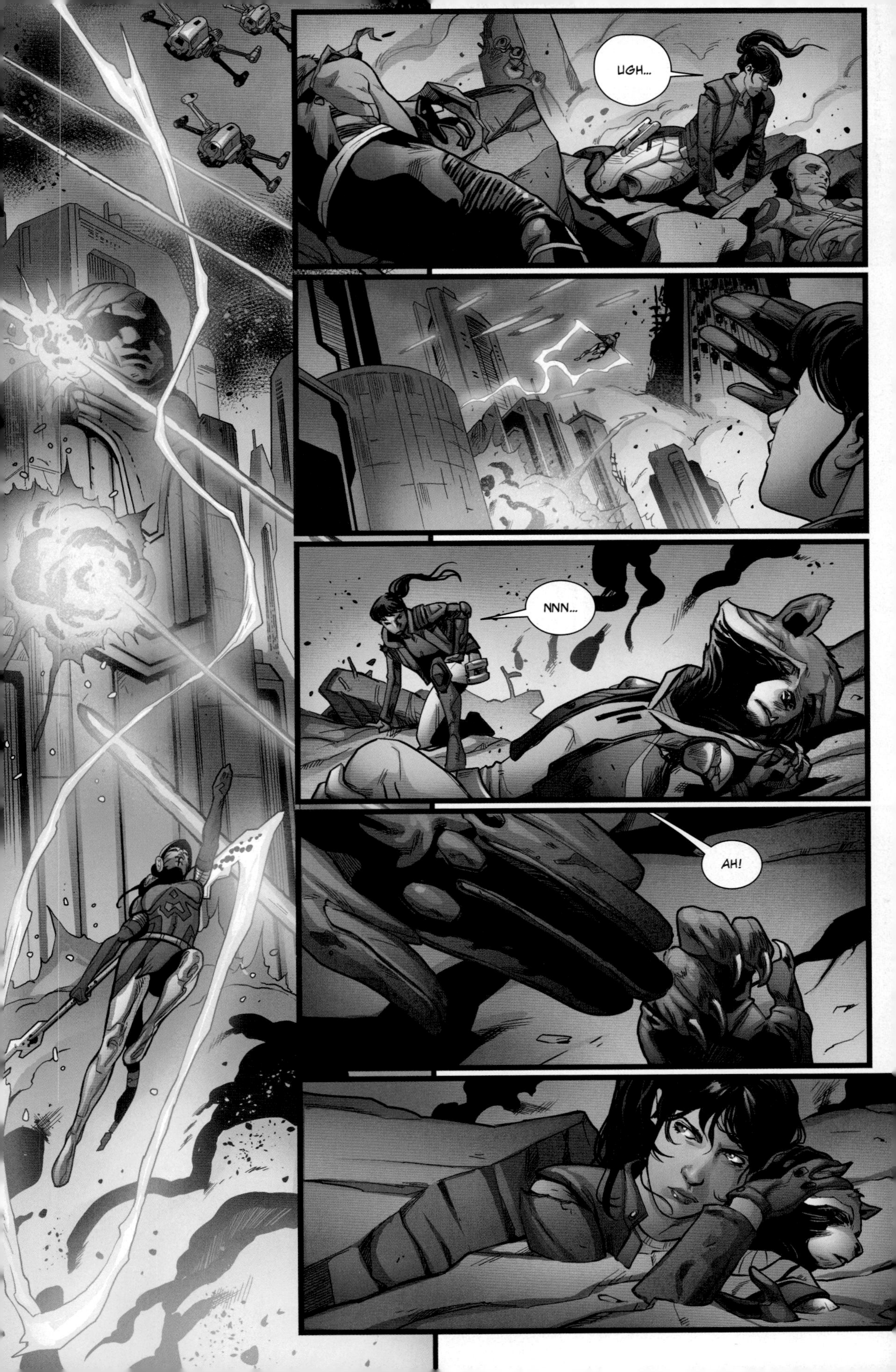
UGH...
NNN...
AH!

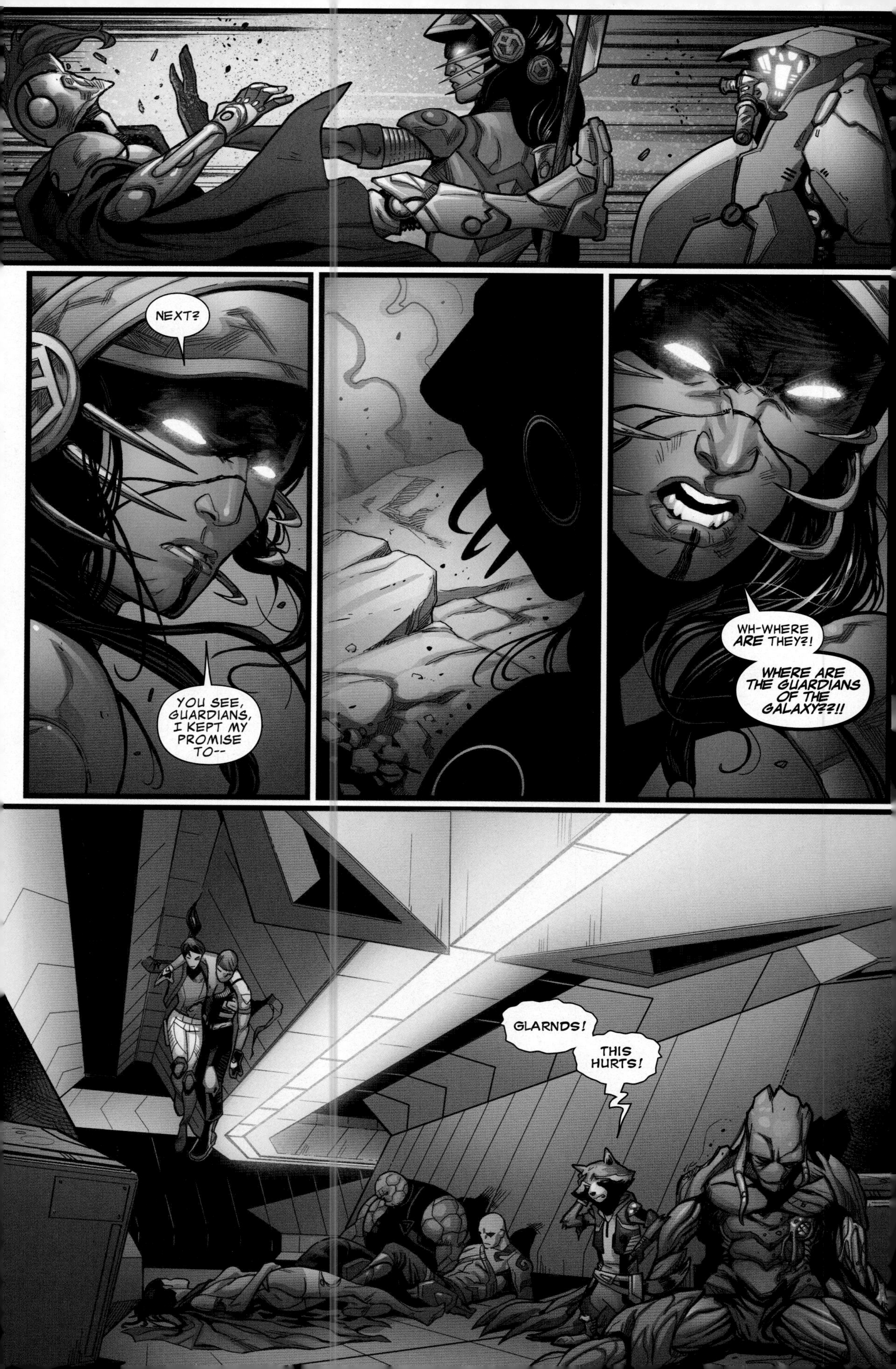
NEXT?
YOU SEE, GUARDIANS, I KEPT MY PROMISE TO--
WH-WHERE ARE THEY?!
WHERE ARE THE GUARDIANS OF THE GALAXY??!!
GLARNDS!
THIS HURTS!

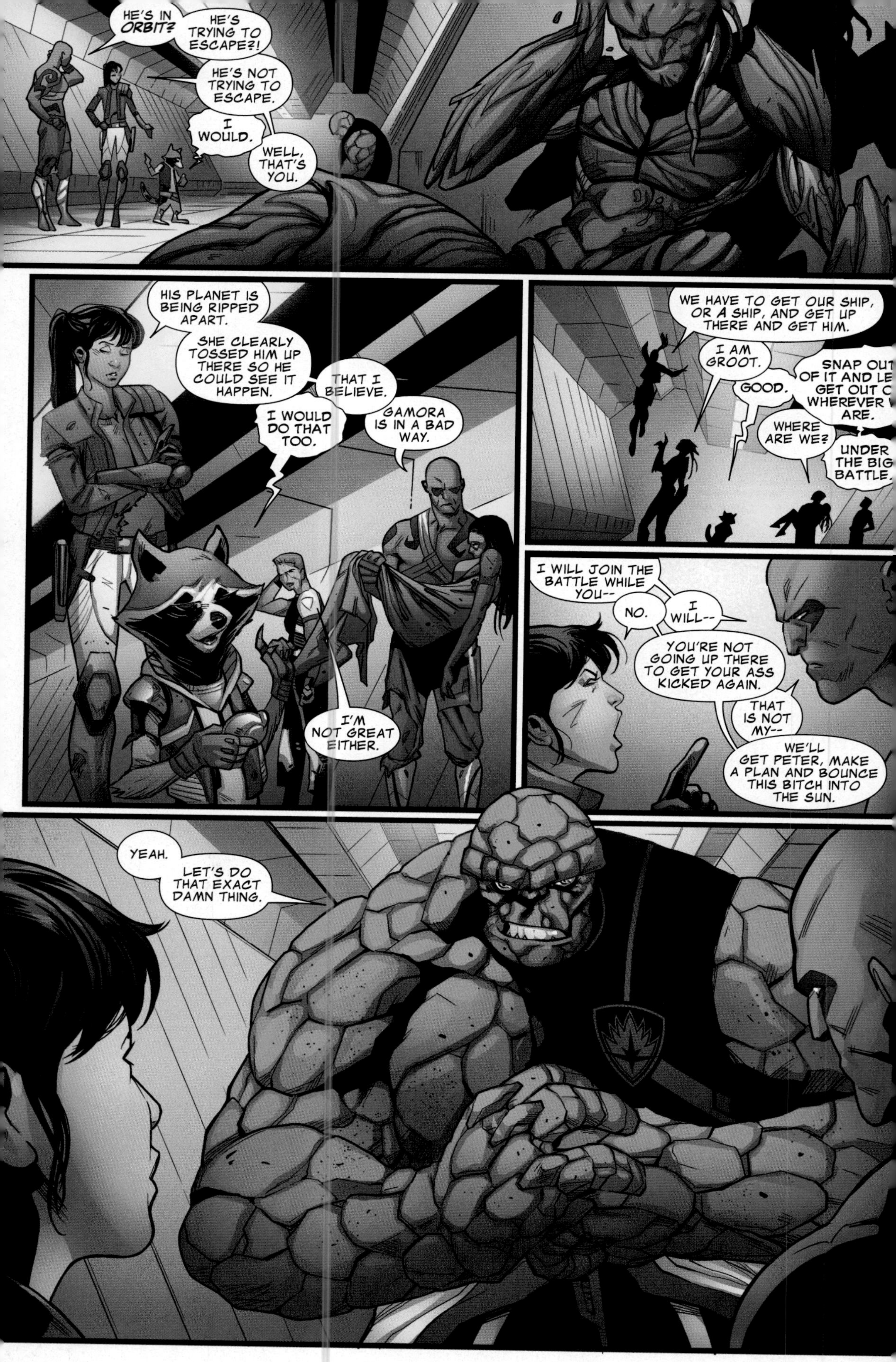
HE'S IN ORBIT?
HE'S TRYING TO ESCAPE?!
HE'S NOT TRYING TO ESCAPE.
I WOULD.
WELL, THAT'S YOU.
HIS PLANET IS BEING RIPPED APART.
SHE CLEARLY TOSSED HIM UP THERE SO HE COULD SEE IT HAPPEN.
THAT I BELIEVE.
I WOULD DO THAT TOO.
GAMORA IS IN A BAD WAY.
I'M NOT GREAT EITHER.
WE HAVE TO GET OUR SHIP, OR A SHIP, AND GET UP THERE AND GET HIM.
I AM GROOT.
GOOD.
WHERE ARE WE?
I WILL JOIN THE BATTLE WHILE YOU--
NO.
I WILL--
YOU'RE NOT GOING UP THERE TO GET YOUR ASS KICKED AGAIN.
THAT IS NOT MY--
WE'LL GET PETER, MAKE A PLAN AND BOUNCE THIS BITCH INTO THE SUN.
YEAH.
LET'S DO THAT EXACT DAMN THING.

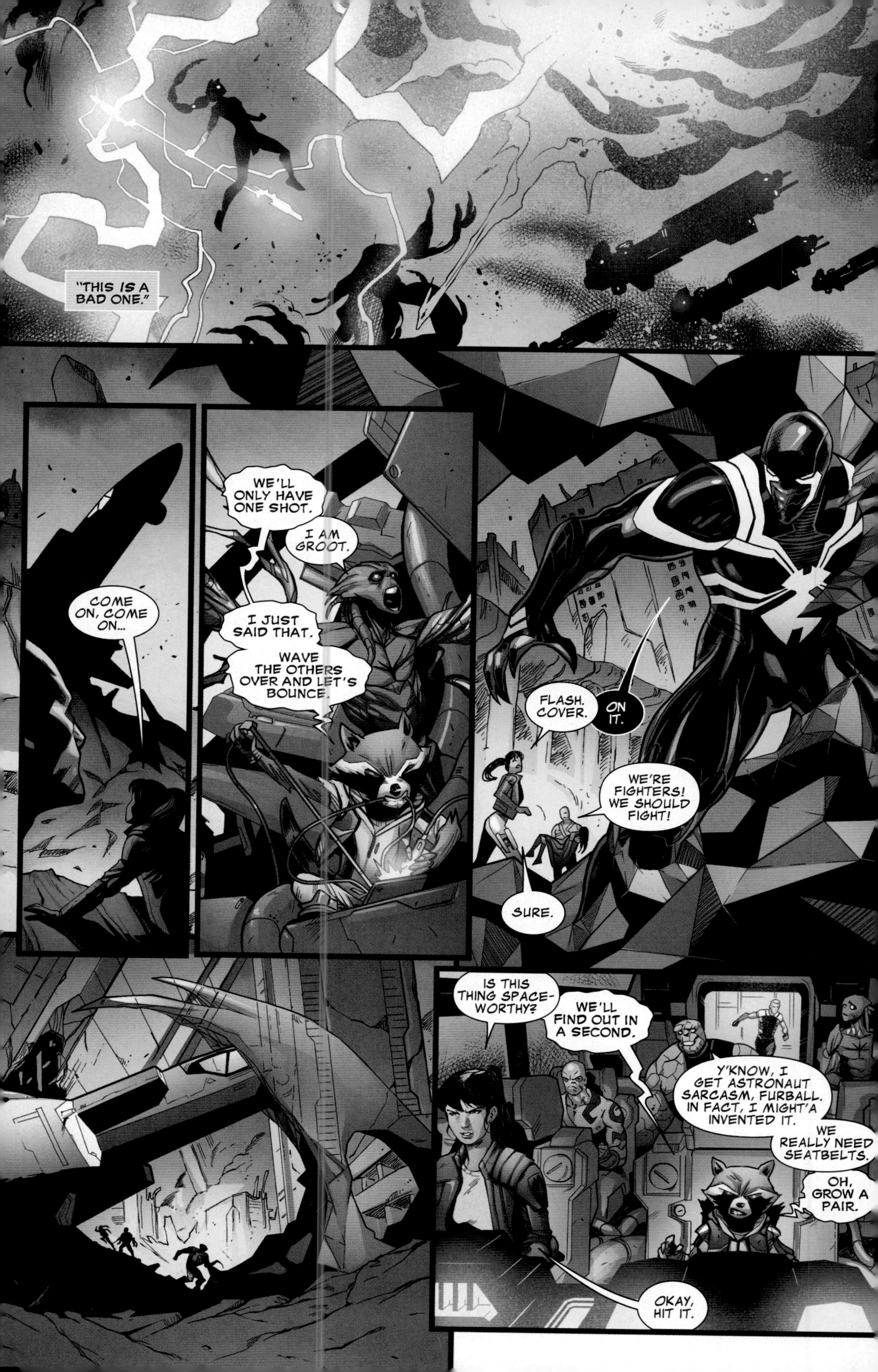
"THIS IS A BAD ONE."
COME ON, COME ON...
WE'LL ONLY HAVE ONE SHOT.
I AM GROOT.
I JUST SAID THAT.
WAVE THE OTHERS OVER AND LET'S BOUNCE.
FLASH. COVER.
ON IT.
WE'RE FIGHTERS! WE SHOULD FIGHT!
SURE.
IS THIS THING SPACE-WORTHY?
WE'LL FIND OUT IN A SECOND.
Y'KNOW, I GET ASTRONAUT SARCASM, FURBALL. IN FACT, I MIGHT'A INVENTED IT.
WE REALLY NEED SEATBELTS.
OH, GROW A PAIR.
OKAY, HIT IT.

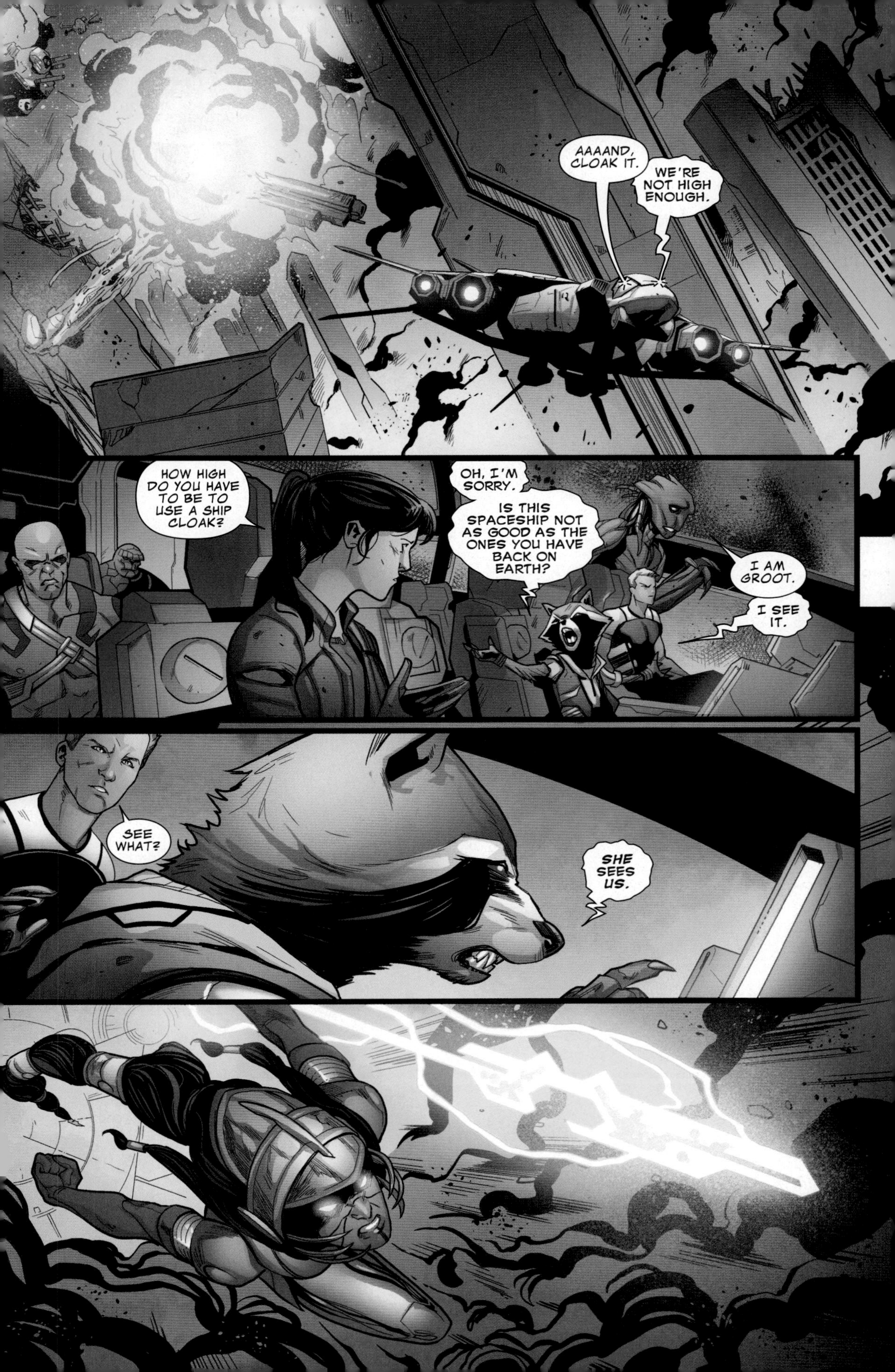
AAAAND, CLOAK IT.
WE'RE NOT HIGH ENOUGH.
HOW HIGH DO YOU HAVE TO BE TO USE A SHIP CLOAK?
OH, I'M SORRY.
IS THIS SPACESHIP NOT AS GOOD AS THE ONES YOU HAVE BACK ON EARTH?
I AM GROOT.
I SEE IT.
SEE WHAT?
SHE SEES US.

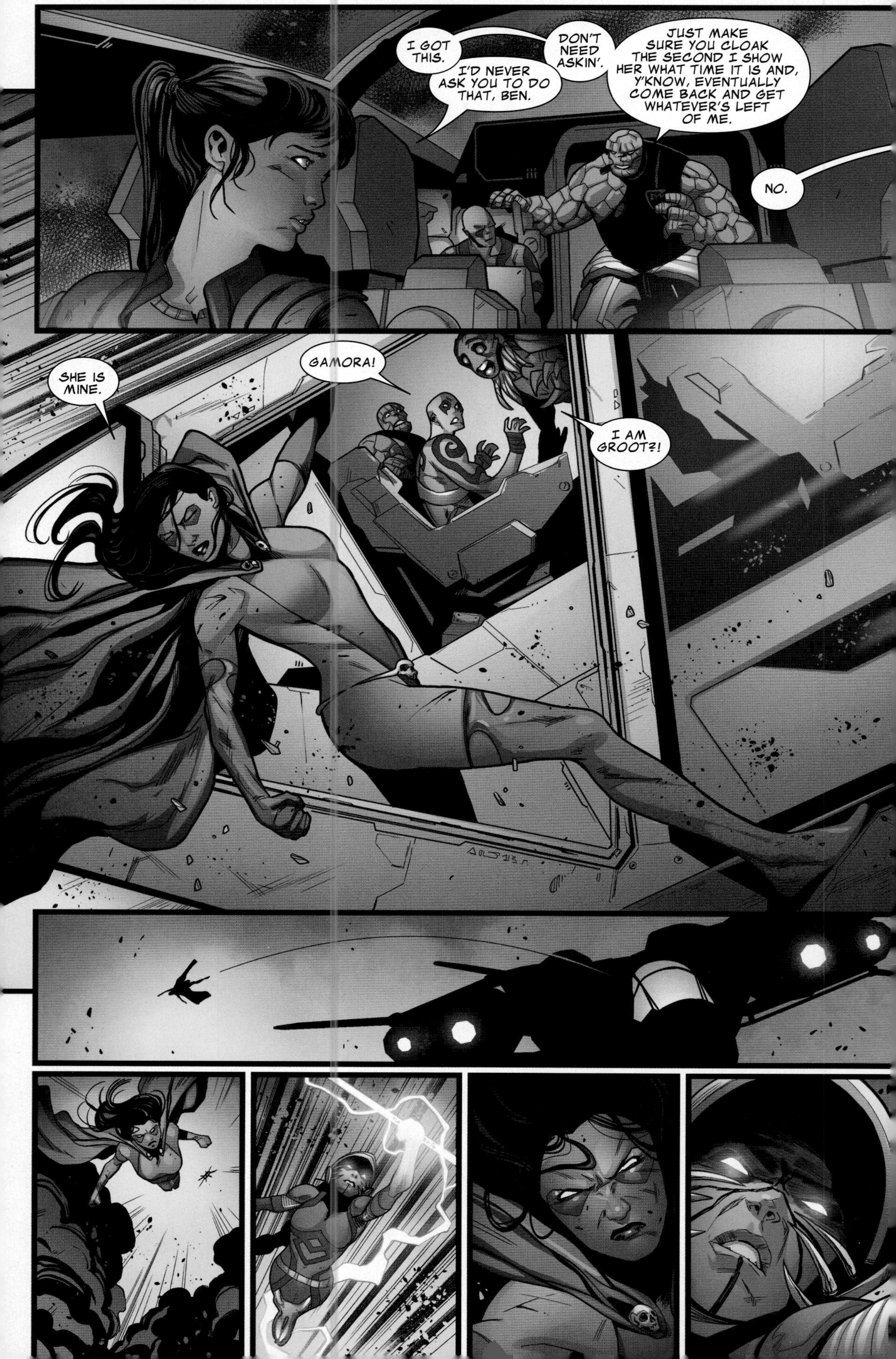
I GOT THIS.
DON'T NEED ASKIN'.
I'D NEVER ASK YOU TO DO THAT, BEN.
JUST MAKE SURE YOU CLOAK THE SECOND I SHOW HER WHAT TIME IT IS AND, Y'KNOW, EVENTUALLY COME BACK AND GET WHATEVER'S LEFT OF ME.
NO.
SHE IS MINE.
GAMORA!
I AM GROOT?!

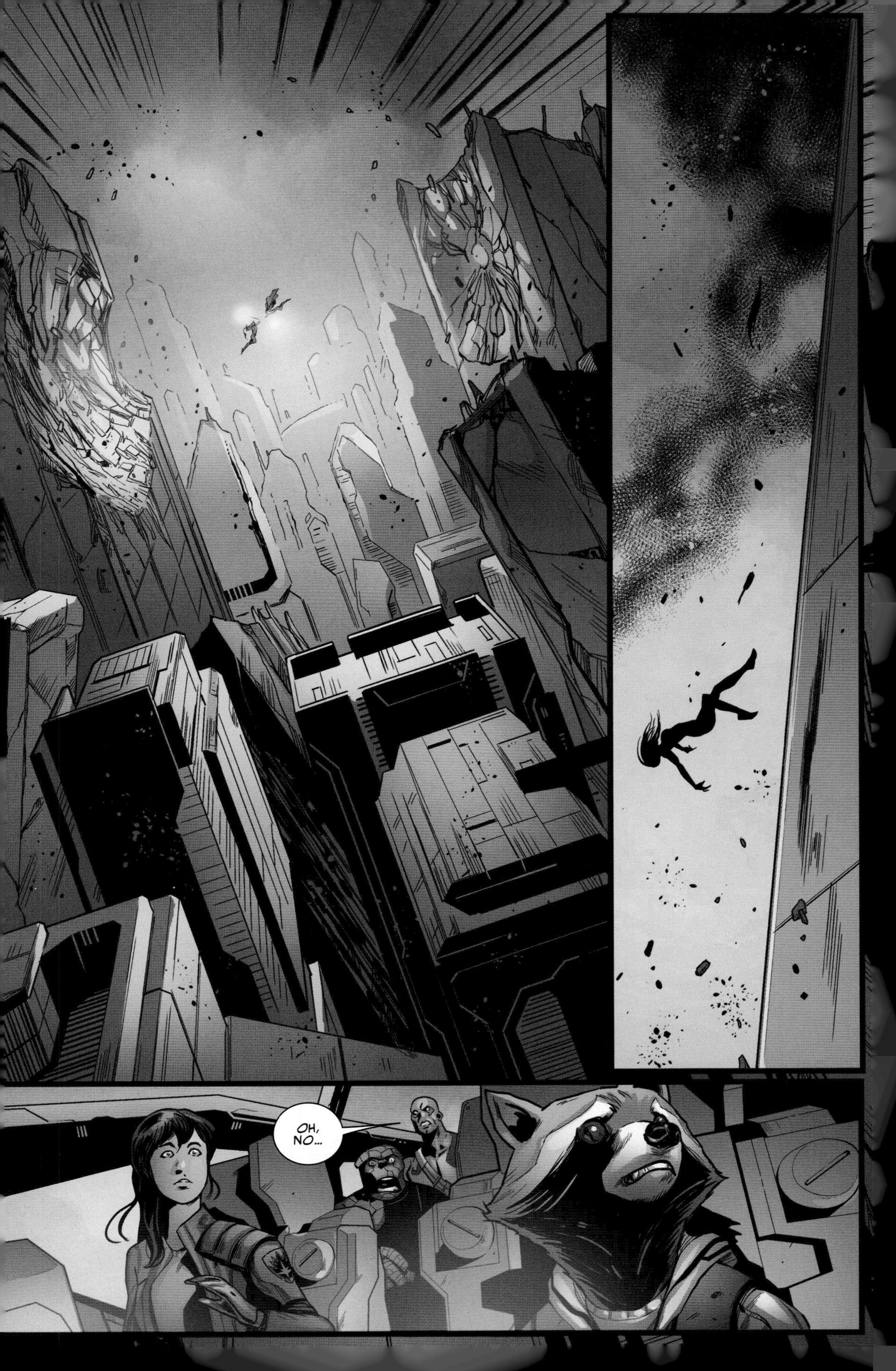
OH, NO...

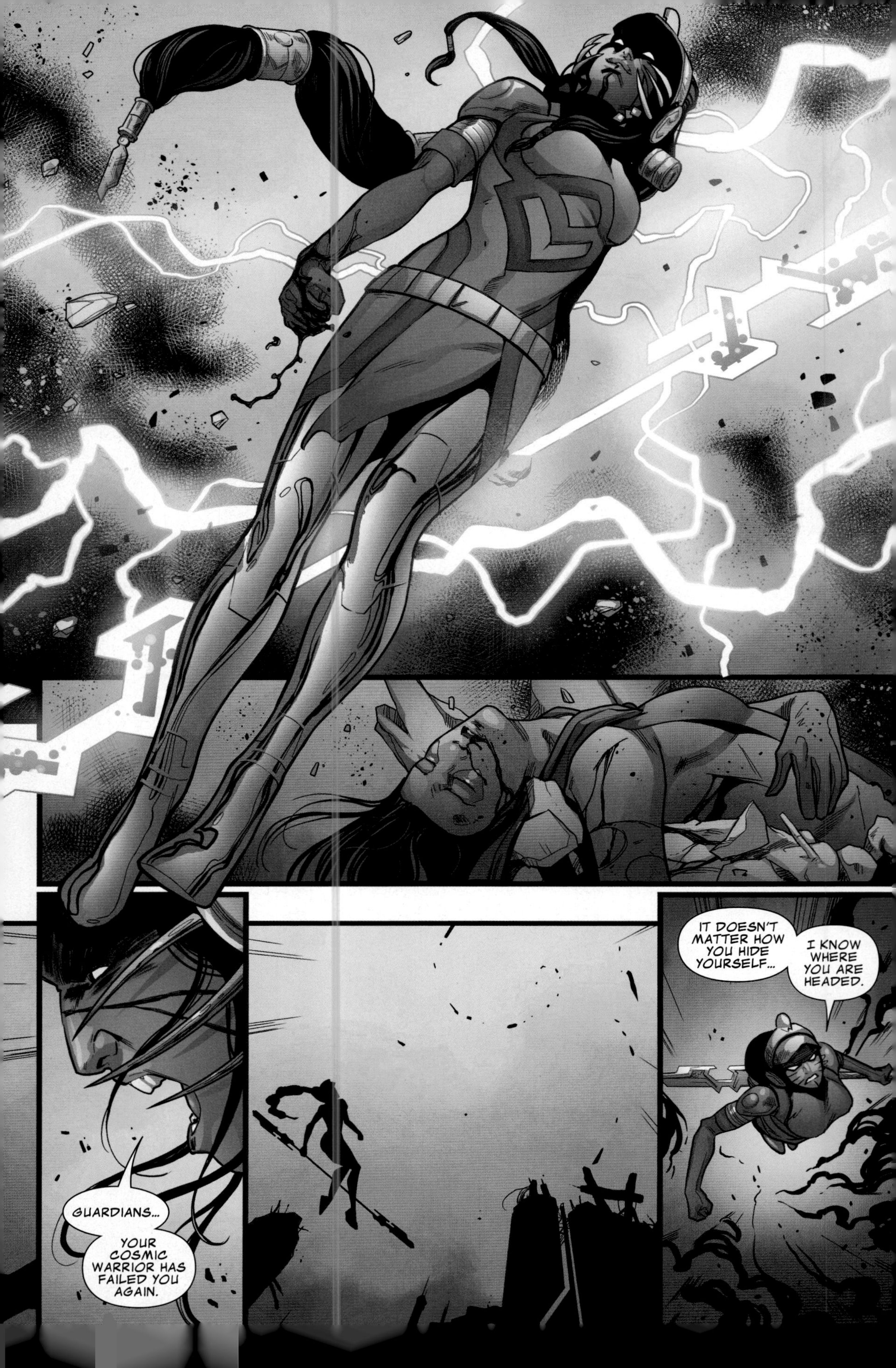
GUARDIANS...
YOUR COSMIC WARRIOR HAS FAILED YOU AGAIN.
IT DOESN'T MATTER HOW YOU HIDE YOURSELF...
I KNOW WHERE YOU ARE HEADED.

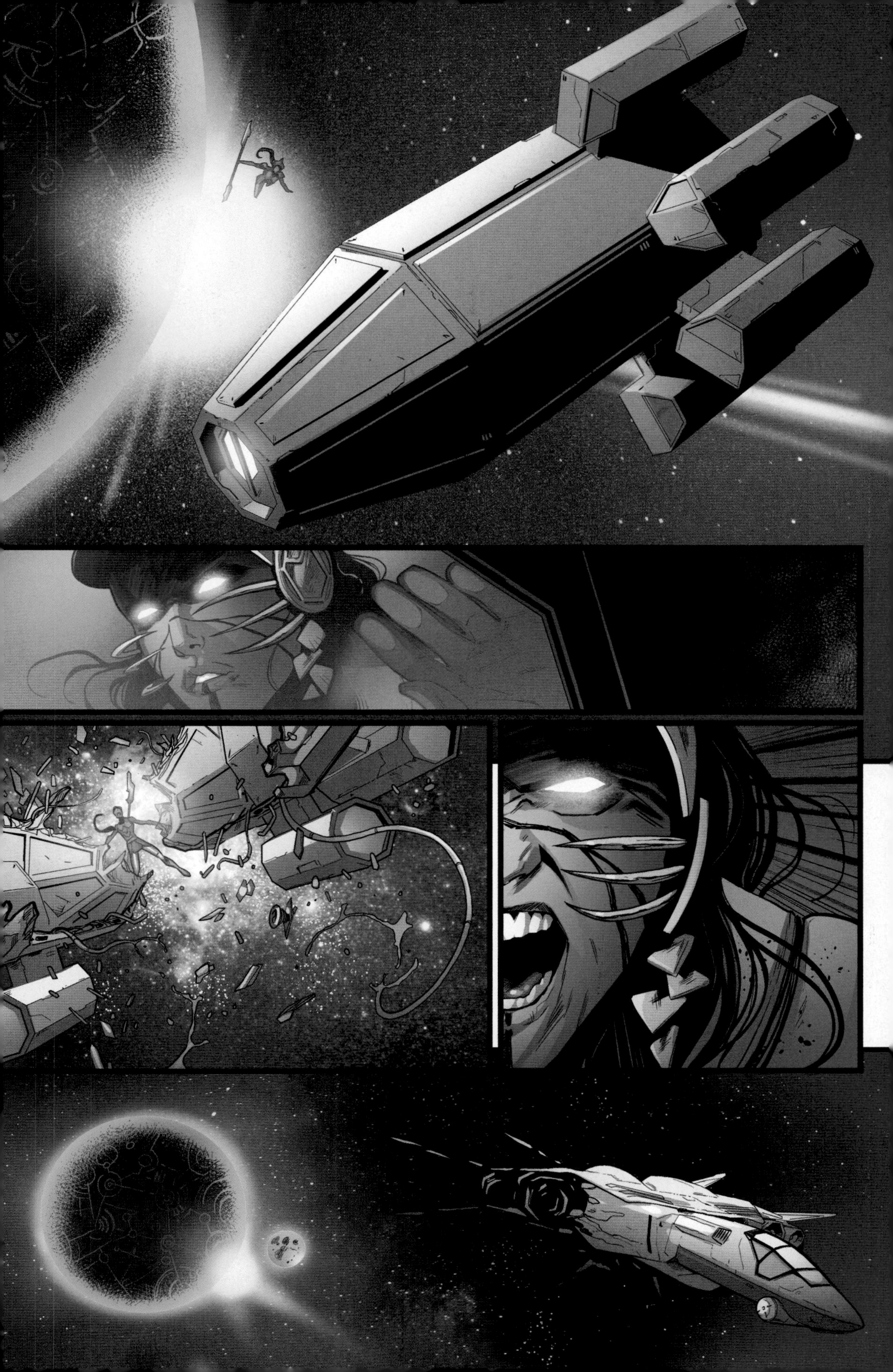

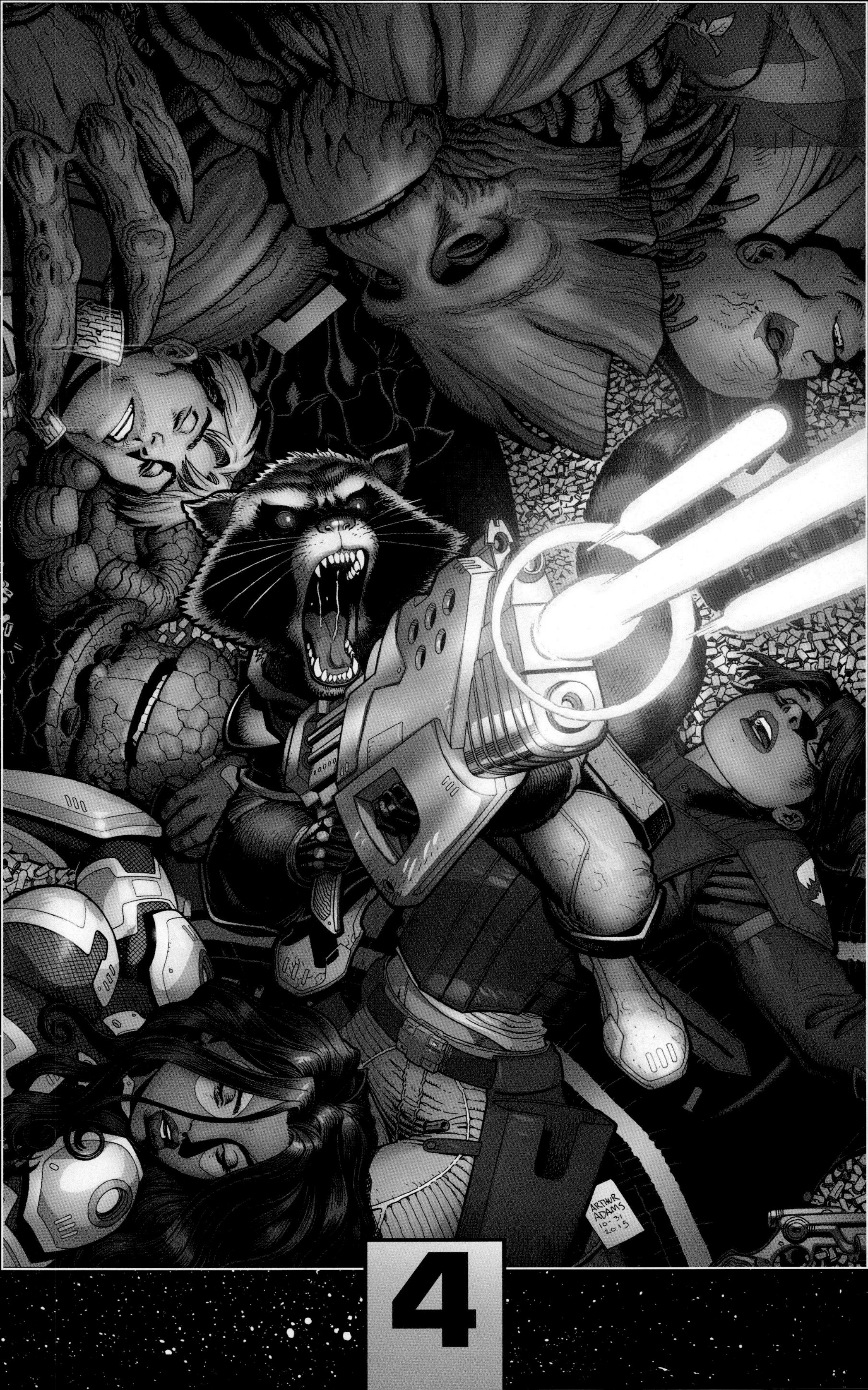
ARTHUR ADAMS
10-31
2015

# 4

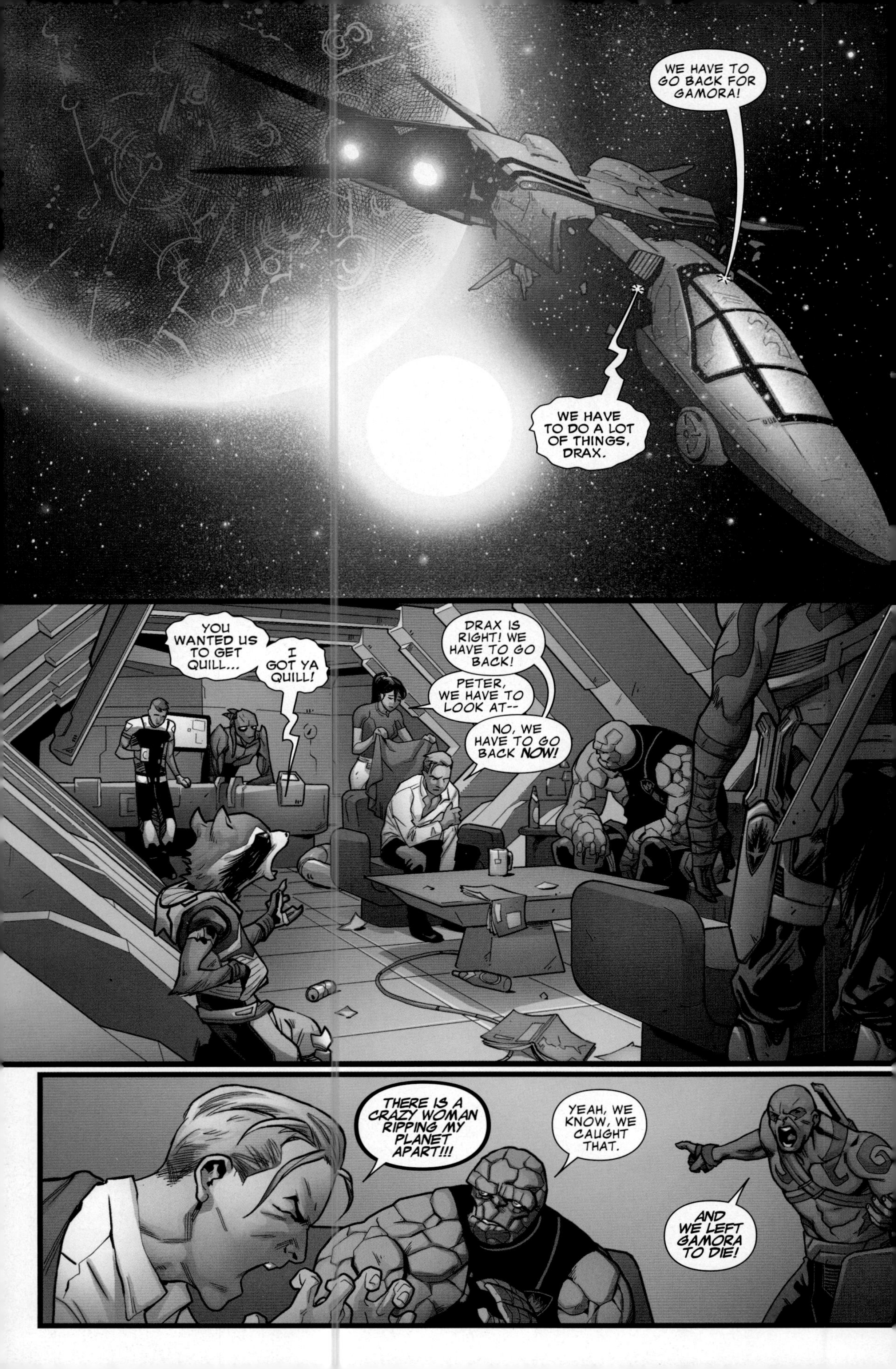
WE HAVE TO GO BACK FOR GAMORA!
WE HAVE TO DO A LOT OF THINGS, DRAX.
YOU WANTED US TO GET QUILL...
I GOT YA QUILL!
DRAX IS RIGHT! WE HAVE TO GO BACK!
PETER, WE HAVE TO LOOK AT--
NO, WE HAVE TO GO BACK NOW!
THERE IS A CRAZY WOMAN RIPPING MY PLANET APART!!!
YEAH, WE KNOW, WE CAUGHT THAT.
AND WE LEFT GAMORA TO DIE!

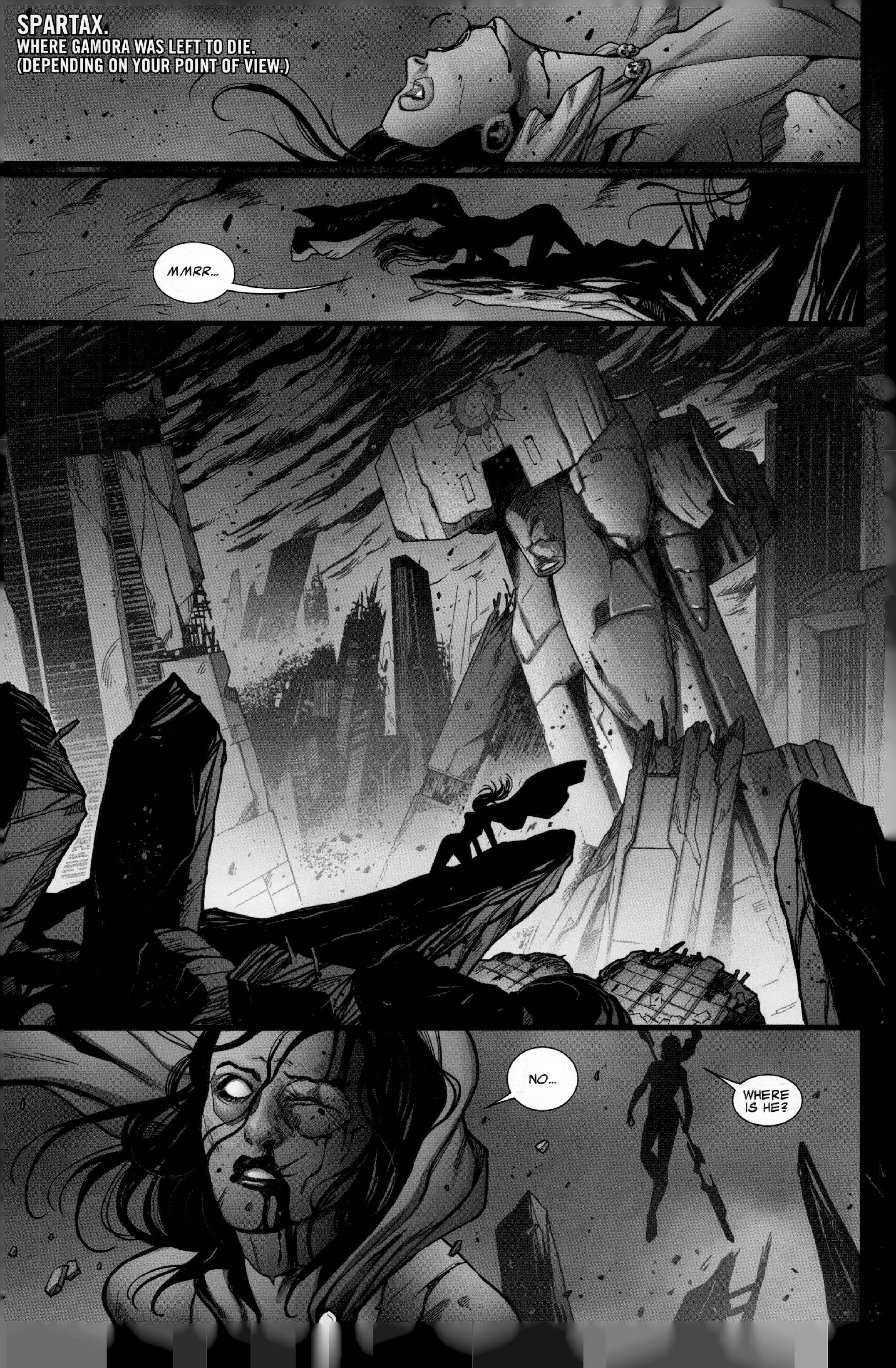
SPARTAX.
WHERE GAMORA WAS LEFT TO DIE.
(DEPENDING ON YOUR POINT OF VIEW.)
MMRR...
NO...
WHERE IS HE?

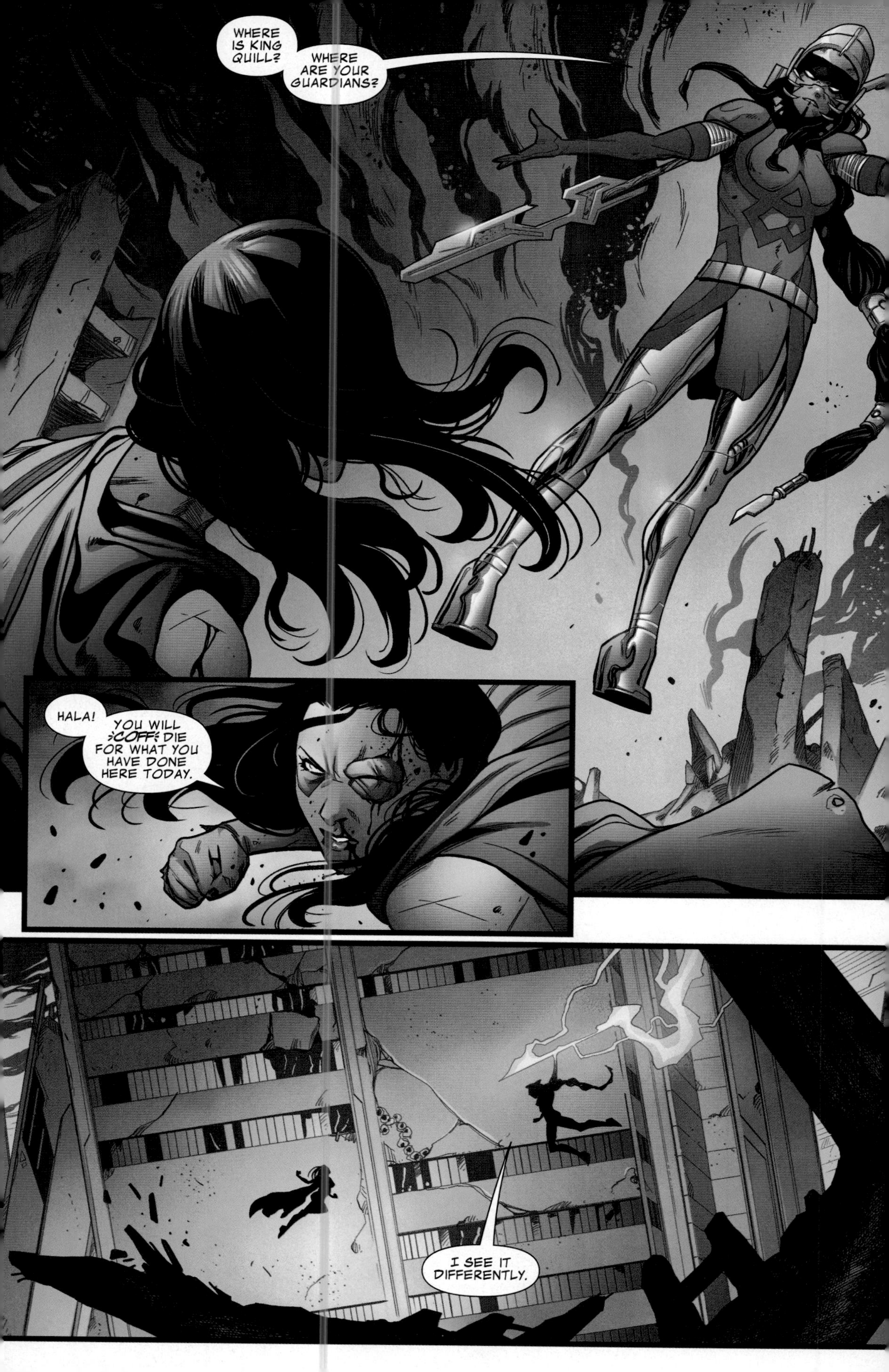
WHERE IS KING QUILL?
WHERE ARE YOUR GUARDIANS?
HALA!
YOU WILL *COFF* DIE FOR WHAT YOU HAVE DONE HERE TODAY.
I SEE IT DIFFERENTLY.

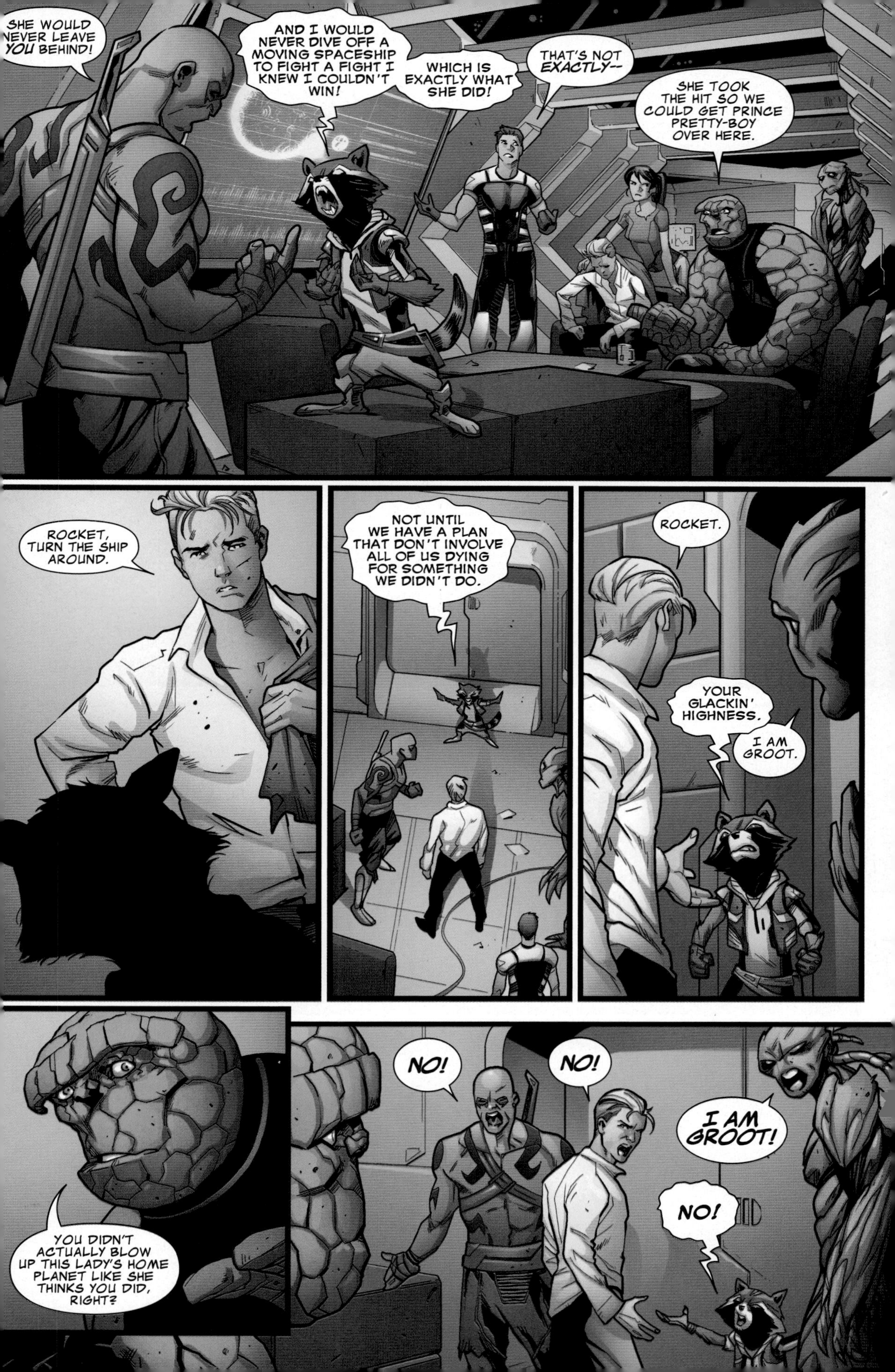
SHE WOULD NEVER LEAVE YOU BEHIND!
AND I WOULD NEVER DIVE OFF A MOVING SPACESHIP TO FIGHT A FIGHT I KNEW I COULDN'T WIN!
WHICH IS EXACTLY WHAT SHE DID!
THAT'S NOT EXACTLY--
SHE TOOK THE HIT SO WE COULD GET PRINCE PRETTY-BOY OVER HERE.
ROCKET, TURN THE SHIP AROUND.
NOT UNTIL WE HAVE A PLAN THAT DON'T INVOLVE ALL OF US DYING FOR SOMETHING WE DIDN'T DO.
ROCKET.
YOUR GLACKIN' HIGHNESS.
I AM GROOT.
YOU DIDN'T ACTUALLY BLOW UP THIS LADY'S HOME PLANET LIKE SHE THINKS YOU DID, RIGHT?
NO!
NO!
I AM GROOT!
NO!

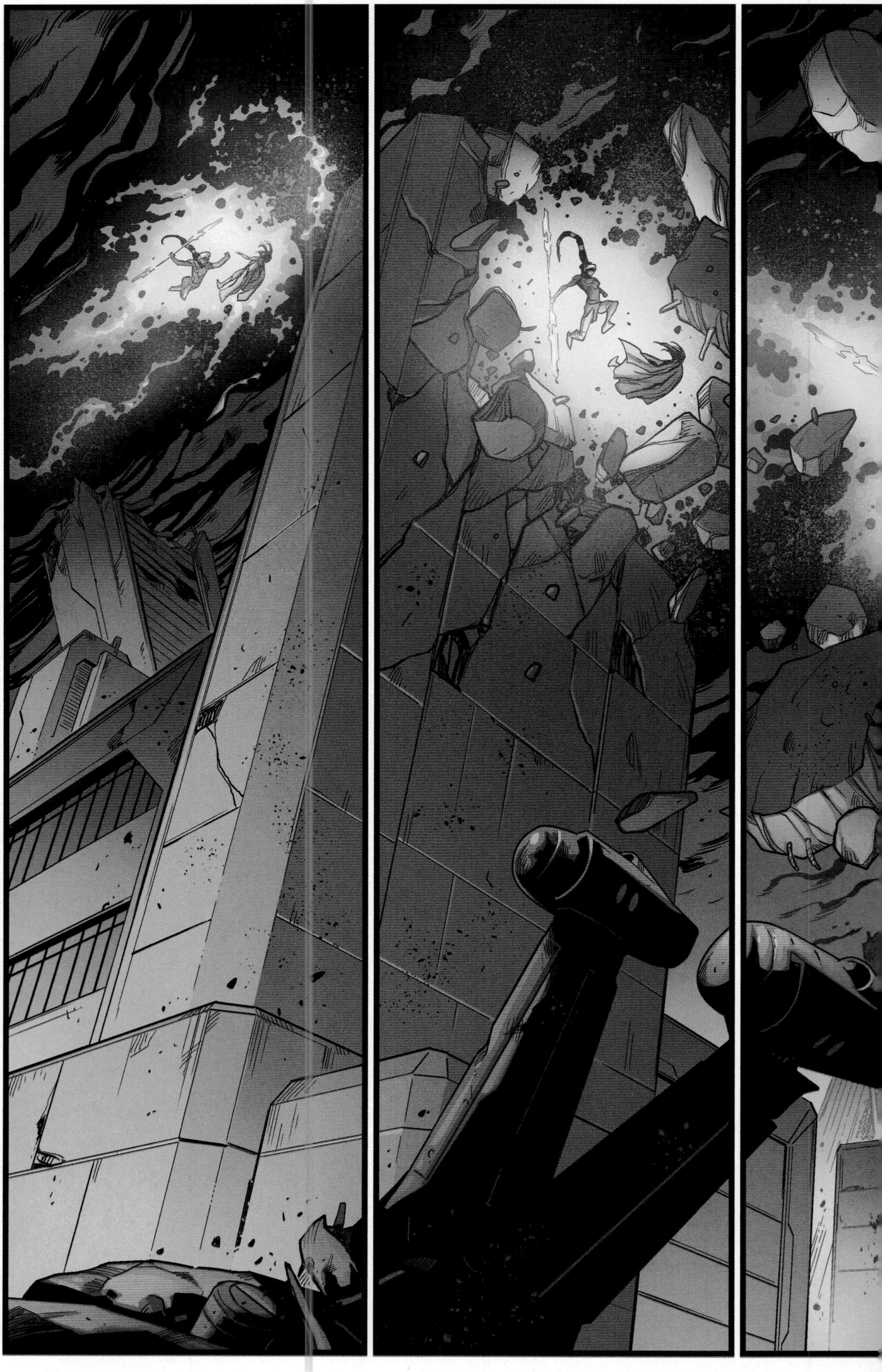

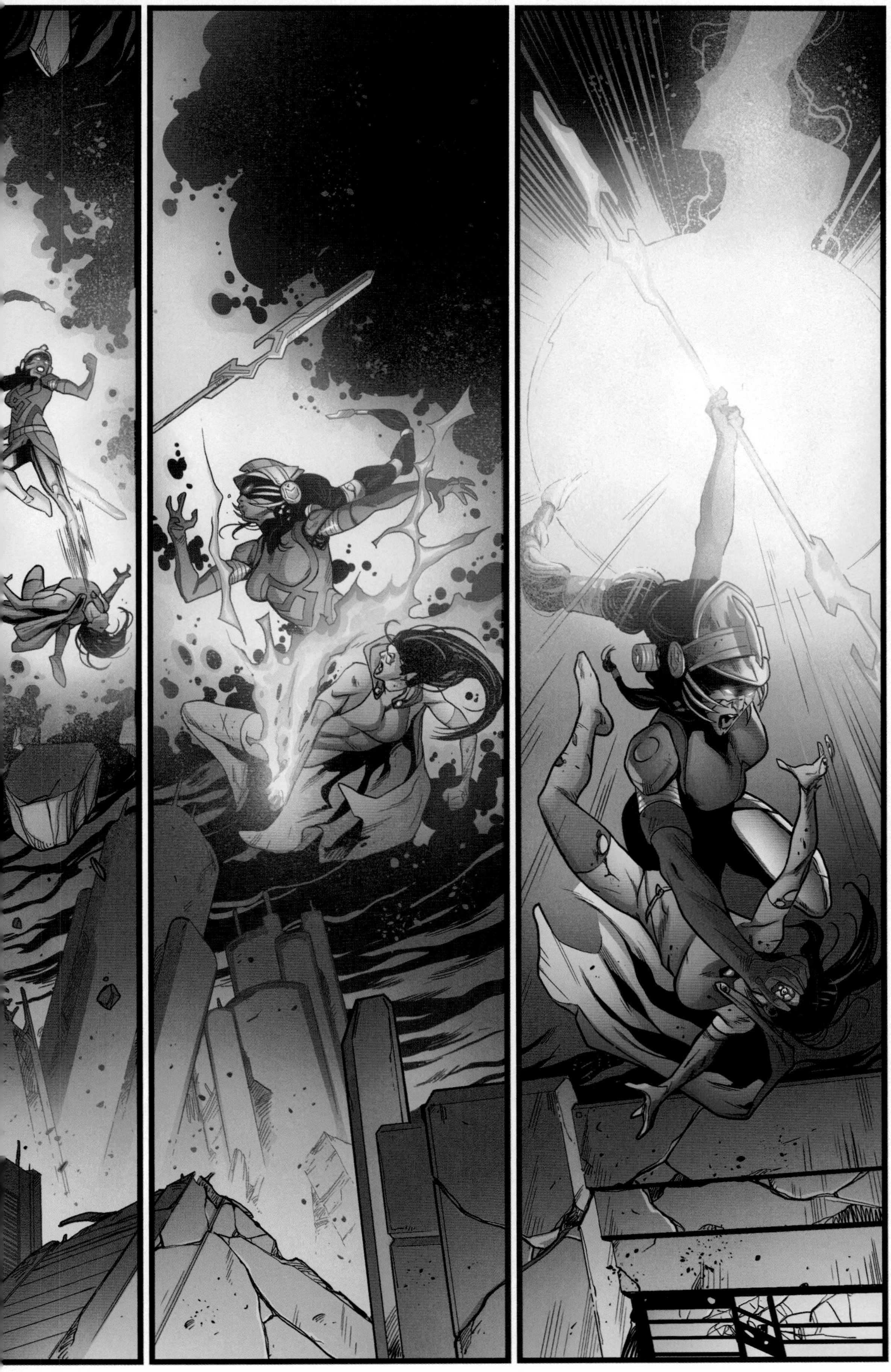

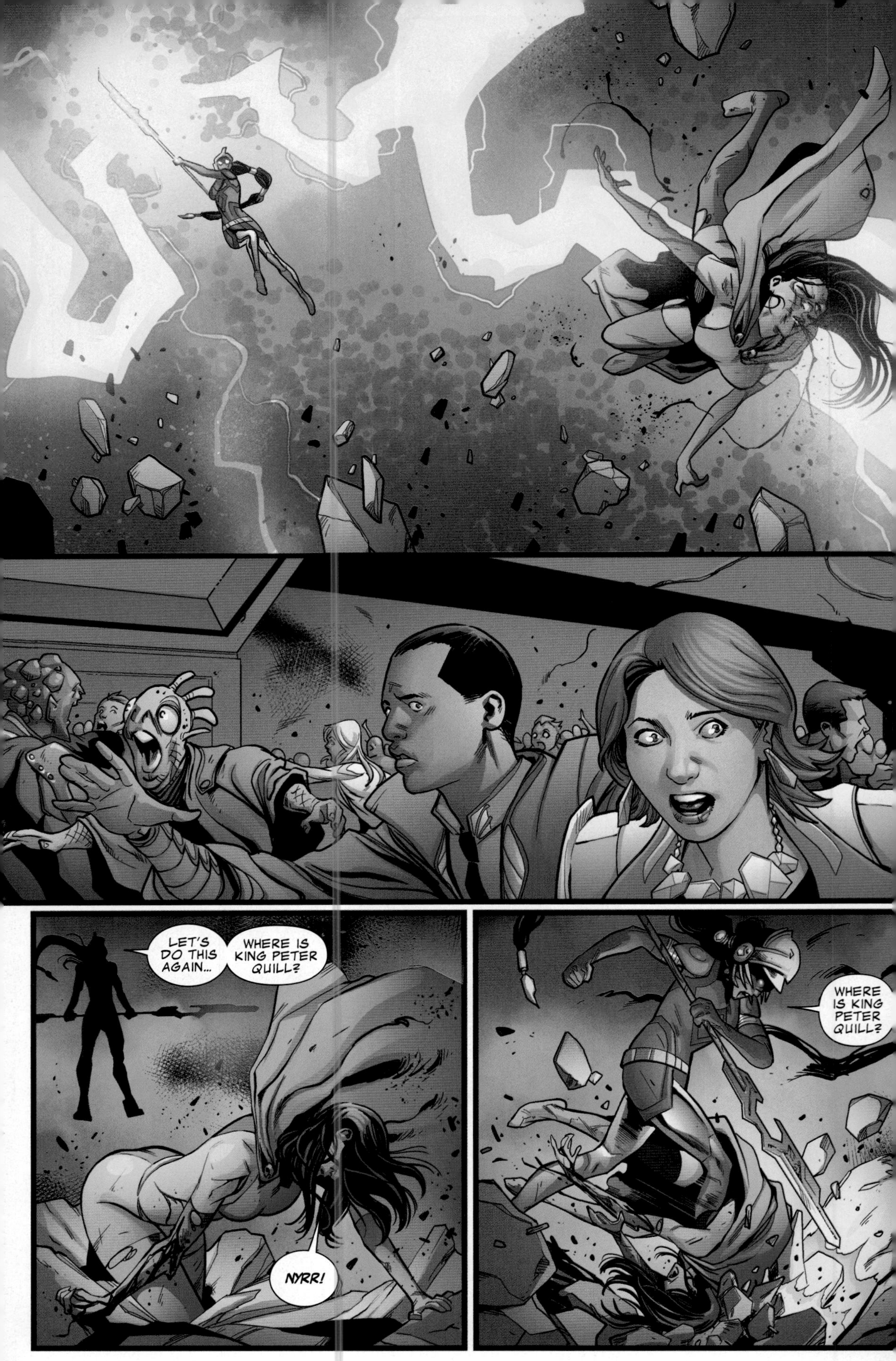
LET'S DO THIS AGAIN...
WHERE IS KING PETER QUILL?
NYRR!
WHERE IS KING PETER QUILL?

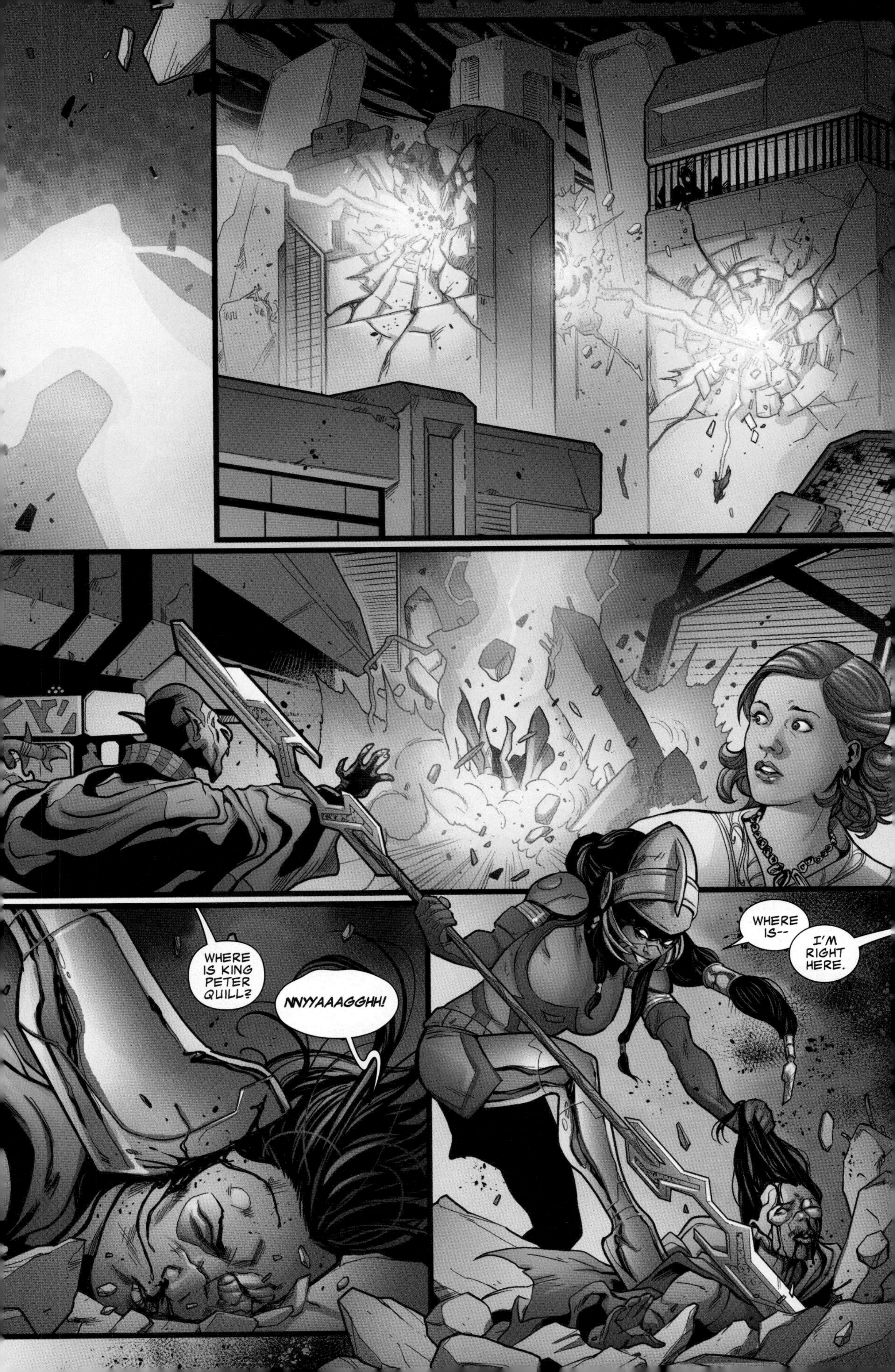
WHERE IS KING PETER QUILL?
NNYYAAAGGHH!
WHERE IS--
I'M RIGHT HERE.

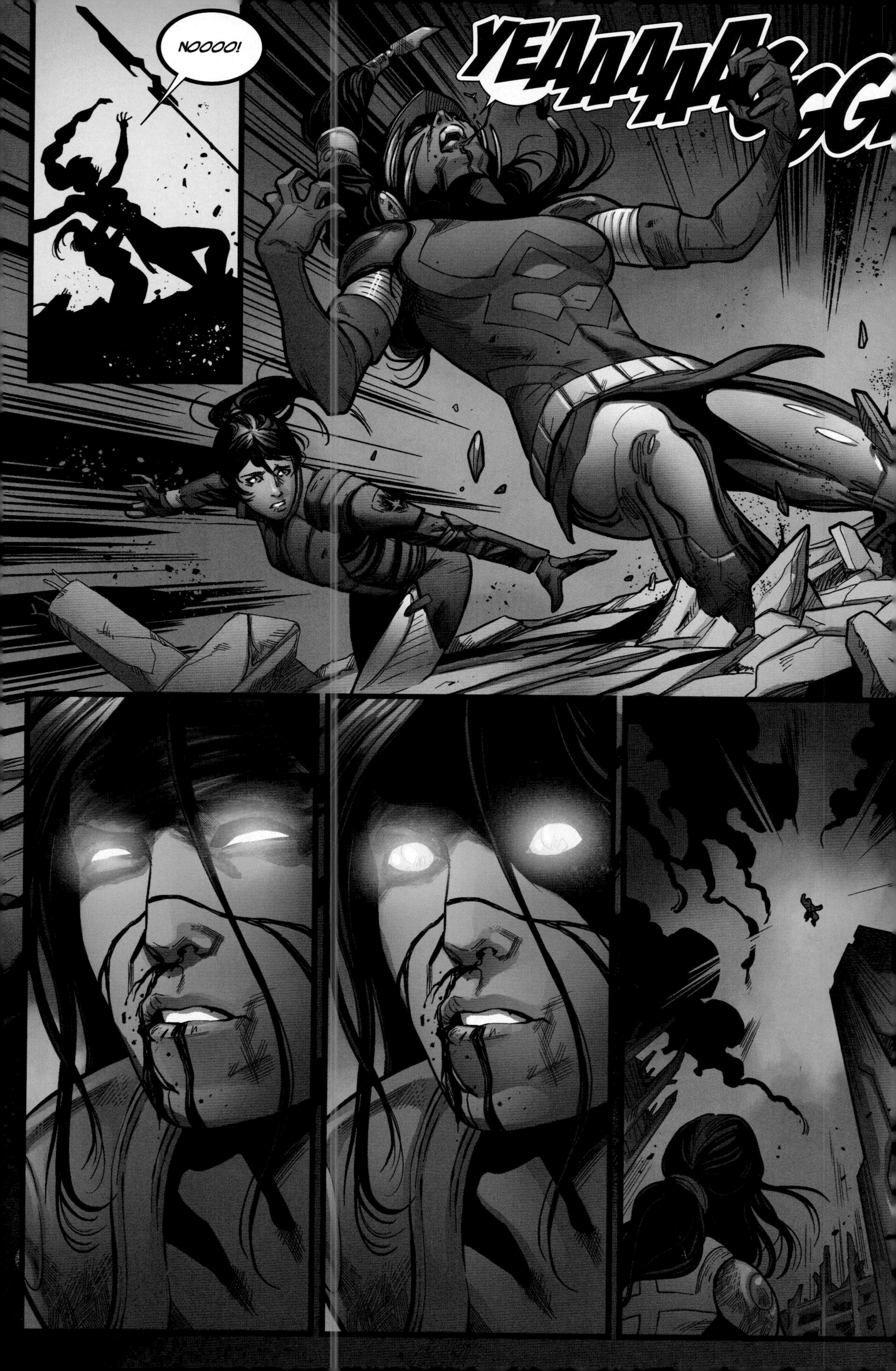
NOOOO!
YEAAAAGG

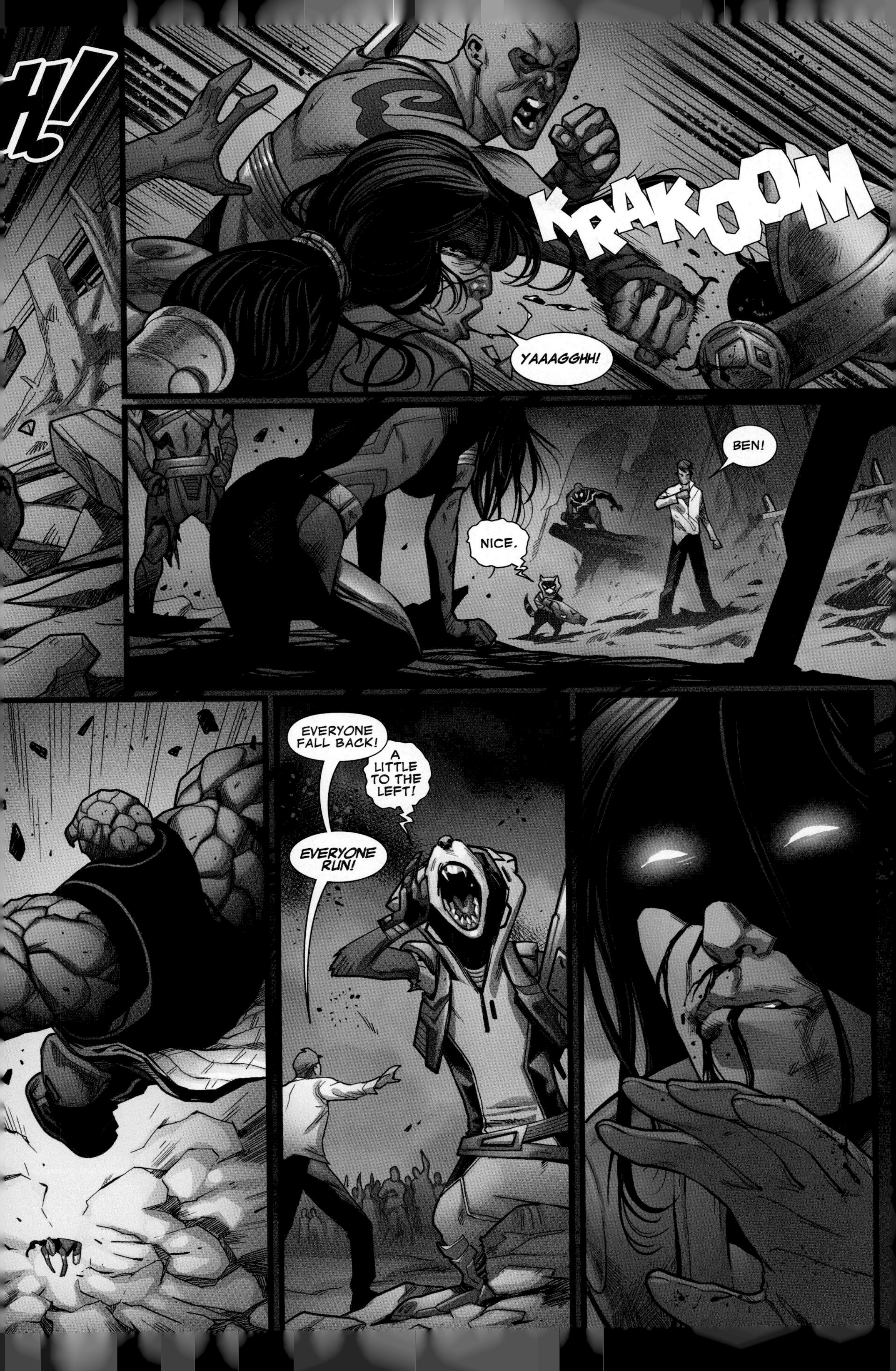
H!
KRAKOOM
YAAAGGHH!
BEN!
NICE.
EVERYONE FALL BACK!
A LITTLE TO THE LEFT!
EVERYONE RUN!

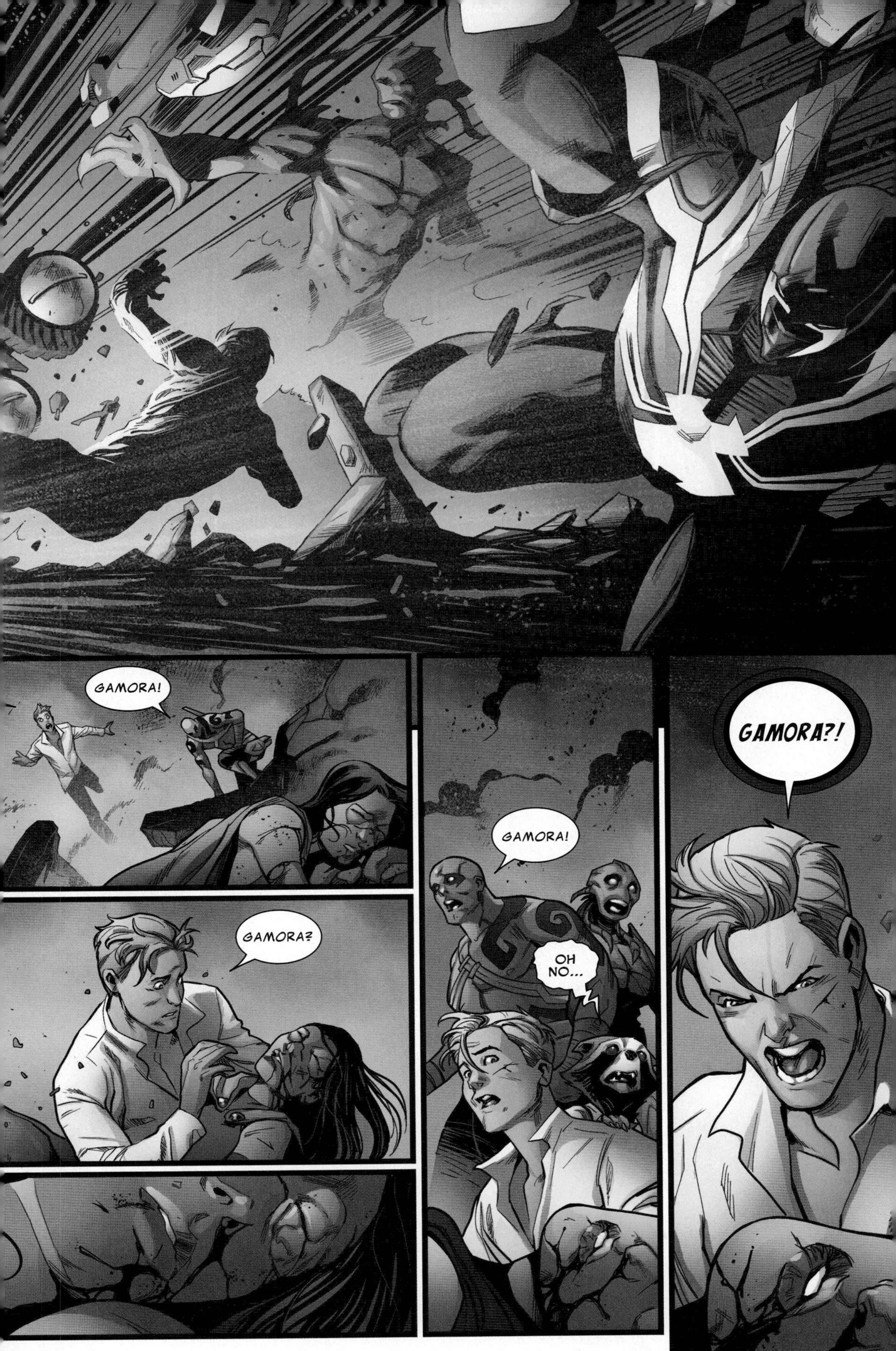
GAMORA!
GAMORA?
GAMORA!
OH NO...
GAMORA?!

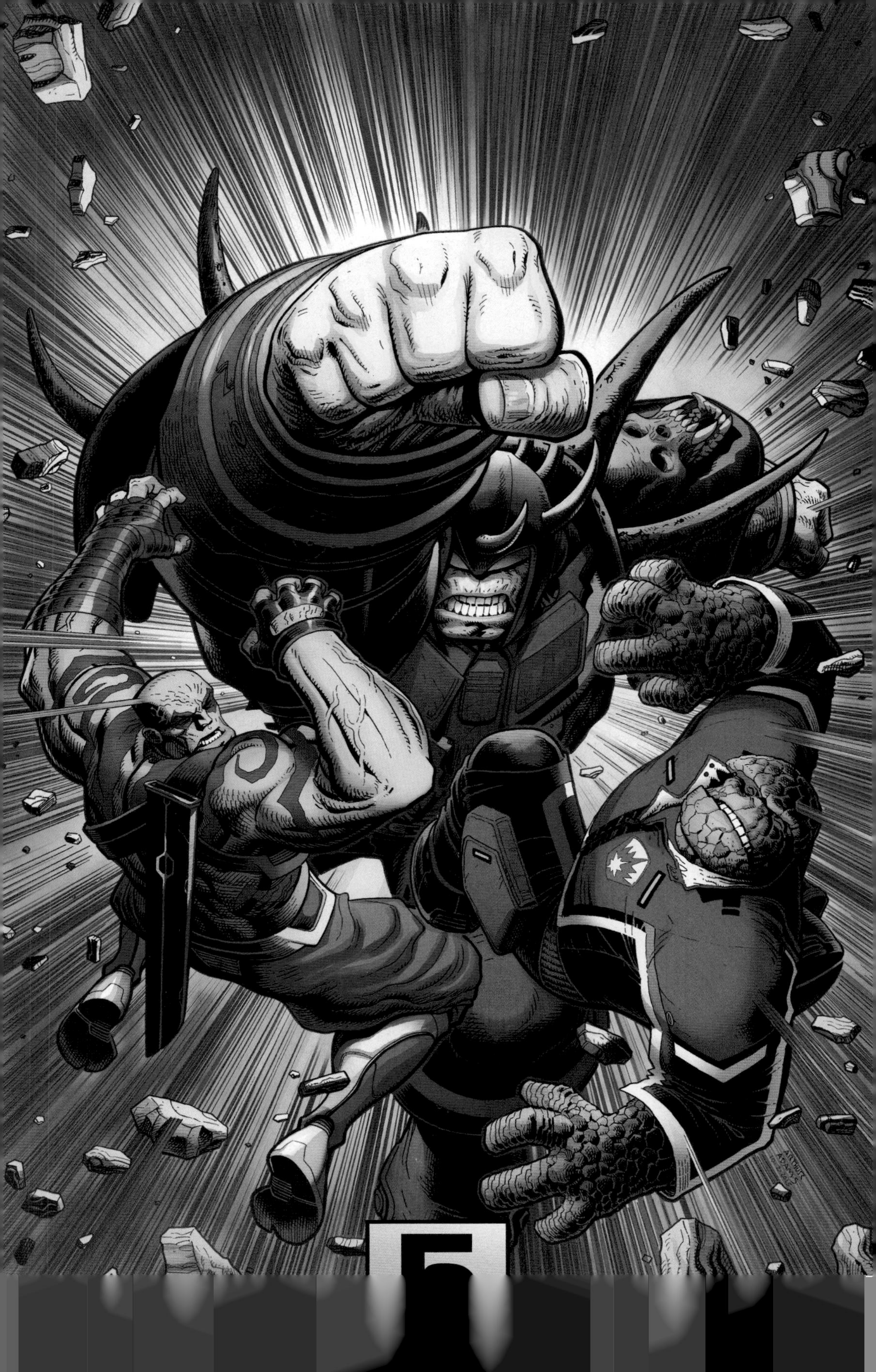
ARTHUR ADAMS
5

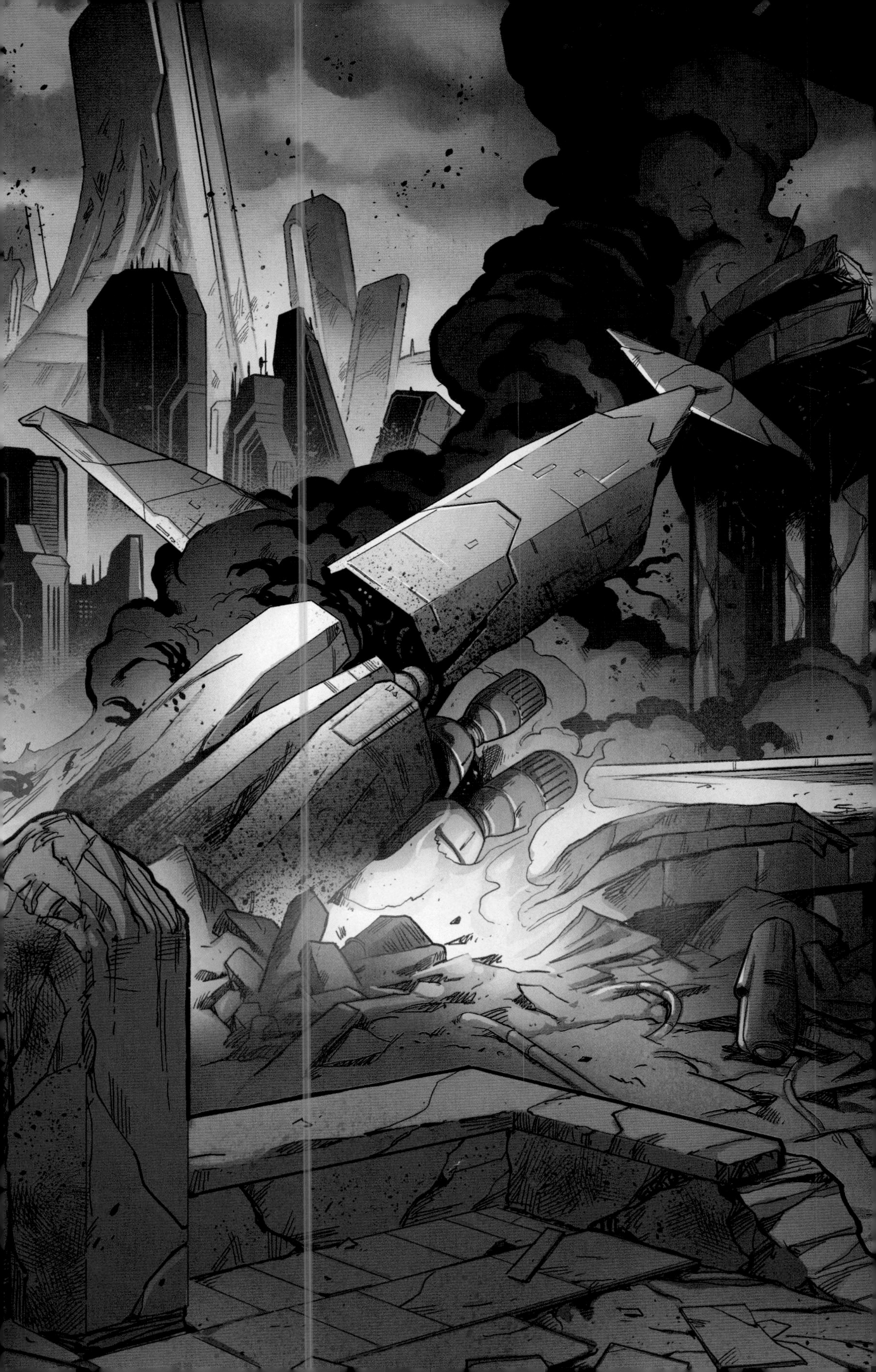

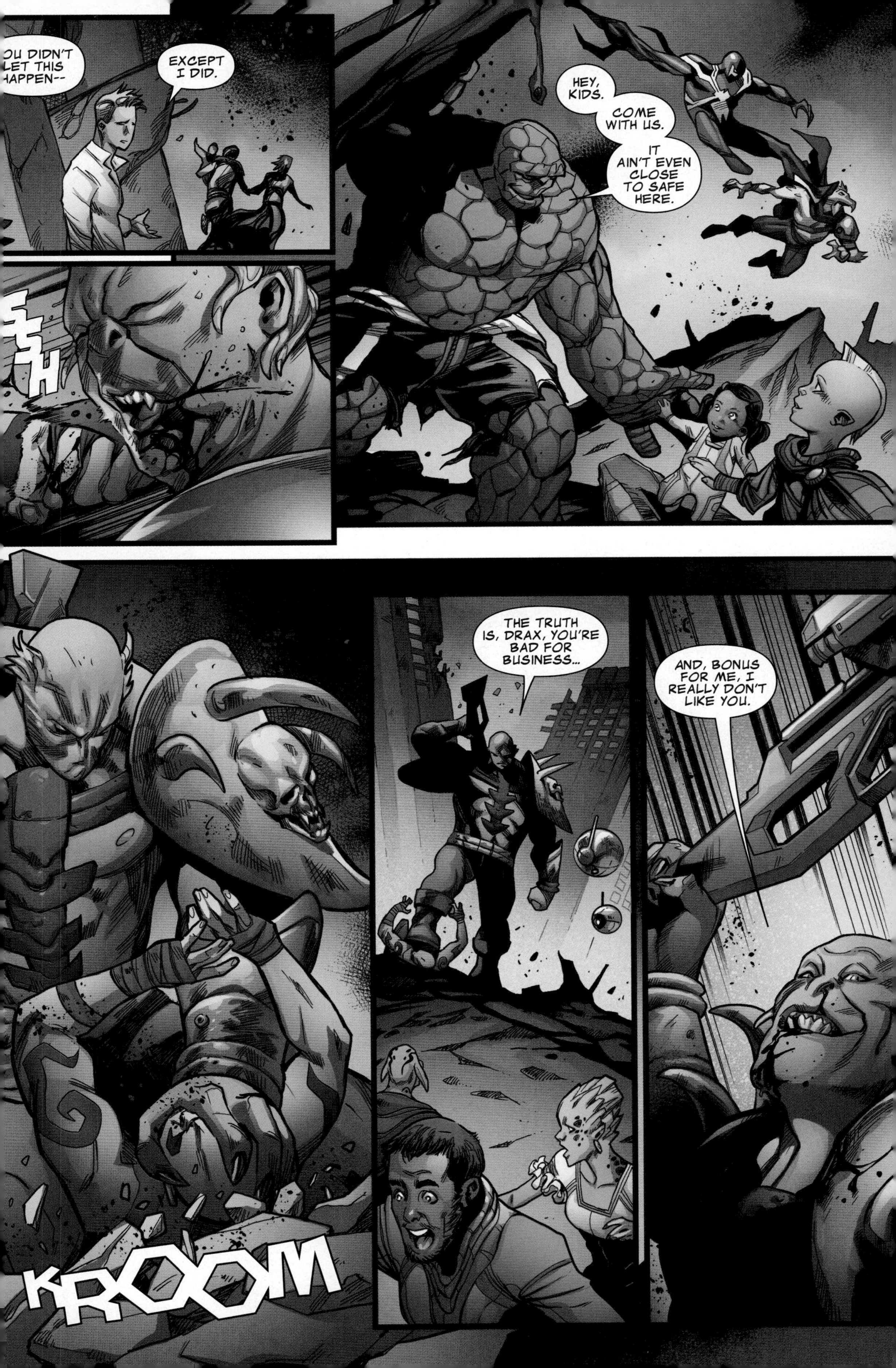
OU DIDN'T LET THIS HAPPEN--
EXCEPT I DID.
HEY, KIDS.
COME WITH US.
IT AIN'T EVEN CLOSE TO SAFE HERE.
KROOM
THE TRUTH IS, DRAX, YOU'RE BAD FOR BUSINESS...
AND, BONUS FOR ME, I REALLY DON'T LIKE YOU.

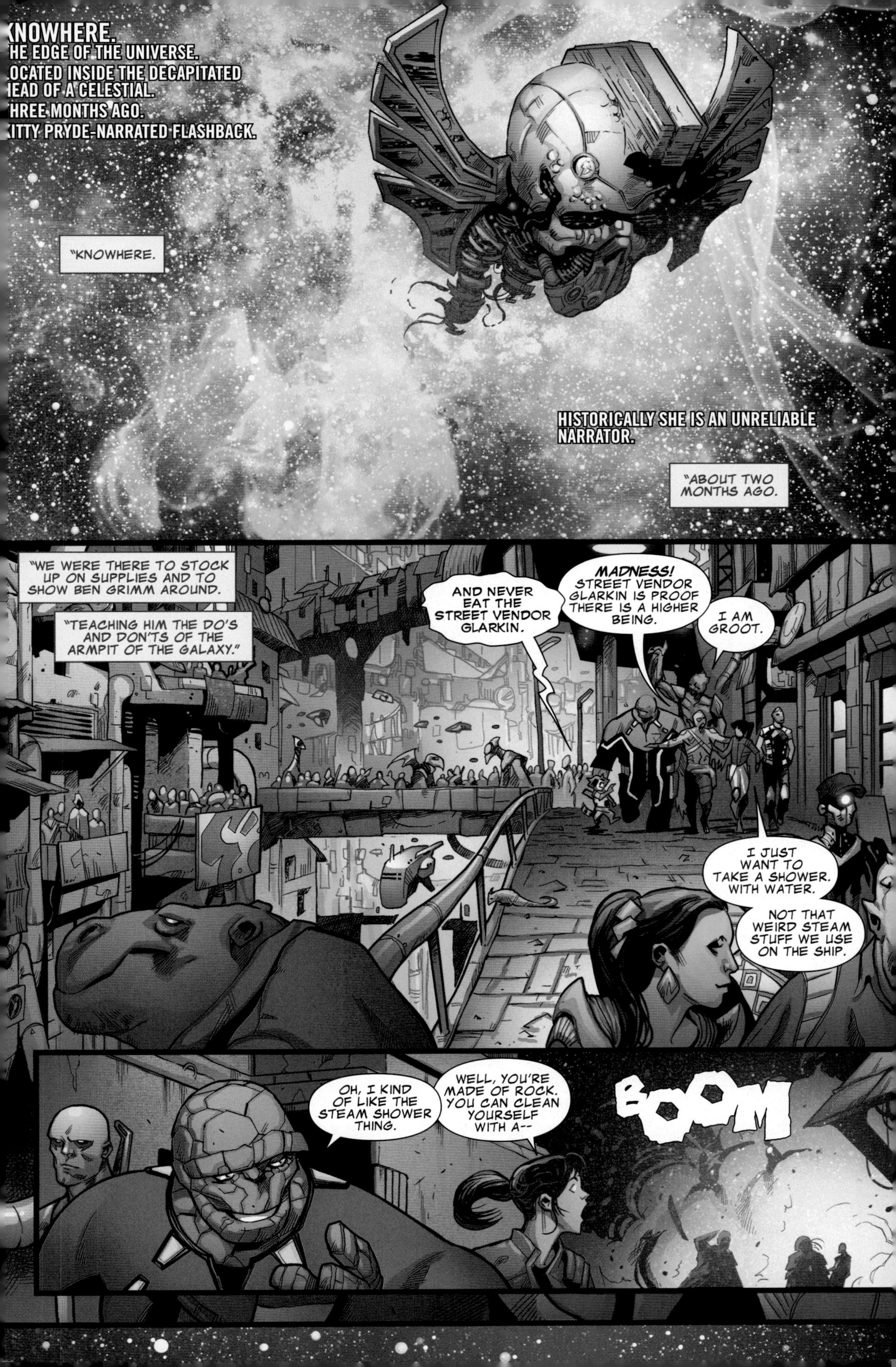
KNOWHERE.
HE EDGE OF THE UNIVERSE.
OCATED INSIDE THE DECAPITATED
EAD OF A CELESTIAL.
HREE MONTHS AGO.
ITTY PRYDE-NARRATED FLASHBACK.
"KNOWHERE.
HISTORICALLY SHE IS AN UNRELIABLE NARRATOR.
"ABOUT TWO MONTHS AGO.
"WE WERE THERE TO STOCK UP ON SUPPLIES AND TO SHOW BEN GRIMM AROUND.
"TEACHING HIM THE DO'S AND DON'TS OF THE ARMPIT OF THE GALAXY."
AND NEVER EAT THE STREET VENDOR GLARKIN.
MADNESS! STREET VENDOR GLARKIN IS PROOF THERE IS A HIGHER BEING.
I AM GROOT.
I JUST WANT TO TAKE A SHOWER. WITH WATER.
NOT THAT WEIRD STEAM STUFF WE USE ON THE SHIP.
OH, I KIND OF LIKE THE STEAM SHOWER THING.
WELL, YOU'RE MADE OF ROCK. YOU CAN CLEAN YOURSELF WITH A--
BOOM

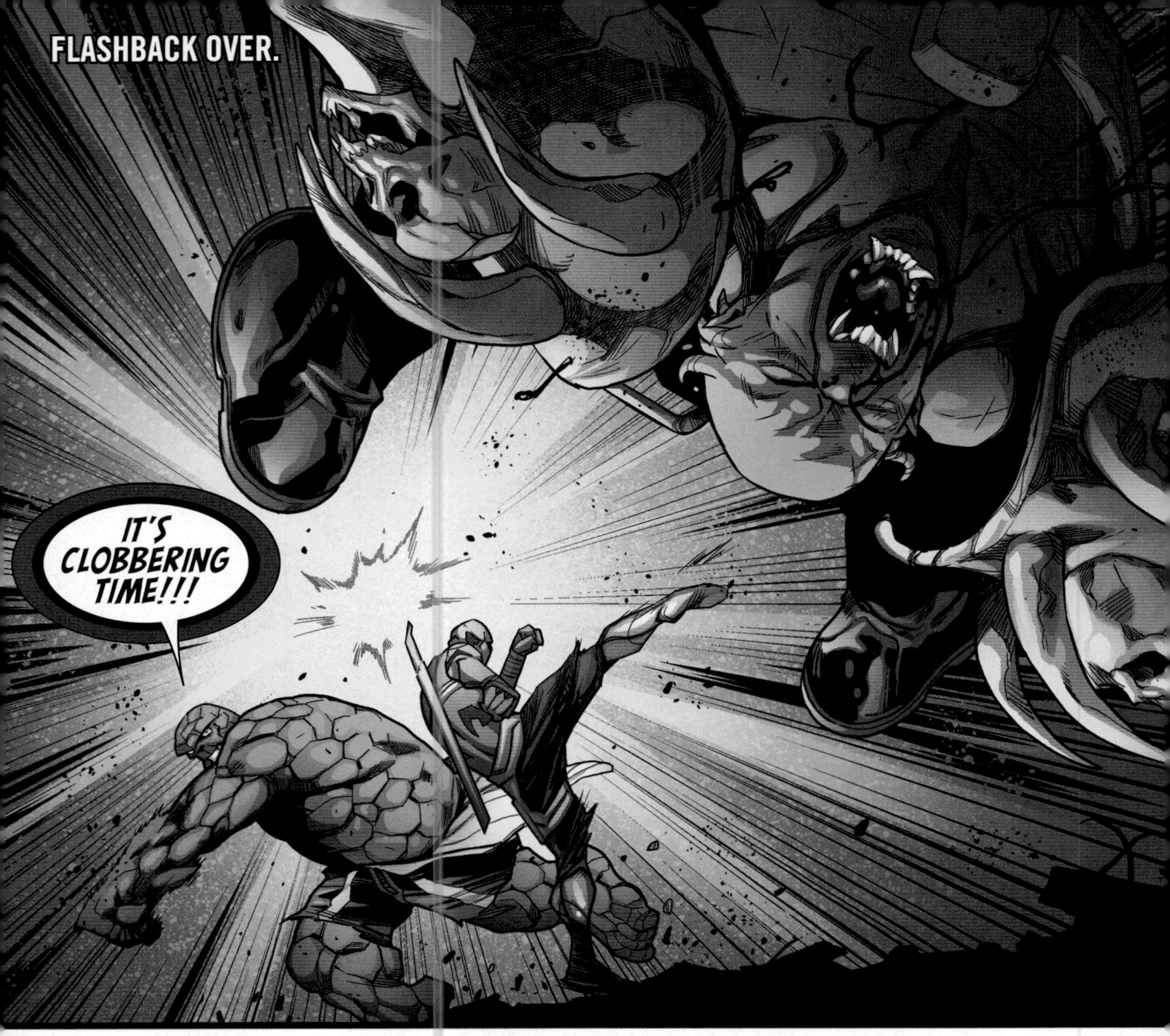
FLASHBACK OVER.
IT'S CLOBBERING TIME!!!

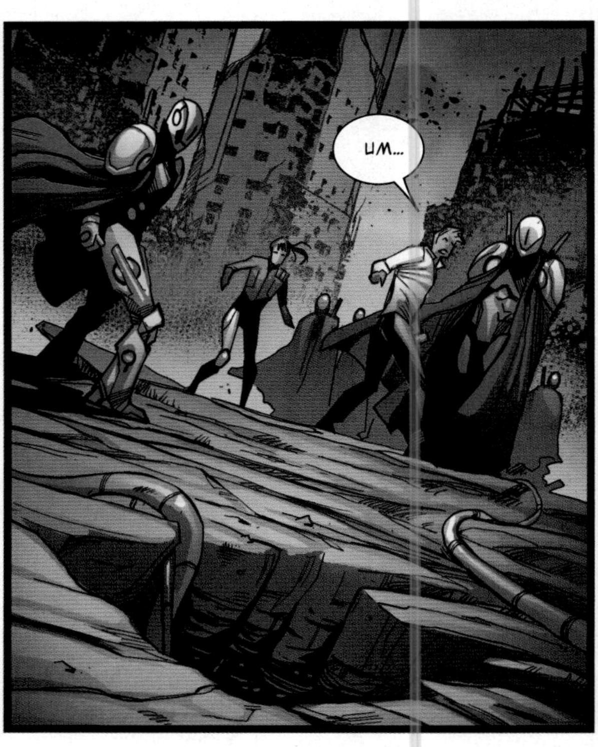
UM...

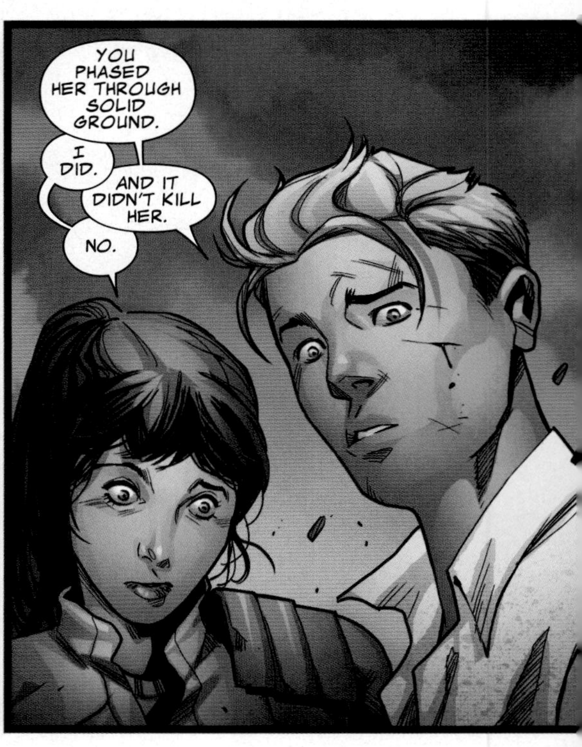
YOU PHASED HER THROUGH SOLID GROUND.
I DID.
AND IT DIDN'T KILL HER.
NO.

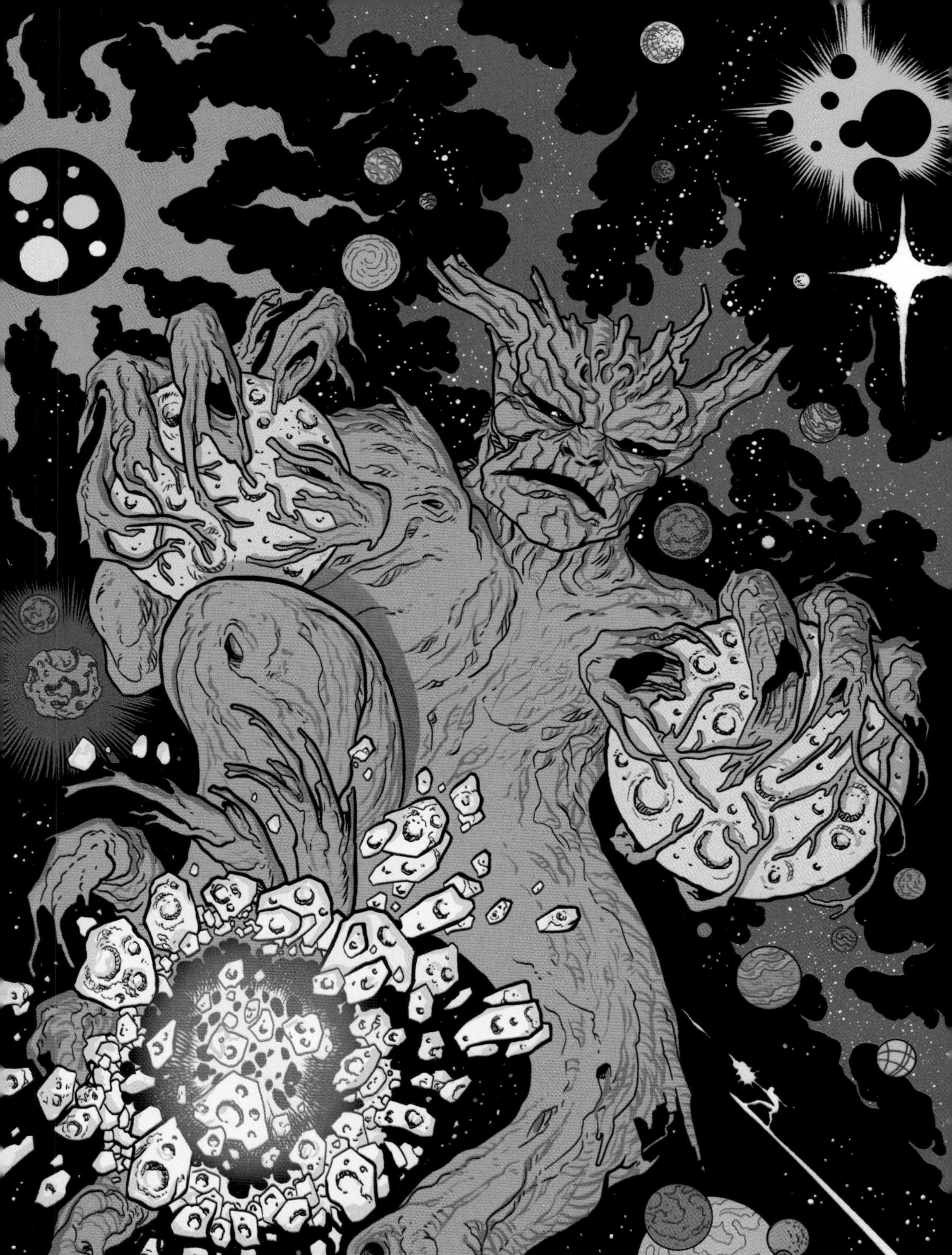
ALL
RED

#1 KIRBY MONSTER

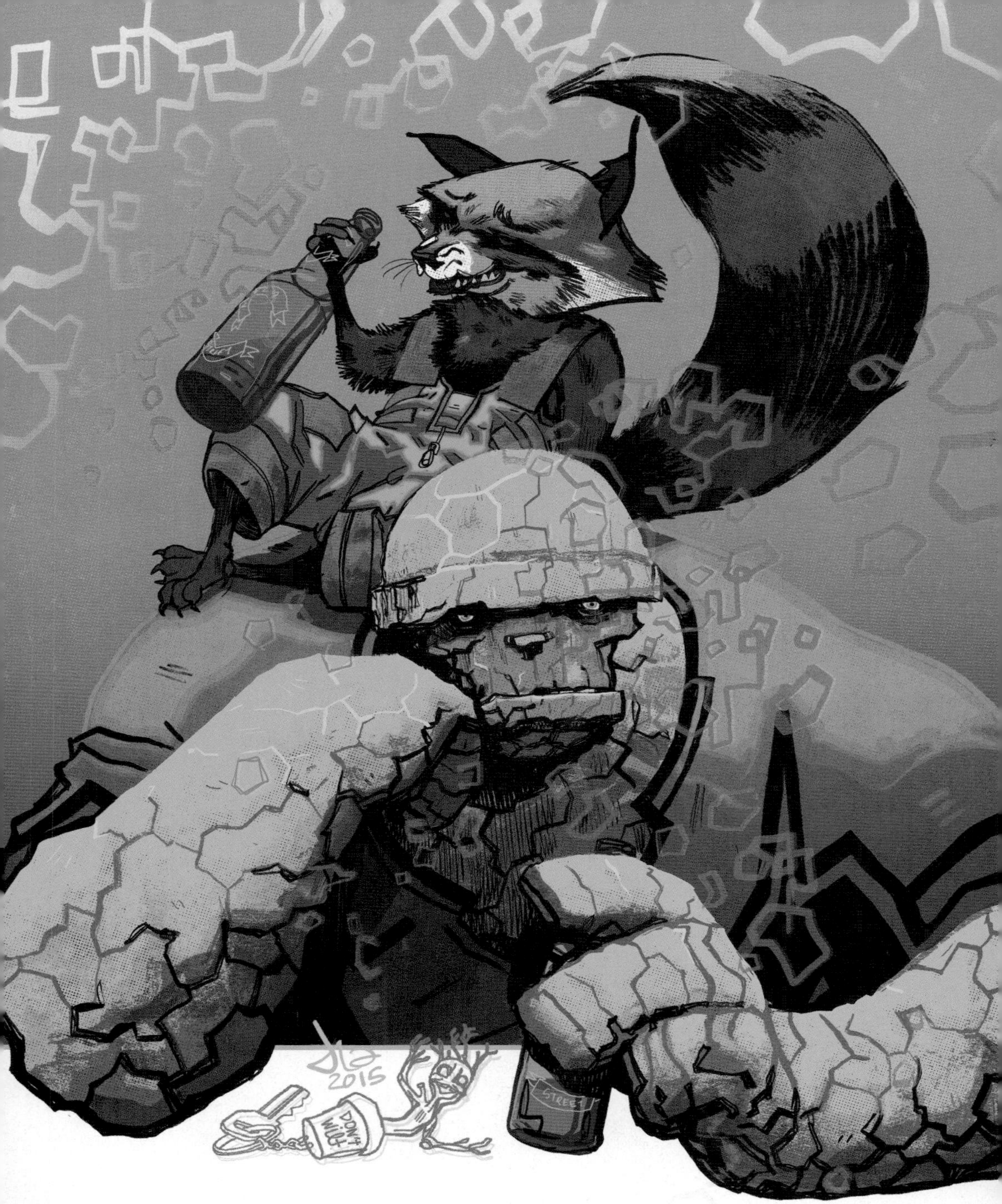
2015
DON'T WILT

#1 VARIANT BY

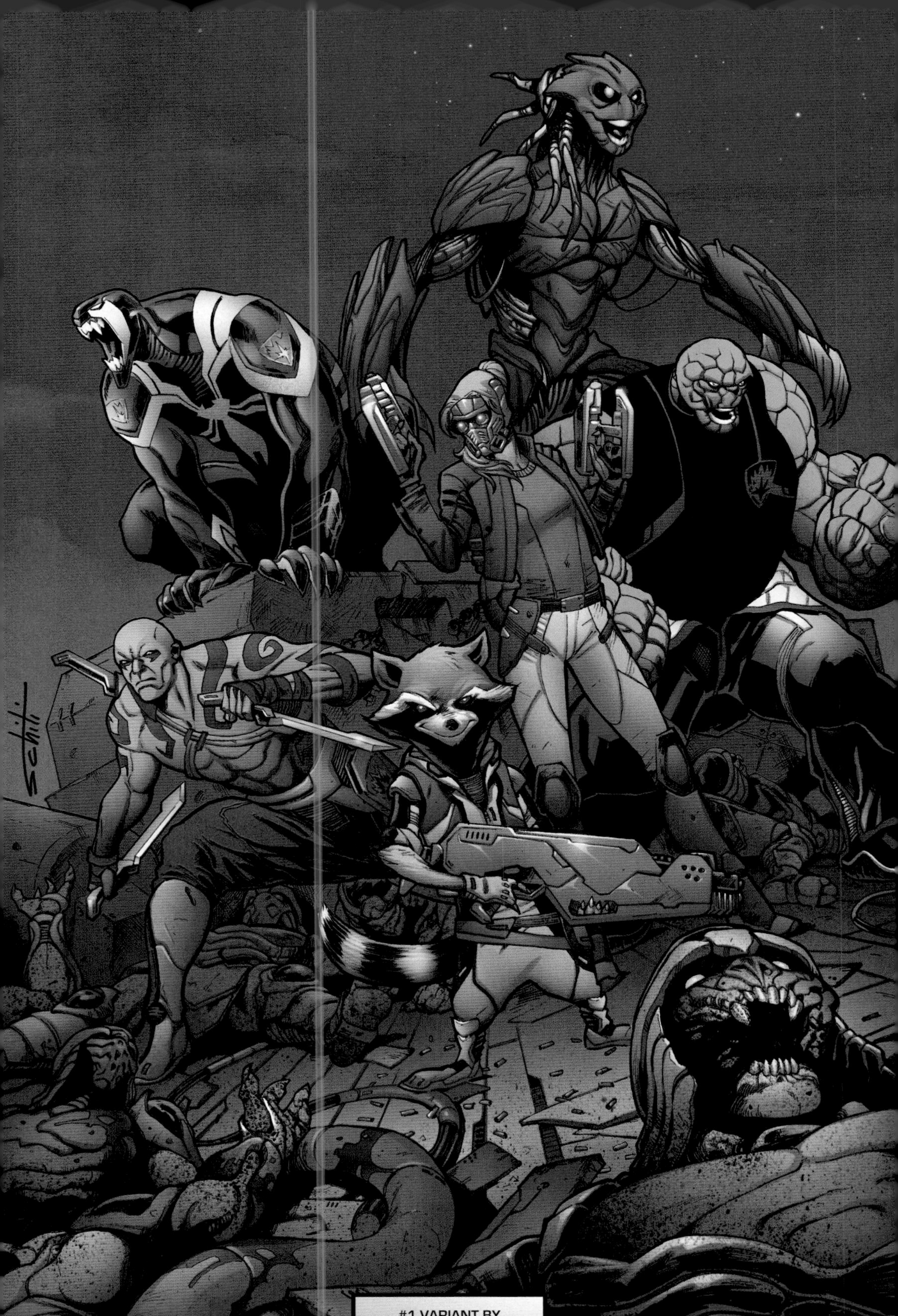

#1 VARIANT BY

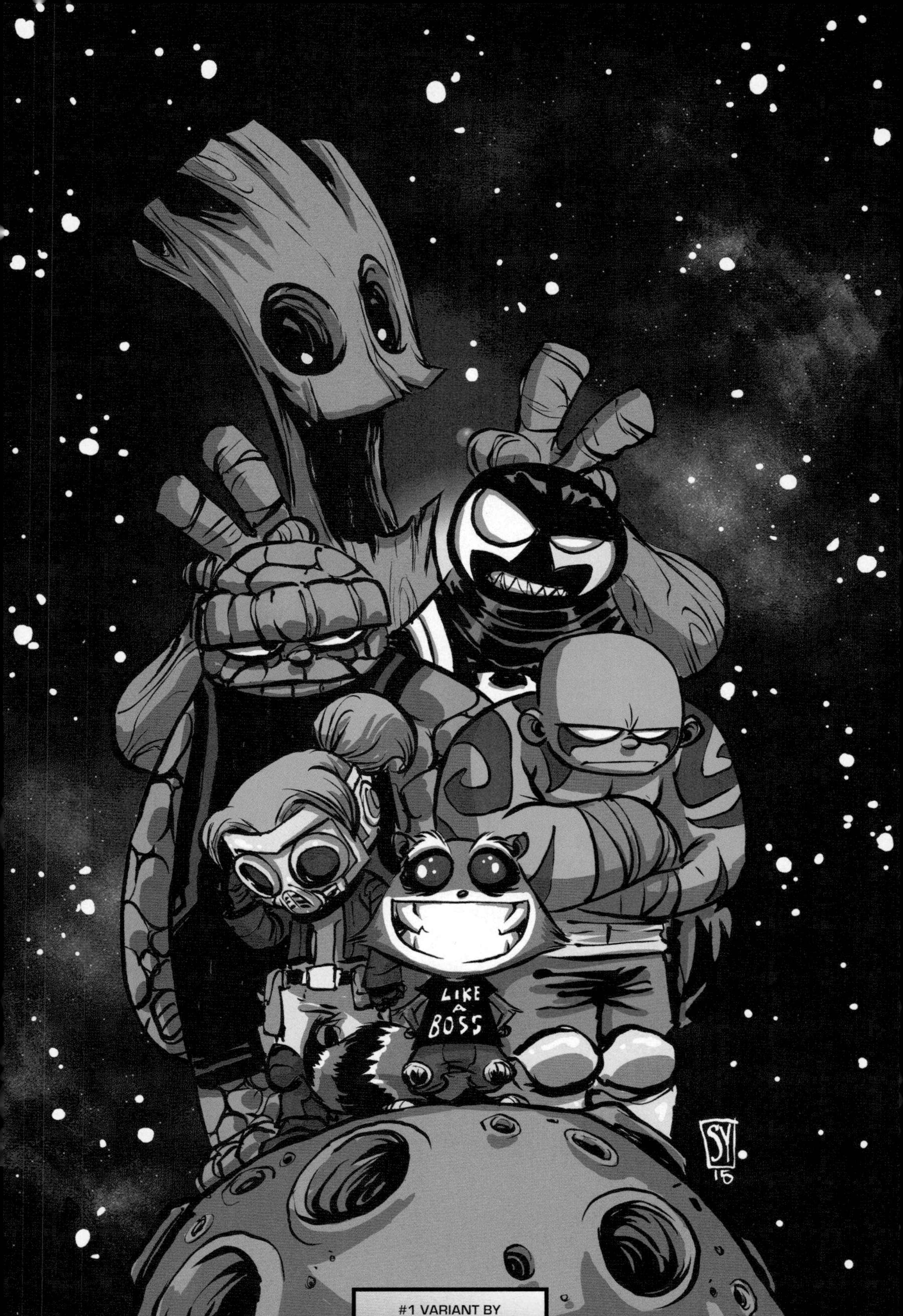
LIKE A BOSS
SY '15

#1 VARIANT BY

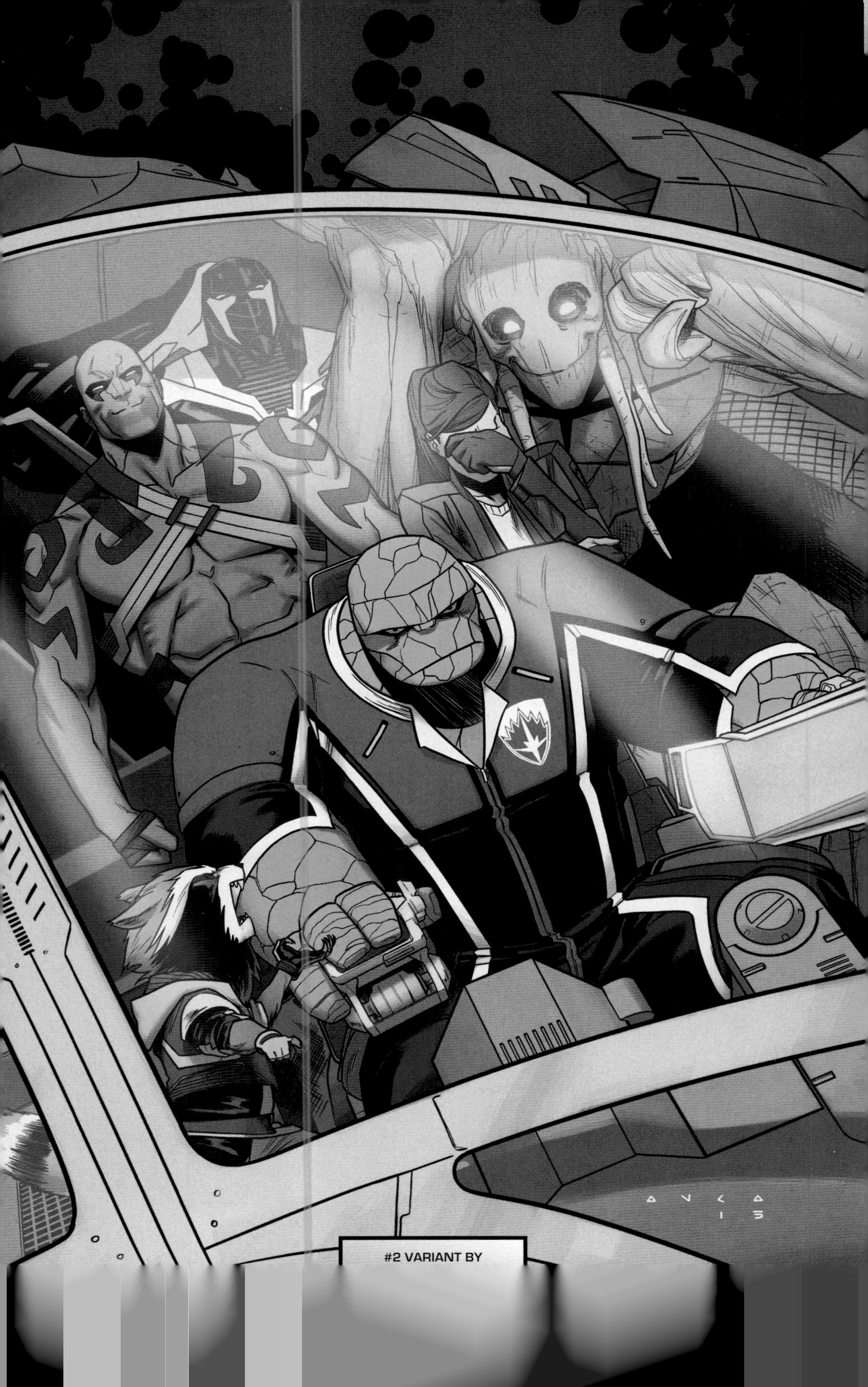

#2 VARIANT BY

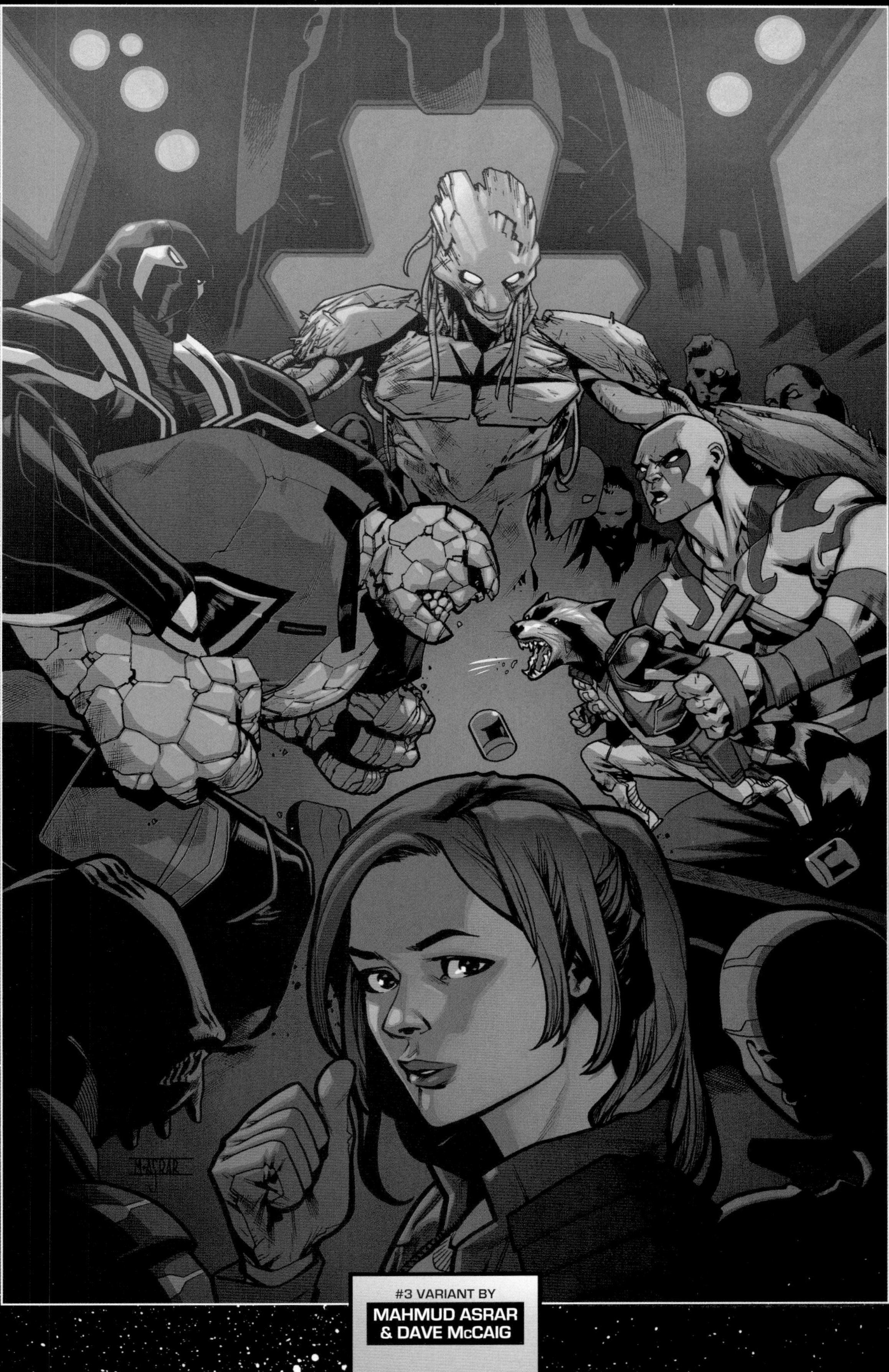

#3 VARIANT BY

**MAHMUD ASRAR & DAVE McCAIG**

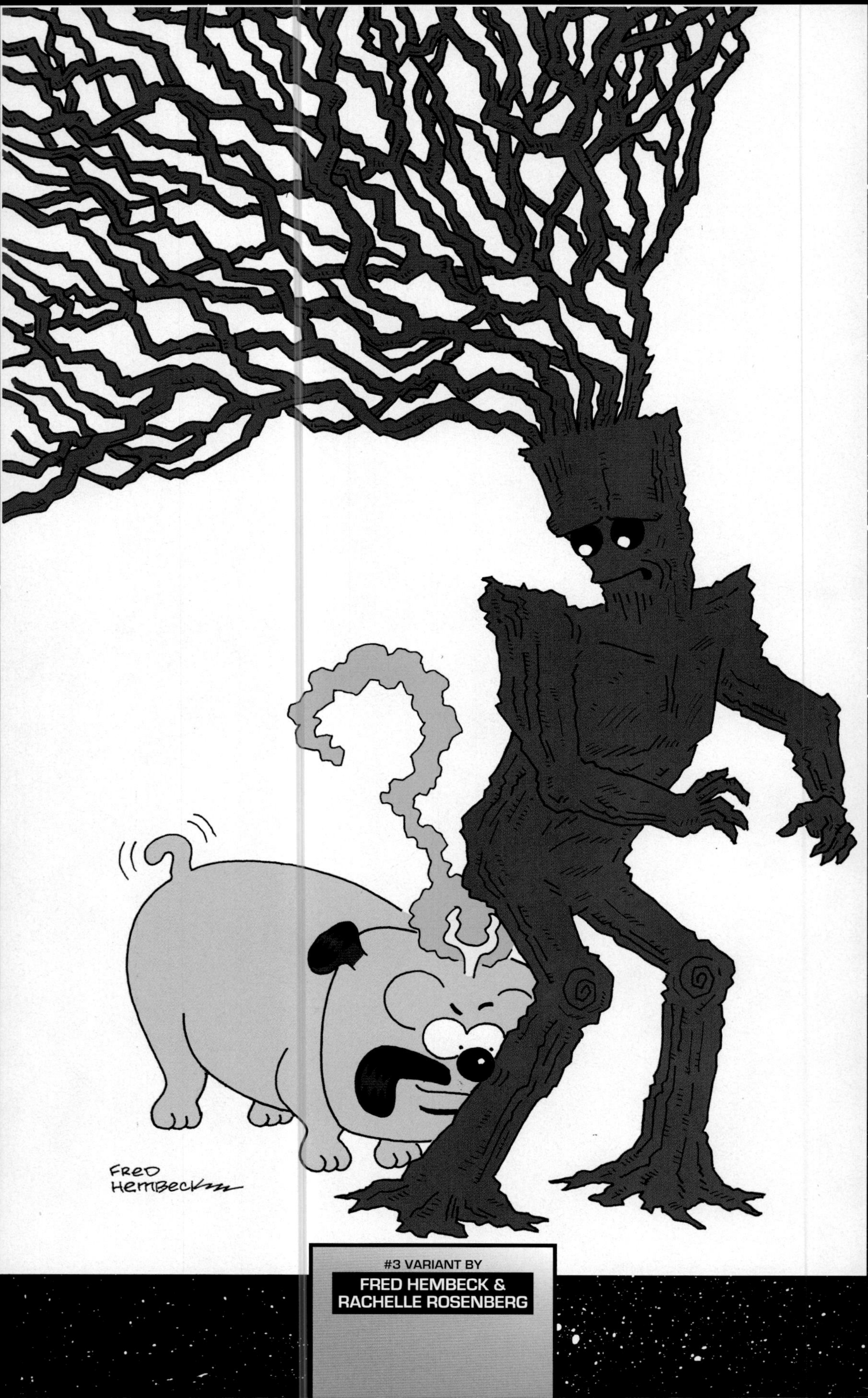
FRED
HEMBECK

#3 VARIANT BY
FRED HEMBECK &
RACHELLE ROSENBERG

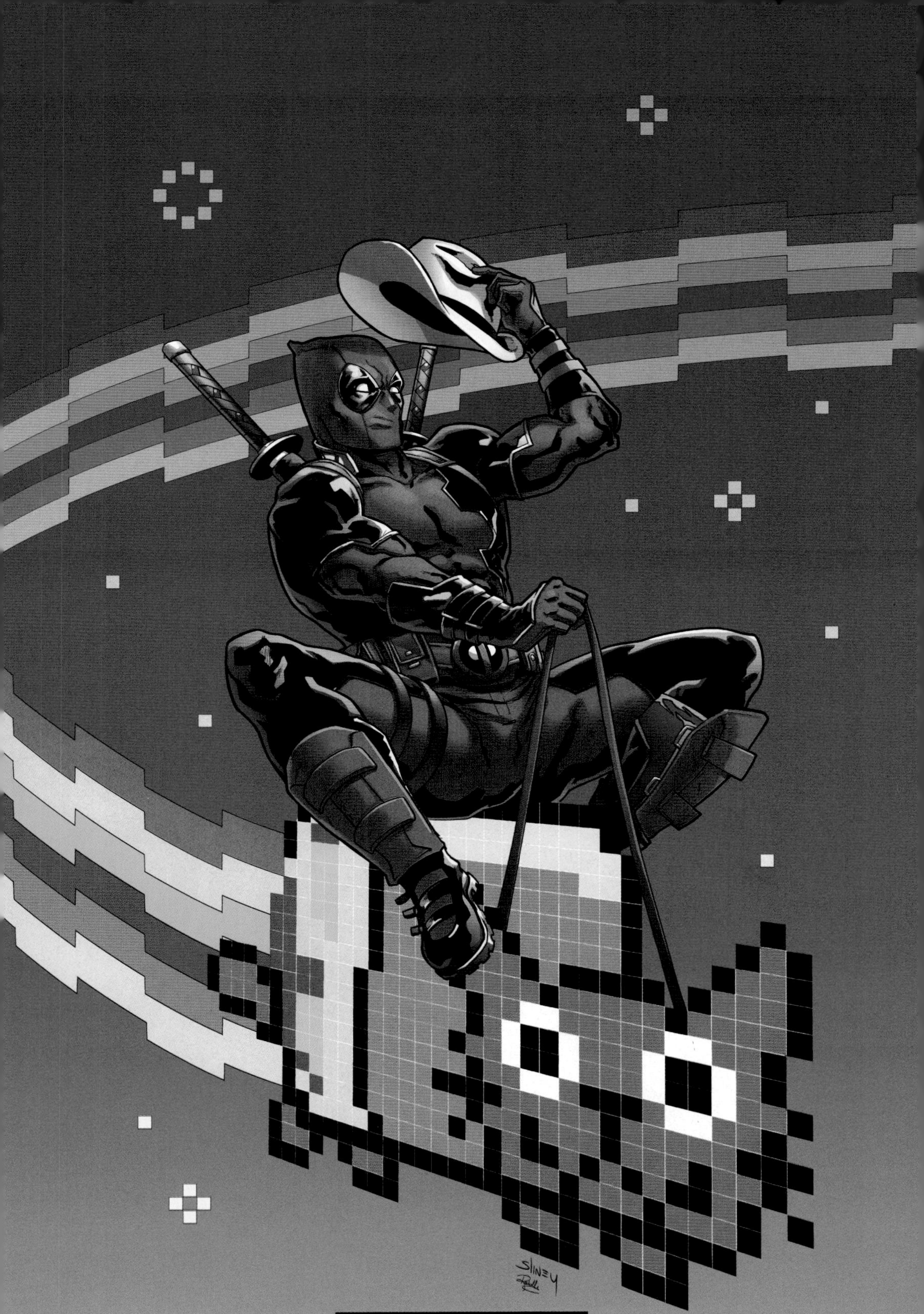
SLINEY

#4 DEADPOOL VARIANT BY

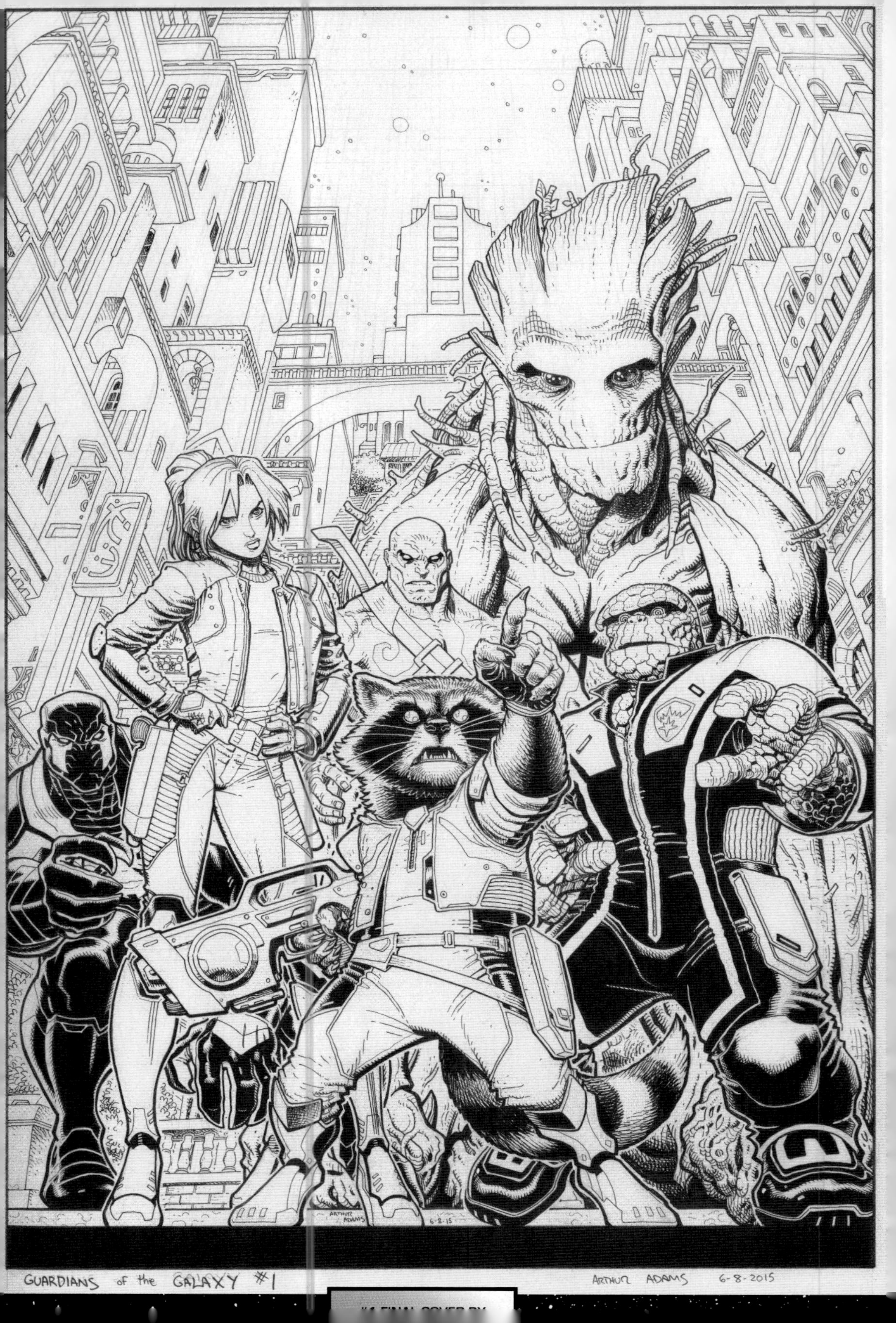
ARTHUR ADAMS
6-8-15
GUARDIANS of the GALAXY #1
ARTHUR ADAMS 6-8-2015

#1 FINAL COVER BY

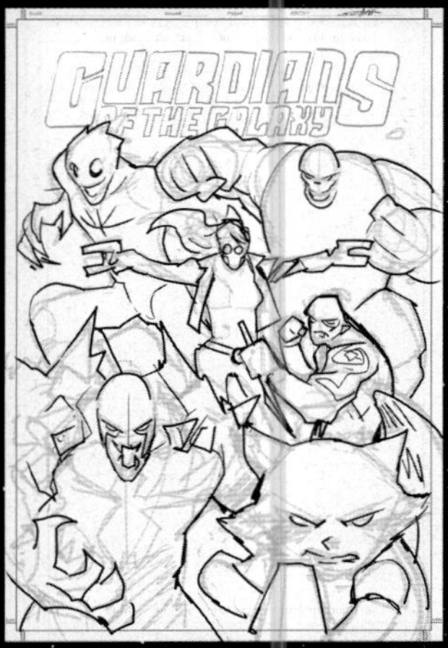
GUARDIANS
OF THE GALAXY

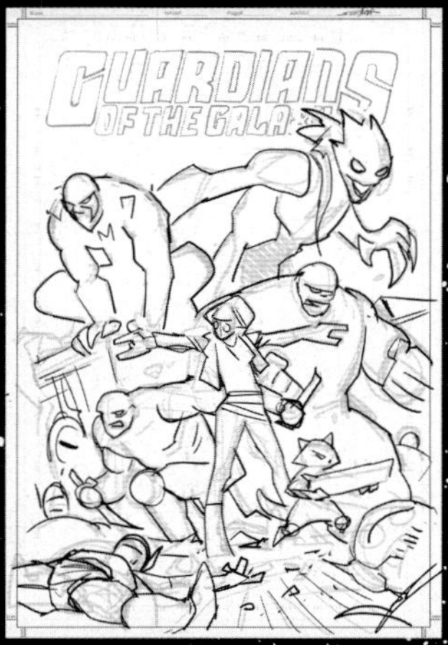
GUARDIANS
OF THE GALA

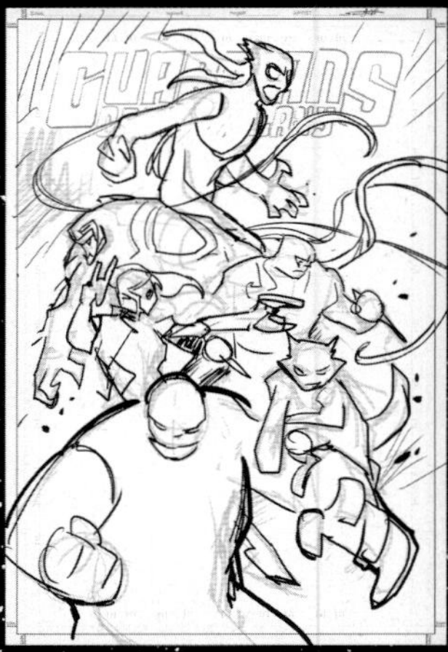

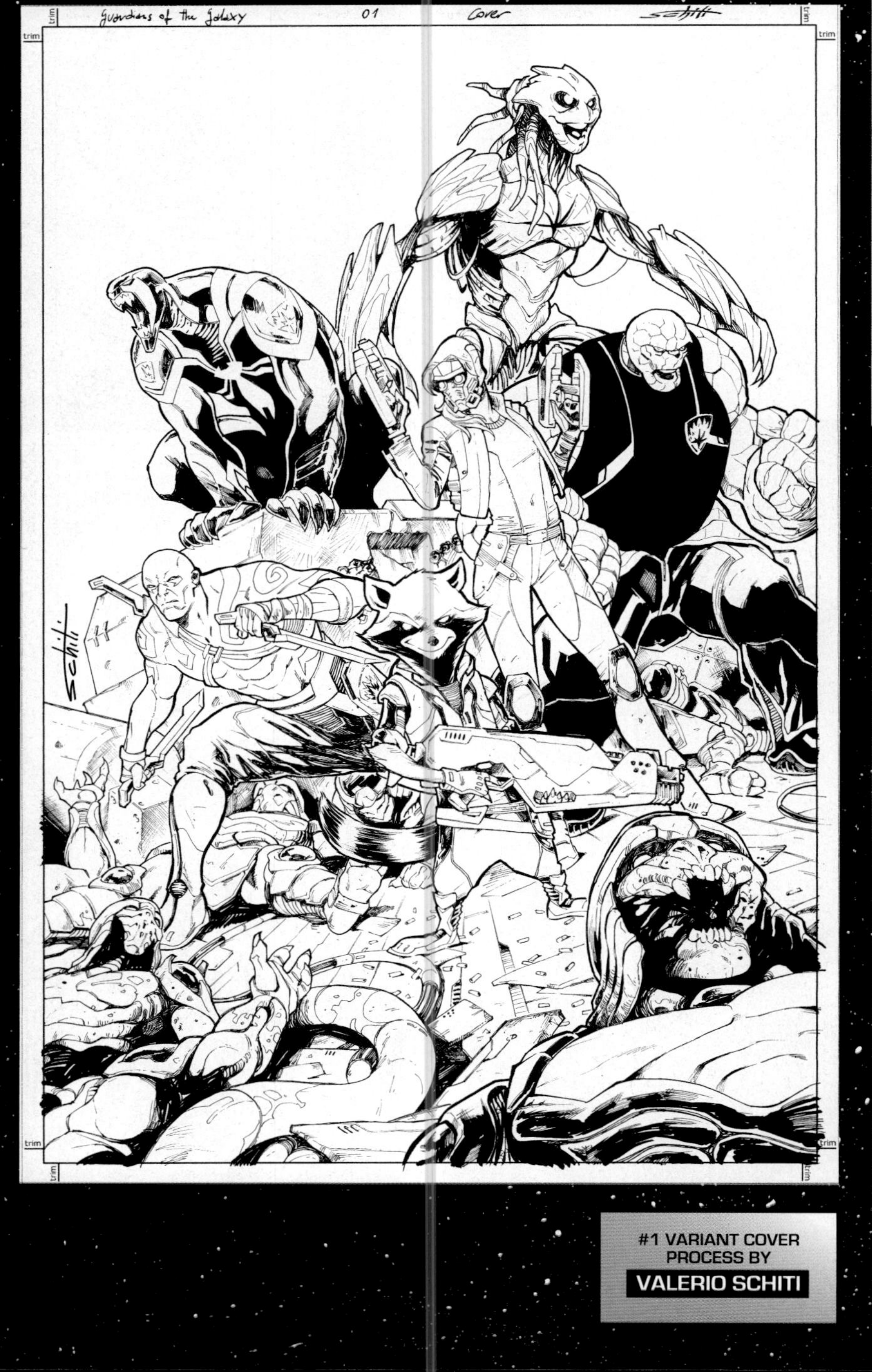
Guardians of the Galaxy
01
Cover
Schiti
trim

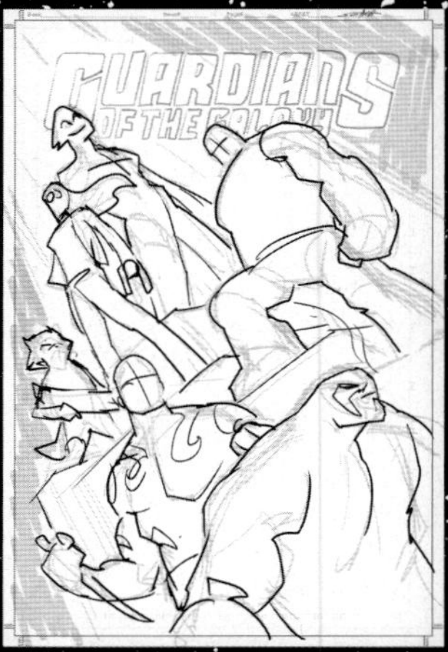
GUARDIANS
OF THE

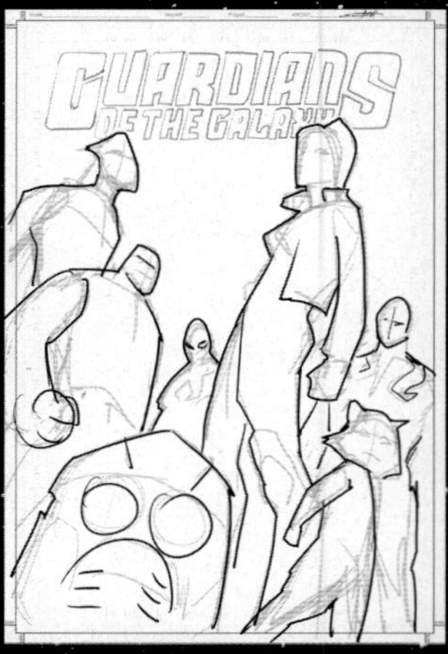
GUARDIANS
OF THE GALA

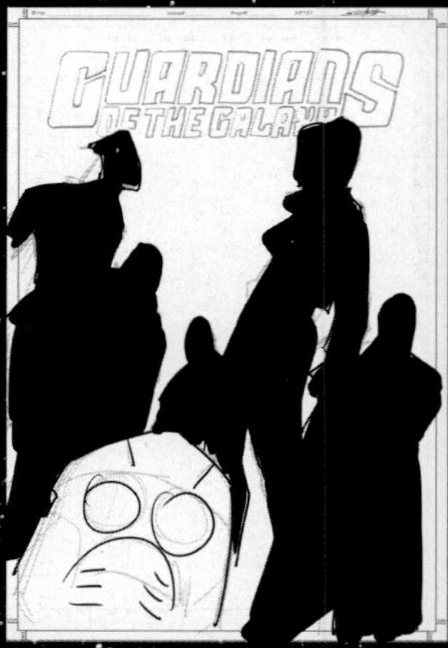
GUARDIANS
OF THE GALA

#1 VARIANT COVER PROCESS BY **VALERIO SCHITI**

## #2 COVER PROCESS BY ARTHUR ADAMS

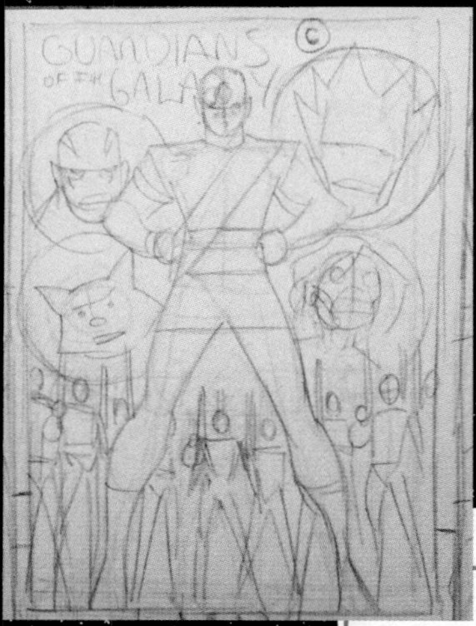
GUARDIANS OF THE GALAXY

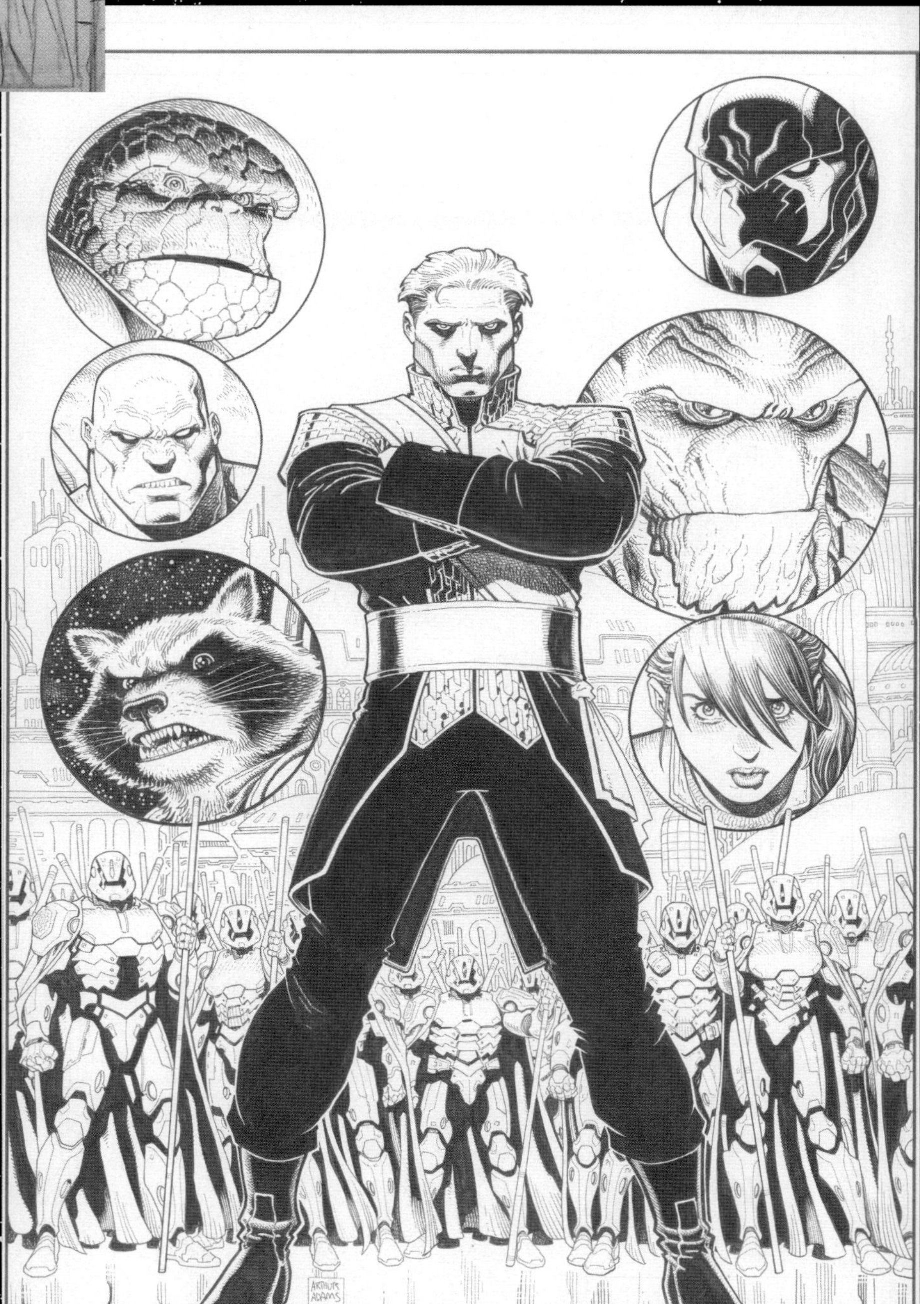
ARTHUR ADAMS 8-6 2015

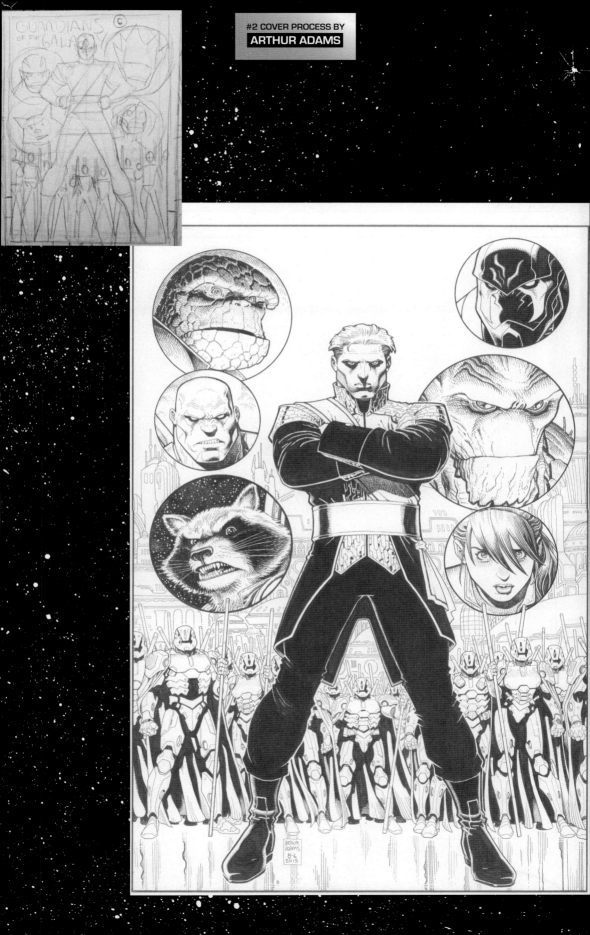

COVER SKETCHES BY
ARTHUR ADAMS

4

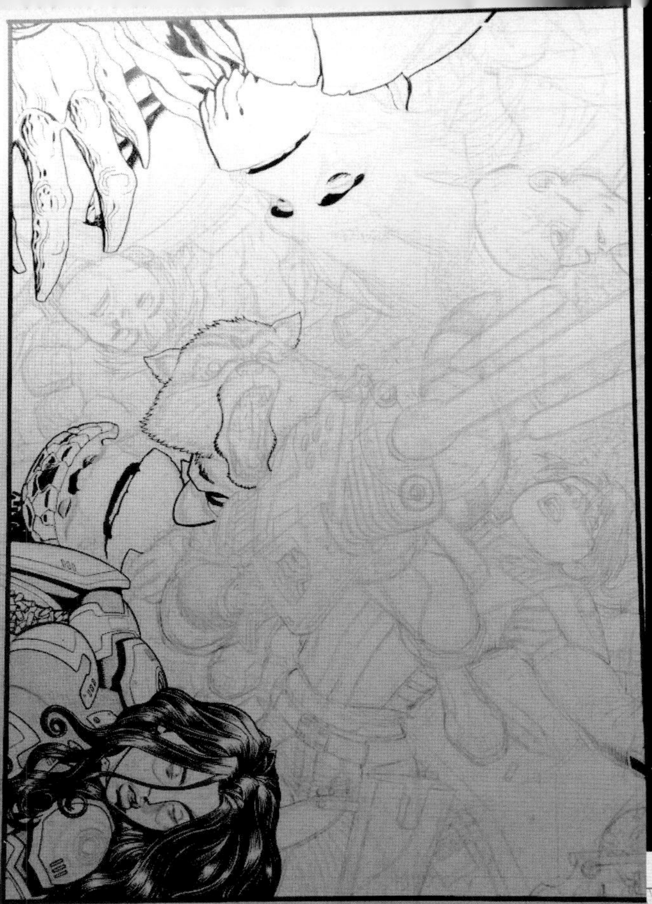

5

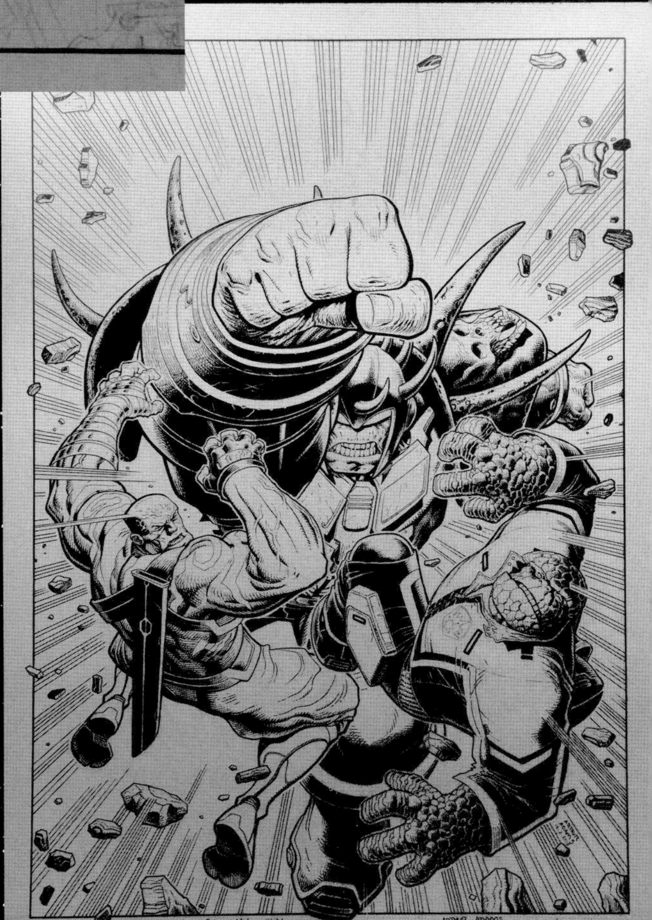
GUARDIANS of the GALAXY #4
ARTHUR ADAMS

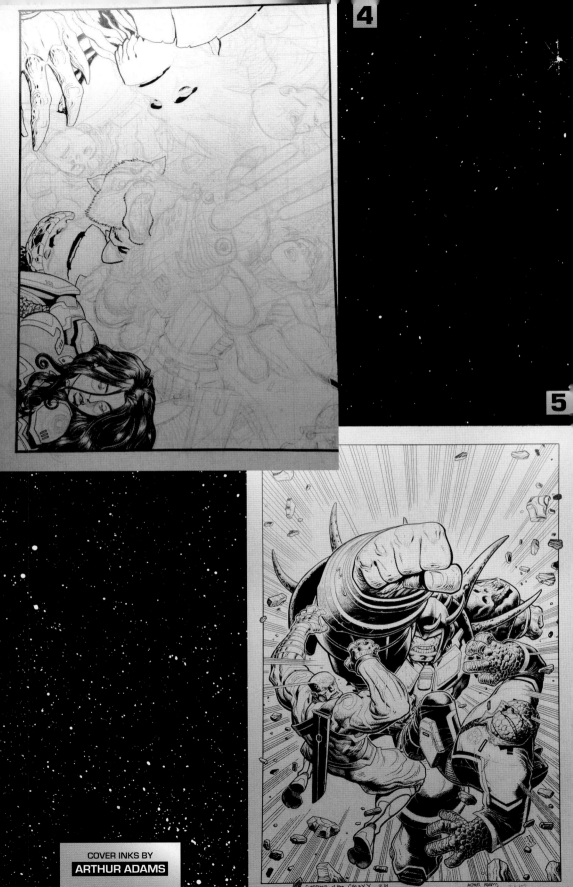

COVER INKS BY
ARTHUR ADAMS

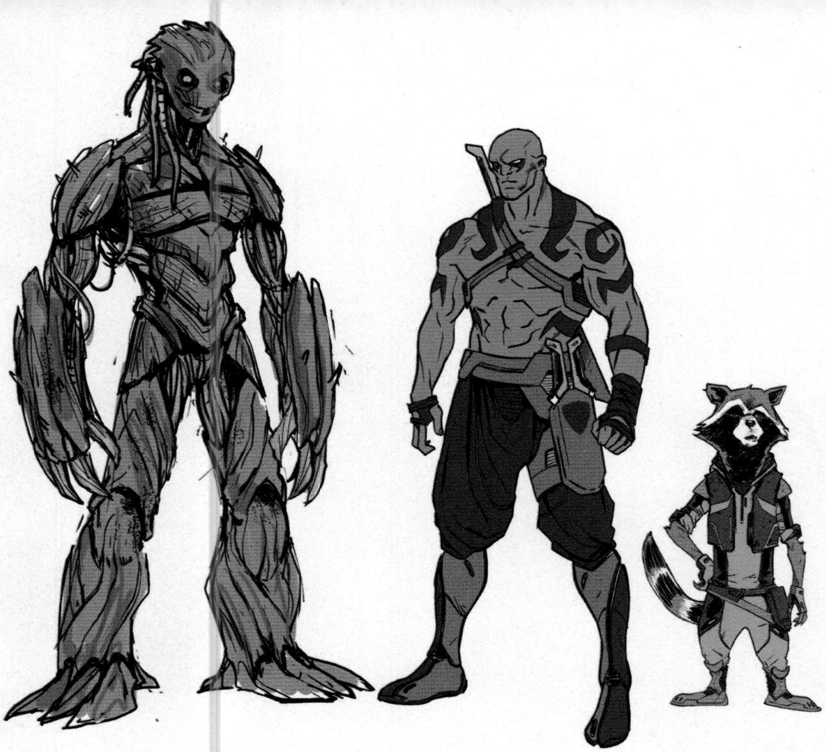

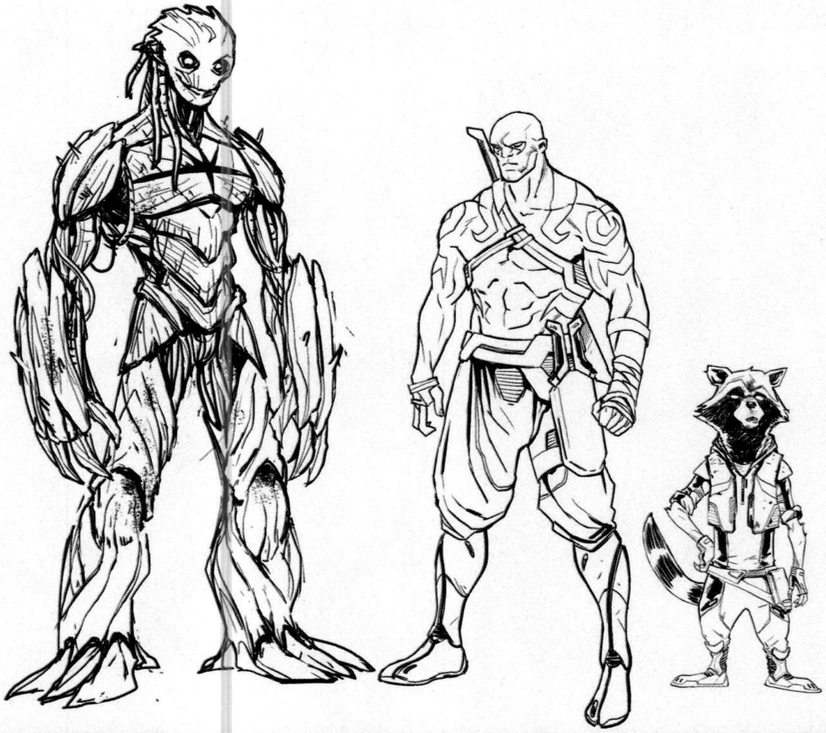

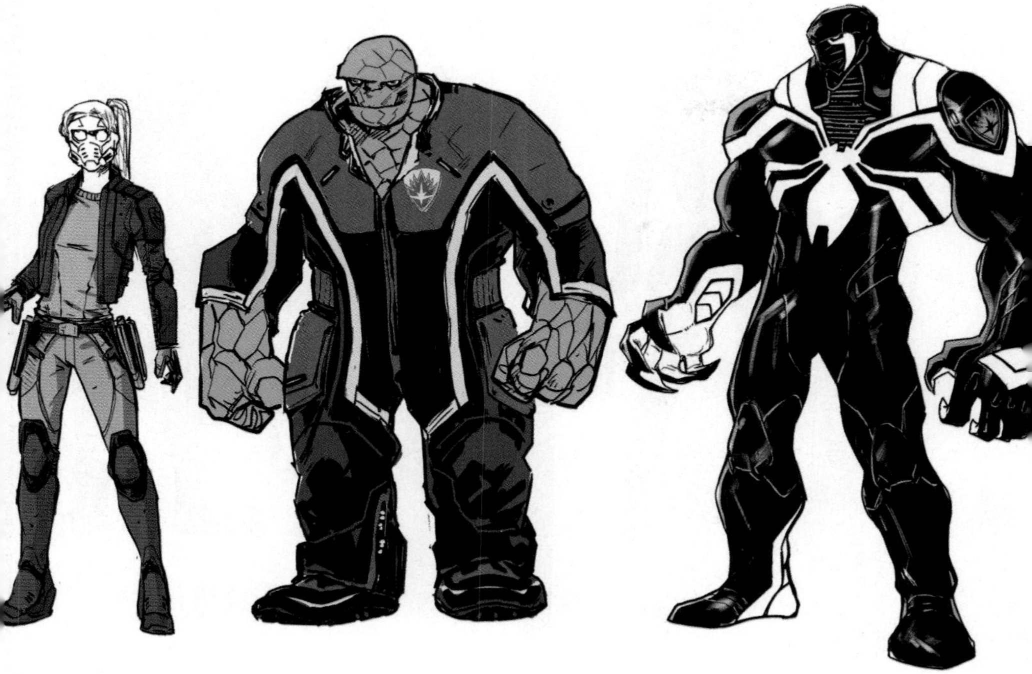

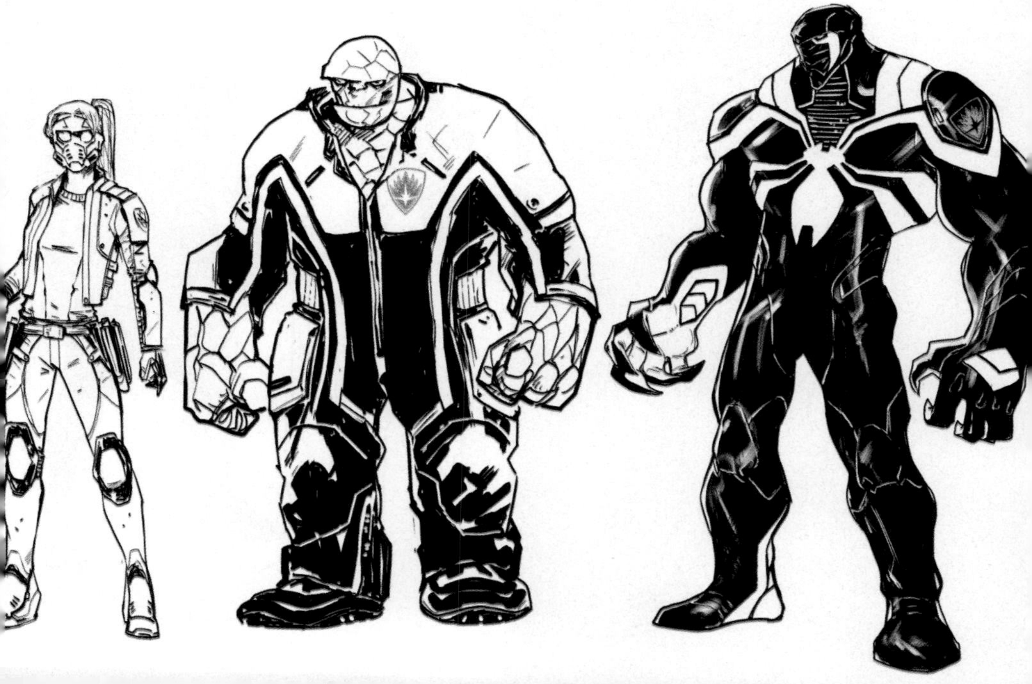

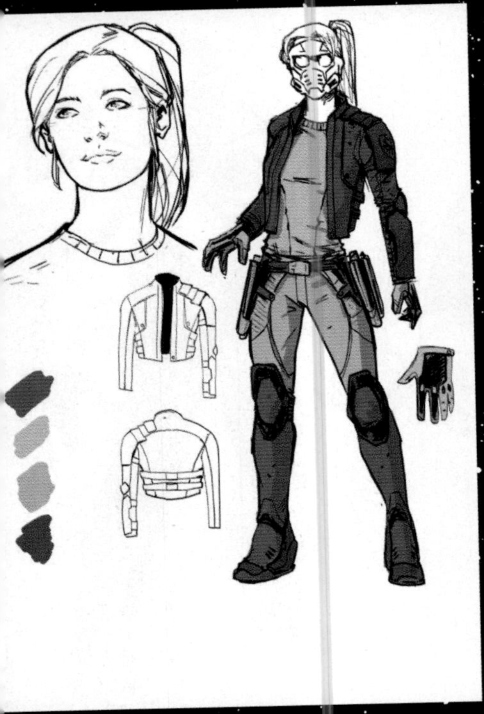

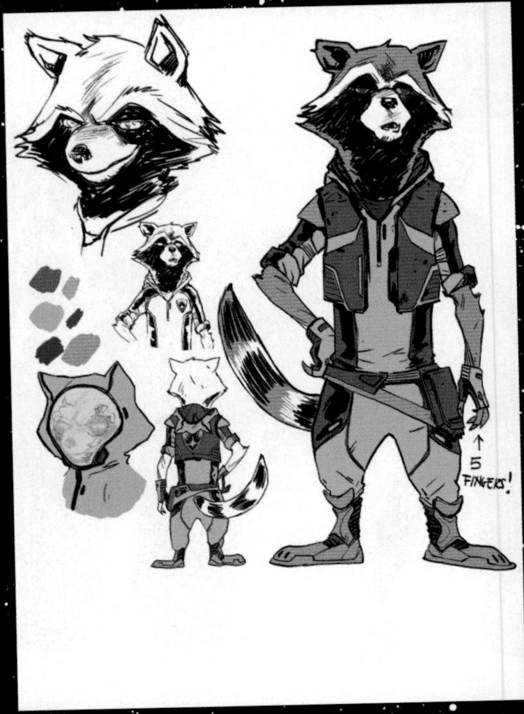
5
FINGERS!

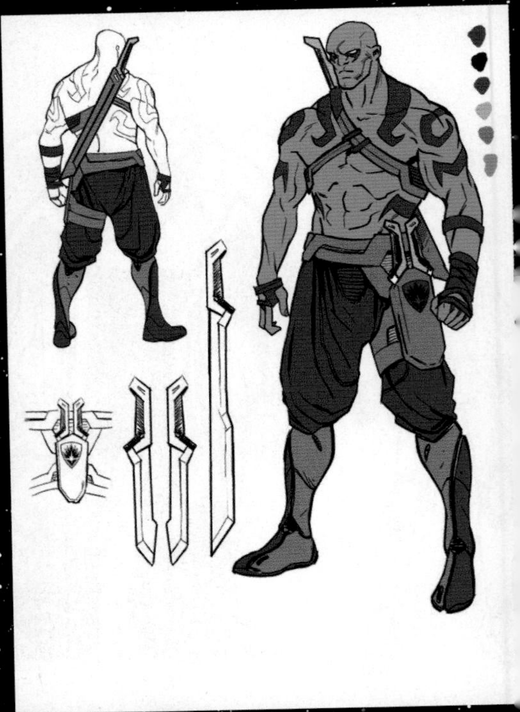

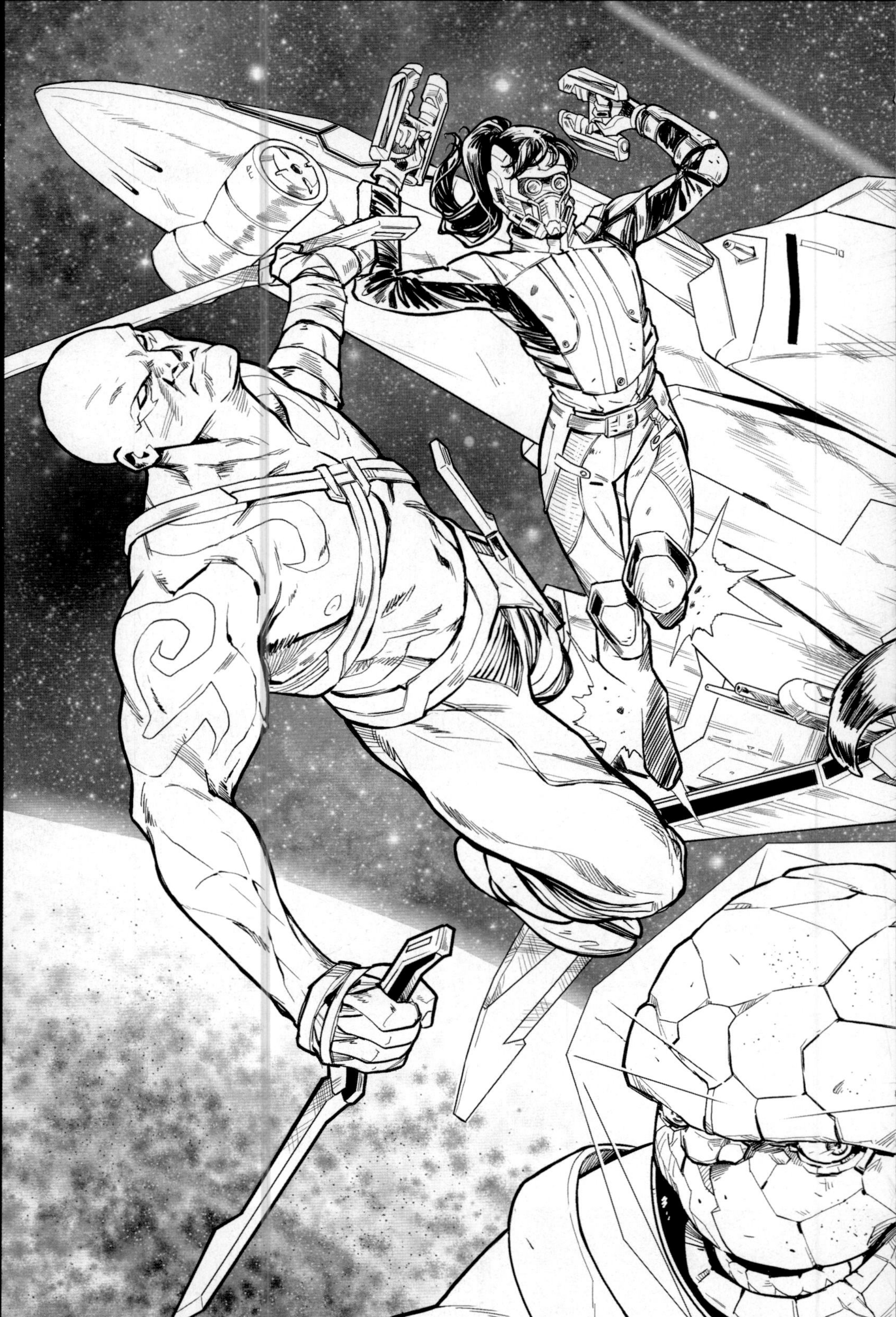

#1, PP. 5-6 ART BY

VALERIO SCHITI

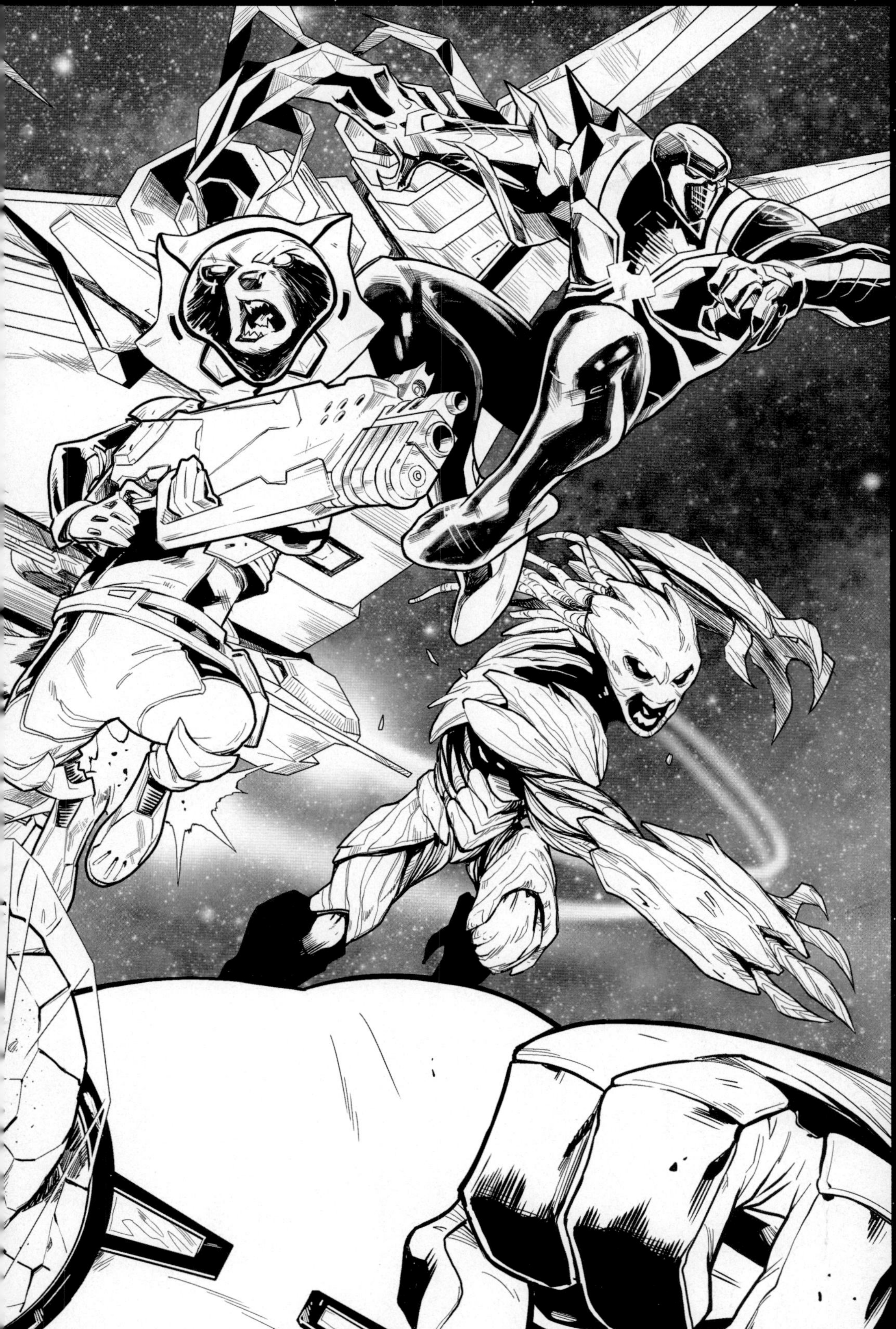